Editor A E J Went

Atlantic Salmon:
its Future

**Proceedings of the second International Atlantic
Salmon Symposium, Edinburgh 1978, sponsored by
The International Atlantic Salmon Foundation and
the Atlantic Salmon Research Trust**

Fishing News Books Ltd
Farnham, Surrey, England

© Fishing News Books Ltd 1980

ISBN 0 85238 103 4

British Library CIP data

International Atlantic Salmon Symposium, *2nd,*
  Edinburgh, 1978
  Atlantic salmon, it future.
  1. Salmon-fisheries – Atlantic Ocean – Congresses
  2. Atlantic salmon – Congresses   3. Fishery
  conservation – Atlantic Ocean – Congresses
  I. Title   II. Went, Arthur Edward James
  639'.97'755   SH346

ISBN 0–85238–103–4

Typeset by Inforum Ltd, Portsmouth

Printed and bound in Great Britain
by the Pitman Press, Bath

Contents

vi

viii

Acknowledgements

The International Atlantic Salmon Foundation and the Atlantic Salmon Research Trust wish to express their great appreciation of the kindness of His Royal Highness the Prince Charles, Duke of Rothesay, for his opening address, which acted as an inspiration to all those who contributed either papers or to the discussions.

To all those who participated the joint sponsors would also wish to offer their grateful thanks. Thanks are also due to those who organized the special exhibition in the David Hume Tower relating to fishing gear, legal and illegal, and research and improvement programmes for the Atlantic salmon, under the direction of Dr L Stewart.

Finally the sponsors would wish to express their appreciation of the efficient and friendly services provided by Mr W Campbell and his staff from the Centre for Industrial Consultancy and Liaison of the University of Edinburgh.

Preface

In 1972 the International Atlantic Salmon Foundation and the Atlantic Salmon Research Trust jointly sponsored the first International Atlantic Salmon Symposium at St Andrews, New Brunswick, Canada, which was devoted in the main to scientific and technical aspects of this important fish. Recognizing the need for further discussions on salmon the same two bodies decided to organize a second symposium, this time in Europe, devoted not so much to scientific and technical aspects but mainly to the role which the Atlantic salmon could and should play in the world of tomorrow.

More than 250 fishermen, conservationists, scientists and students from eleven different countries attended the three-day conference, during which many important aspects of the Atlantic salmon and its future role were described and discussed. Everyone at the Symposium recognised that, if the Atlantic salmon is to survive, positive action was necessary within all those countries which produce and/or fish for the species.

During the Symposium a number of speakers pointed out that modern developments, including those arising from the Law of the Sea Conference, made it imperative that new international approaches be adopted to solve the increasing number of problems relating to the conservation of Atlantic salmon stocks. At the close of the Symposium resolutions were unanimously adopted calling for the establishment of an International Convention for Atlantic salmon by the countries which produce and/or fish for the species.

Opening Address

*by His Royal Highness the Prince Charles, Duke of Rothesay,
who was introduced by Lord Home*

Many of you, perhaps, may wonder why on earth I am here
today making the opening address to this Symposium. It is a
question that I have asked myself frequently in the last few
weeks, having seen the list of people attending this gather-
ing. As usual, I find myself preaching to the converted – an
amateur amongst a frightening array of professionals. But
I am an amateur who has had an almost lifelong admiration
and fascination for the Atlantic salmon – an amateur who
has enjoyed countless hours of absorbing concentration,
excitement, tranquillity and appalling despair on all sorts of
memorable rivers. There is no doubt that in this sense I am
most fortunate – and I have no hesitation in admitting it.

The main reasons for my being here are, firstly, that I
actually *wanted* to come. Secondly, that I feel it is the least I
can do in return for all the pleasure, excitement and happi-
ness this magnificent fish has given me (and will, I hope go
on giving me . . .). Thirdly, and most importantly, I am here
because I desperately want to see the salmon survive as a
species – not just because I want to catch them in the most
difficult way conceivable, but because their disappearance
would be a tragedy of major proportions and would matter
to us all.

There are a considerable number of people, I suspect,
who upon hearing the mention of salmon immediately
think of a rich man's sport. However erroneous that may be
nowadays it is still an indication of how valuable a resource
the salmon is and what enormous prices it can command.
The very fact of its value – commercially, gastronomically

and from the sporting point of view – is liable to be its undoing. Gone are the days when the apprentices of Attercliffe (in Sheffield) petitioned the Crown that they be not made to eat salmon more than twice a week. Instead, apparently, they can't get enough of it on the Continent and are prepared to pay enormous, inflated prices for the genuine article. Pressures on any resource nowadays and particularly on a wildlife one, are becoming almost intolerable as a result of man's curiously insatiable greed and his equally curious and apparent inability to understand the necessity for sensible conservation and wise management. There is no *proof* that stocks are being depleted seems to be the perennial cry. It is only when the catches, and not only of salmon, are reduced to almost nothing that self interest stimulates some kind of action – and the awful thing is that it *could* be too late in certain cases.

I cannot help thinking it is highly appropriate that we should be meeting here in Scotland on this occasion, for it is probably true to say that the Scottish achievement in the conservation of salmon is almost without equal. Other countries have succeeded in depleting their salmon runs through over fishing, pollution, water abstraction, uncontrolled poaching, hydro-electric schemes and other obstructions. Scotland have lost the odd battle in this constant fight against the salmon enemies, but on the whole the losses have been made good with new fish ladders, sewage works, hatcheries and improved management practice. In many other countries it would seem that netsmen and anglers use their money to oppose each other, but in Scotland, under the District Fishery Board structure, the traditional netsmen and anglers have united their funds to fight the common foe. It is surely a sound practical approach to the whole problem.

In another sense it is perhaps *not* so appropriate that we should be meeting in Scotland. Except for one or two notable exceptions, this year has seen record runs of salmon in many of Scotland's rivers and, what is more, has seen the return of the spring salmon and a corresponding slight decline in the large run of grilse, which seems to have been a common feature of recent years. No doubt there are all

sorts of reasons for this encouraging state of affairs – one of which is probably the increased vigilance of fishery protection patrols in Scottish waters. In Ireland, however, I am told that the situation is very different indeed. In the 1977 report of the Irish Salmon Research Trust we are told that the production of smolts in fresh water which gave rise to the 1977 grilse run was normal, but that the low level of returning grilse was directly attributable to mortality in the sea. But by far the most disturbing part of this report is the sentence which says that *present survival rates are less than half that required for a self-sustaining population.* This is surely an extremely serious situation in a country where 90-95 percent of the annual catch is made by commercial fishermen and where, in 1970, anglers produced over 40 percent of the *income* from the salmon fishing industry as a whole, but caught less than 10 percent of the fish. The situation has reached the stage now where the drift netters themselves are finding that there is little to catch. With Irish stocks in serious jeopardy, it is a plain object lesson for us all and also an object lesson for England, which has already lost much of its salmon stock in years gone by, to the extent that they are probably little more than one tenth of Scottish stocks.

It is, of course, only too easy to list all the frightful problems that exist in relation to the Atlantic salmon, but another matter to actually *do* something about solving these problems. One thing is absolutely certain and that is that the pressures on the salmon will go on increasing at a steady pace.

There will inevitably be more and more people who want to fish and yet the available water remains the same – *unless* further determined action is taken to fight pollution and to restore our former salmon rivers to their original glory. There is no doubt, either, that prices will continue to rise – unless some form of price stabilization is achieved. Prices certainly affect the level of commercialization which is now being seen amongst rod fishermen, owners and river managers and thought ought to be given as to whether this trend is in the long-term interest of salmon. It is all very well rod fishermen and owners complaining bitterly about netting at sea, but it doesn't help if attempts are then made to maximize the short-term income from fisheries by, for instance, splitting beats into smaller lengths, putting on more and more rods and charging higher and higher prices which in turn encourage many of those fishing to adopt what must be some of the less sporting methods of catching fish.

I find myself becoming more and more convinced that if we are going to do something to cope with the enormous demand for salmon, it is absolutely essential to perfect the techniques of salt-water farming of salmon so that when a reasonable production level is obtained (say 2,000 tons per annum from the United Kingdom and Ireland) there will be a sensible alternative to the hunting of salmon at sea. It is interesting to think what could be achieved if some of the technological effort which is put into devising bigger and better boats, carrying longer and deeper nets of light indestructible material, fishing by day and night for longer periods in rougher conditions . . . if this effort could be diverted into farming fish satisfactorily.

I suppose, inevitably, the main concern amongst all of us here is that there should be an adequate stock of salmon to breed in our rivers – not just because we want to catch them in the rivers or in the estuaries, but because unless they can breed in our rivers no-one *at all* will have any salmon. For that reason it is important to recognize the damage that can be done by indiscriminate drift netting at sea. Scotland recognized this a long time ago. *England doesn't appear to have done so* and Ireland is *beginning* to recognize it. If regulations are made, then the most difficult problem is how to enforce them, particularly when fishery protection vessels are so scarce. It is true that air patrols have been a considerable success in Scotland, but with so many regulations coming into force nowadays (affecting other sorts of fish, apart from salmon, which need protecting) I cannot understand why it is not possible to utilize a number of the fast trawlers, which I saw lying redundant and rusting in the fishing ports of Humberside, for temporary fishing protection duties.

One final point – before I drive you all demented with boredom. Most of the countries which are lucky enough to play host to the Atlantic or Pacific salmon will have had legislation in existence for a long time in order to regulate their salmon fisheries. Scotland, for instance, has a long history of conservation-orientated legislation going back at least to the reign of William the Lion in 1175. Nowadays, however, *under the present state of affairs*, it would appear that the legislation may not be altogether sufficient. For instance, it seems generally agreed that the powers of the District Salmon Fishery Boards in Scotland, and the funds and the staff available to them, *are no longer adequate* and should be replaced by Area Fishery Boards. Whatever the case, it seems important to make the regulations apply to the present situation.

Having cast a rather bad fly over this assembly to open the Symposium, I can only hope that you all rise extremely well during the rest of the week and have a most successful and fruitful meeting.

1 A general review of the state of the salmon fisheries of the north Atlantic

Sir Richard Levinge, Salmon and Trout Association

Introduction

The salmon fisheries in Great Britain and Ireland are very different from those of the north American continent, Iceland and Norway. Due to our temperate winter climate, fresh salmon can and do run from the sea into our rivers almost throughout the year. For example, the River Tweed on the east coast border of England and Scotland is one extreme which enjoys a run of fresh salmon for 11 months of the year. The short 'spate' rivers of northwest Scotland and west Ireland are another extreme with a run of salmon (mainly one sea-winter fish or grilse) in the summer months only.

For obvious reasons such a wide seasonal distribution is impossible in countries with an arctic-type winter climate. For example, Canada has no spring run of salmon. The so called 'spring fish' caught in May are in fact kelts or spent fish.

It is important to remember this difference – because our UK fisheries are subject to seasonal trends which tend to distort the overall picture.

Present state of Atlantic salmon fisheries

At the outset I can report definitely that the state of the Atlantic salmon fisheries is now quite healthy. There are black areas still, however, where mismanagement and greedy exploitation are endangering the local survival of the species. There are also success stories where the salmon population is on the increase, or is even being restored to rivers where pollution, over fishing, power demands, *etc*, had completely eliminated the species.

I think, on balance, the success stories outweigh the black areas. I would mention here, for example, that such has been the improvement in the water quality of London's River Thames that a study team under Mr Ian Allan has confidently been able to recommend that an attempt be made to reintroduce salmon to the Thames. In fact a very small experimental planting of parr and smolts was made in 1973-76 and one adult salmon appeared in July of 1978 at Shepperton Weir – 16 miles upstream of London Bridge (the first salmon in fresh water in the Thames for 160 years). There are also most encouraging signs that the massive programme, financed by the US Government, to restore the Atlantic salmon to the rivers of the northeast maritime states is beginning to bear fruit. For example, this year the hitherto barren Connecticut River had a return of 60 adult fish. Unfortunately, few of these survived in captivity as potential breeding stock.

International agreement to restrict exploitation

The great threat to the Atlantic salmon in 1972 was the extensive and expanding exploitation by drift nets operating in the high seas on the feeding grounds, most especially by fishermen from countries having little or no salmon bearing rivers of their own and no responsibility or care for the conservation of the species. The Davis Strait off the coast of Greenland was the principal area of exploitation where immature salmon, originating largely from Canada, but also from Great Britain and Ireland, were being slaughtered. Other potential areas, round The Faeroes, for example, were being prospected for exploitation. An international agreement was later reached with these objectives:

First, to phase out the Davis Strait fishing by 1976 and fix a quota of 1,192 tonnes for the Greenland onshore fishing.

Secondly, the agreement of the member countries of the Northeast Atlantic Fisheries Commission (NEAFC) to establish 200 mile 'boxes' beyond their own territorial limits in which there would be no salmon fishing.

Credit for this must go initially to the vigorous offensive mounted by the Atlantic Salmon Association (ASA) under its much loved and admired director, the late T B (Happy) Fraser. Subsequently, the Atlantic Salmon Research Trust (ASRT) and International Atlantic Salmon Foundation (IASF) sponsored a conference in 1969, in London, to evaluate and assess this threat. Ultimately, the Governments of the USA and Canada backed by IASF and ASA put on diplomatic pressure to stop the Davis Strait slaughter. Now the old cliché, 'one swallow does not make a summer', is very wise; so it is with reservation but pleasure that I report to you a most significant improvement in the run of two and three sea-winter salmon in both Canadian and UK rivers coincident with the final closing of the Davis Strait drift net fishery in 1976.

Canada

The reports from the IASF for the rivers of Quebec and New Brunswick show very significant improvement in 1977 and 1978 both in numbers and size of salmon – but here we must remember that the Canadian authorities reacted, to their great credit, by imposing drastic, even draconian, legislation to preserve their dwindling stocks. For example: a temporary but still continuing ban on commercial fishing in coastal water of part of Quebec and of New Brunswick, prohibition of the sale of salmon, and a reduction in the rod limit to two fish per rod day. As a result of this severe limitation, this marked improvement must be an understatement of the true position as the escapement of the salmon to the spawning beds is probably now restored to an adequate level.

In the absence of general and reliable techniques for counting the escapement of salmon to breed, I consider that the success or otherwise of rod fishing provides the best criterion. Kept within reasonable restraint, rod fishing cannot lead to over exploitation, but it does reflect the number of fish in a river.

The continued existence of an extensive commercial fishery off Newfoundland (and to a lesser extent off Labrador) is perhaps a blot on the otherwise excellent record of

Canadian salmon conservation. It is indiscriminate, taking salmon homing to all rivers of Canada and to the northeast states of the USA. The size of this fishery is considerable – the average yearly catch for 1910 to 1969 was 3,521 thousands of pounds and in 1973 to 1975 it rose to 4,463 thousands of pounds. It is of the same magnitude as the Irish drift net fishery to which I will refer at length later on, but we must remember that the Canadian fishery is a huge one comprising most if not all the rivers in the provinces of Labrador, Newfoundland, New Brunswick and in Quebec on the north and south shores of the St. Lawrence, the Gaspé Peninsula and the Bay de Chaleur. Maybe Canada can support this fishery but if it is taking, as tag returns show it does, a large proportion of salmon homing to the northeast states of the USA, then it is doing grave damage to the enormous efforts of the most praiseworthy programme of restoration of salmon to the rivers of Maine, Connecticut and New Hampshire. Also we must remember that the existence of large national drift net fisheries does much to damage the case against a ban on high seas fishing.

The other main problem in Canada, and especially in the Quebec Province, is illegal fishing and abuses of the established rights of the Indian population. IASF estimates that not less that 1,000 salmon per week are being taken, and sold, illegally from the Restigouche estuary alone.

Great Britain
Turning to the rivers of Great Britain, especially the Scottish rivers (and Scotland contains most of the major UK salmon rivers), in 1978 they have enjoyed a remarkable change in their fortunes. For the past decade the run of spring two and three sea-winter fish had declined to almost nil in many rivers – they had become largely dependent for their stocks on summer and autumn running fish with a preponderance of one sea-winter fish (grilse). 1978 has produced a great run of true spring salmon, two sea-winter fish, but also a substantial proportion of large three sea-winter springers such as we have not seen for ten years or more. I reserve judgement on this, but the circumstantial evidence at this time is reasonably convincing and hopeful.

Most certainly, it justifies beyond all doubt the elimination, hopefully for all time, of high seas fishing. But above all we must not become complacent – the threat of a future escalation of high seas fishing is ever present. The existing international agreements are at risk from the uncertainty of the protracted 'Law of the Sea' negotiations. We in the UK are also under pressure from our European Economic Community (EEC) partners to open our waters to them. The UK Government has taken a strong, and in my view wholly commendable line in resisting this. While the main concern is with white fish, especially pelagic fish, salmon must come under this general umbrella.

I have mentioned the continual decline in the spring salmon run up to 1978 and the possibility that this may have been largely due to the slaughter of this particular race of salmon in the Davis Strait but there is no doubt that we have also been going through a cyclic change, with increasing runs of summer salmon and grilse. What to me is even more interesting is that the size of grilse has increased significantly; grilse attaining eight pounds or more by midsummer are frequent, and scale readings show that most of these fish have been feeding and growing at sea as quickly in winter as in summer and the normal narrow 'sea-winter' mark is absent or very slight. As the criterion for distinguishing salmon and grilse is six pounds, *Table 1* may well be an underestimate of the grilse catch. It would seem to me that the migration and feeding habits of our salmon may have undergone a change – the fish finding new and perhaps richer feeding grounds closer to home – accelerating their growth and maturity.

Table 1 Numbers of Scottish salmon and grilse caught in east coast rivers (annual averages)

	salmon × 100	grilse × 100	total × 100	grilse %
1952-56	1,373	547	1,920	28·5
1957-61	1,425	737	2,162	34·0
1962-66	1,409	1,126	2,535	44·4
1967-71	1,250	1,548	2,798	55·3
1972-75	1,173	1,438	2,611	55·1

The major problem and menace to salmon stocks in our waters is from illegal drift netting at sea – the prize is high and, because of the difficulty of policing such a wide area, the risk of detection and prosecution is too slight.

There is only one significant legal drift net fishery – off the northeast coast of England. This in itself is not large enough to be a menace. But its existence is provocative. It is an incitement to illegal fishing and a source of annoyance to the Scots because, as shown by a recent Ministry of Agriculture, Fisheries and Food investigation, most of the fish taken by this fishery are homing to Scottish waters. Fortunately for the Scottish salmon, a recent agitation to extend drift net fishing to Scottish waters met with a very dusty, but well reasoned, answer in Parliament by the Secretary of State for Scotland.

Ulcerative dermal necrosis (UDN) too is still present. This disease develops especially on salmon in fresh water in spring and autumn which could indicate that the causative organism is either temperature sensitive or conditioned by hours of daylight. The spring outbreak is lethal and few infected fish survive. The autumn outbreak is less lethal and infected fish may well survive to spawn. It is particularly sad that this year, when we have at last enjoyed a good run of spring salmon, UDN in some rivers has taken a severe toll – no doubt because of the denser population of fish.

Ireland

Now I come to the blackest spot in the north Atlantic fisheries. Ireland was once a model of a well-managed and enormously prolific salmon fishery in spite of the inborn proclivity of its people to poach an odd salmon by hook or by crook, mainly by crook. I'm going to deal with the Irish fishery in some detail as it serves as an awful warning and example of a rake's progress.

There was always a public right of drift netting in certain limited and legally defined areas, principally off the northwest coast, operated by farmers with small hand-powered boats as an increment to their livelihood from poor and infertile land. Financial support was given by the government to enable inshore fishermen, primarily for white fish, to purchase larger and more powerful boats. Of course these state-subsidised fishermen lost no time in exploiting the salmon and made huge killings, to the envy of fishermen all along the west and south coasts. Political pressure then built up to extend the legal drift netting areas. After going through the motions of public enquiries *etc*, a greatly extended drift fishery was opened up, thus giving a boost to the political image of the party in power.

Diagrams from the 1975 Report of the Inland Fisheries Commission show:

1 The number of licensed drift nets rose from approximately 650 in the decade 1952-1962 to approximately 1,100 in the decade 1965-1976. It remains at this level.
2 From a few isolated areas, virtually the whole of the north, west and south coasts of the Republic of Ireland became opened up to drift netting.
3 The total salmon catch rose from around 2,000 million pounds per annum, prior to 1961, to peak at 4,000 million pounds in the period 1970-1975. During the period 1961-1975 the drift net catch rose from about 20 percent of the total to 70 percent of the total, while the estuary draft net catch fell from 50 percent to 20 percent. The rod catch share of course declined most of all, falling from about 15 percent to less than 5 percent.

There are now signs that the 'golden eggs' are no longer for the taking; with no significant reduction in the number of nets, the drift net catch has declined in the last two years by 12 percent, and 1977 was generally a good year for salmon elsewhere in the British Isles. Meanwhile, especially where the drift nets place a cordon across some of the large bays into which several rivers open, there are tragic examples of individual rivers which have become virtually denuded of salmon. They are only surviving on the small numbers of late running fish which arrive after the total closure of netting in August. Ireland does operate a system of registering and licensing salmon dealers, so it is difficult for commercial fishermen to dispose of catches made outside the legal season. These late running fish contribute little to the rod fishing or to the tourist revenue of Ireland. Unfortunately, however, it is not purely an Irish concern. Ireland lies across the path of salmon homing to Scottish, English and Welsh rivers.

Drift netting at sea is a most indiscriminate method of exploitation. The wider the area over which it operates, the more difficult it is to control and police. There is evidence that Irish fishermen have been extending their activities beyond territorial limits, contrary to NEAFC agreement, taking both feeding and migrating salmon of UK origin. The huge escalation of this drift net fishing, and the difficulty of controlling and policing it, have resulted in a state of anarchy along the Irish coast. The regulations controlling dimensions of nets, positioning of nets, weekly close period and so forth, are openly flouted. The few protected areas still left off the west coast are now being fished openly but illegally.

Table 2 Growth of the drift net industry in the Republic of Ireland (annual averages)

	total catch × 1,000 lb	draft %	drift %	rod* %	others %
1957-61	1,680	52·4	18·2	17·6	11·8
1961-66	2,840	48·2	26·2	12·4	13·2
1966-71	3,200	44·4	44·8	6·4	4·4
1971-74	4,000	22·3	67·3	4·3	6·1

*rod catch 1957-61 296,000 lb, 1971-74 172,000 lb

There is a most important lesson to be learnt from this. Ireland never had any voluntary body concerned to protect its salmon fisheries – nothing comparable to IASF, ASA, Salmon and Trout Association (STA), ASRT, *etc*. When the proposal to extend the drift net fishing came up, there was no organized opposition. I know this only too well as it fell on my shoulders to attempt to organize and to collect funds, at the shortest notice, for professional representation to provide legal and technical opposition at the public enquiry. But political expediency prevailed.

I have dwelt at some length on this because I want to

Table 3 Growth of new drift net fisheries in the Republic of Ireland

		licencees	numbers of fish caught by drift netting
Cork	1969	*30*	*2,056*
	1975	*134*	*90,445*
Kerry	1969	*4*	*nil*
	1975	*9*	*4,692*
Galway	1969	*25*	*287*
	1975	*38*	*28,080*
Connemara	1969	*7*	*68*
	1975	*30*	*4,533*
Bangor	1969	*15*	*1,373*
	1975	*25*	*24,770*

bring home a very important lesson – that all concerned in salmon conservation, and especially those with interest in salmon waters, whether they be proprietors, lessees or holders of licences to catch salmon, must support their national organizations concerned with salmon conservation.

The record of the USA and Canada of their support of IASF and ASA is exemplary. I regret to say that with a few notable exceptions support is poor in the UK, most especially from many of the major proprietors of enormously valuable salmon fisheries.

Iceland
Now to turn to a real success story – the superb record of Iceland, an exemplary model of salmon conservation which we would all do well to study and, within the limits of our own national conditions, copy.

In Iceland, the salmon is regarded as the property of the riparian owners, though the state lays down regulations within which they may exploit the resource. There is no commercial fishing at sea. There are limited rights of commercial fishing in estuaries, mainly in glacier fed rivers on which rod fishing is restricted or impossible because of the nature of the water.

Under the enlightened management of the Director of Fresh Water Fisheries, Mr Thor Gudjonsson, national rearing stations on a self-financing basis have been established. As a result, the rod fishing catch, which reflects the escapement of breeding salmon, is increasing at the rate of 7 percent per annum, with a consequent growth of the revenue to the State from tourism arising from salmon fishing. Today the Icelandic salmon fishery is a major contributor to the country's economy – one that grows from year to year – as well as a major recreational activity of the Icelanders. The total salmon catch for Iceland is small considering the size of the country and its numerous rivers – about 220 tonnes – only 40 percent of which is from the nets. It could be argued that there is a case for taking a larger crop by controlled netting confined to the river mouths or by using traps to take an agreed percentage of the run. This could benefit the Icelandic economy without unduly reducing the stock for angling and breeding. It is possible, especially when fresh water conditions are arduous for juvenile fish, to have too many salmon and much of the resource may be wasted.

Norway
The Norwegian fishery is an important one, perhaps more for the size than the numbers of its fish and with its huge coastline and massive winter snowfall, it has a goodly number of salmon rivers, but great waterfalls place barriers on the length of available nursery areas and the harsh winter climate freezes up headwaters and tributaries. Norway's salmon is a precious resource – one that should be carefully husbanded.

Table 4 Average annual catches in Norway (tonnes)

	homewaters	driftnet	long-line	total
1960-64	1,812	nil	nil	1,812
1965-69	1,729	278	467*	2,474
1970-75	1,472	310	570	2,352
			*1967-69	

It is probable that Norwegian salmon mainly migrate to rich feeding grounds fairly close to home round the north-west coasts; the short migration route coupled with the richness of these feeding grounds probably explains the rapid growth of these salmon where three sea-winter fish can achieve 50 lbs or more.

In addition to the traditional fishing by hang net in the fjords and by rod and line, a coastal drift net fishery became established in 1965.

In 1967 the feeding grounds were located, principally in an area off the Lofoten Islands, and a new fishery using baited long lines was opened up. To permit the capture of fish on their feeding grounds, where many of them have not reached full growth or maturity, seems to me to be a profligate waste of precious resources. So the pressure of exploitation has been increasing.

Norway, especially in the southern districts, suffers from a new threat – airborne pollution carried from the industrial regions of Europe and deposited by rainfall into Norwegian watersheds. The effect of this is to pollute rivers with SO_2, so that the pH of many rivers has fallen drastically to below five with consequent disastrous effects on their ecology. Salmon have virtually disappeared from several of the most seriously affected rivers.

Not content with poisoning their own rivers to destruction, certain European countries are now poisoning their neighbours' waters by total failure to establish proper controls over pollution. One can only hope that these offending states will never be permitted to exploit salmon at sea.

A great deal of research and development work is being carried out in Norway on salmon farming. Indeed, Norway has ideal conditions for this husbandry.

France
Alas poor France – the few remaining salmon bearing rivers (mainly in Brittany) show a continual decline (2,900 fish in 1972, 740 in 1976). Evidence from tagging shows that the villain is almost certainly the Greenland fishery. Certainly, it is no fault of France, where resolute voluntary bodies, and the state with a grant of 70m francs, are fighting hard to maintain and restore their rivers.

Salmon farming
Following the Norwegian example, salmon farming is now

in an advanced development stage in the west coast of
Scotland, Ireland and Brittany. If farming becomes a viable
activity, and reduces the pressure on the wild *Salmo salar*, we
must all give it unqualified blessing, provided that it is
confined to *Salmo salar*, and that no short cuts are taken with
Pacific salmon unless and until it can conclusively be proved
that there will be no conceivable risk of colonization of our
rivers with alien species.

Conclusion

I make three suggestions for the continued conservation of
our salmon:

First – everyone who has a stake in salmon fishing and
conservation must support to the utmost, by cash and personal endeavours, those voluntary bodies which seek to
maintain and improve the lot of *Salmo salar*. It is no use
relying on 'the Government' – with the honourable exception of Iceland.

Secondly – our aim should be to limit the exploitation of
salmon to their home rivers and estuaries.

Thirdly – let us recognize that we have a lot to learn –
research and development is greatly needed. This again
requires the financial support of all who wish to hand on to
posterity a heritage of one of nature's most superb creatures.

2 The future of the Atlantic salmon – an international issue

D L McKernan, Institute for Marine Studies, University of Washington, Seattle

Introduction

Much has been written about Atlantic salmon. Symposia have been held; scientific papers have been written describing its life history and habits, and books have been published tracing its history into antiquity. That the species still persists at all is something of a modern miracle, considering intense exploitation at sea, in estuaries, and within fresh water rivers as it returns to spawn in its natal streams. From Anthony Netboy's recent book, *The Salmon*, comes an appropriate quote from Frank Buckland's *Land and Water*:

> Perhaps the most unfortunate thing in the world is the salmon. Everybody and everything, from the otter to the fisherman, persecutes him. He is naturally an inhabitant of the sea. He runs up rivers, and would almost jump into the pot in the kitchen fire if allowed but every effort is put forth to keep him at a distance.

Man's effect on the Atlantic salmon resources has been far more than just reducing the supply and spawning escapement by fishing. Since the adult salmon must ascend the rivers of its origin to lay its eggs in the clean gravel of the stream and since the young salmon which hatch must find biologically productive waters in which to spend from one to three years before descending to the sea, pollution of the salmon rivers and the erection of physical barriers to the upstream and downstream migration of the salmon can and have reduced or eradicated the runs in many major salmon-producing rivers of the north Atlantic. This destruction of the freshwater habitat has been most pronounced in the rivers of France, Belgium, the Netherlands and Denmark, as well as in most of the highly productive salmon rivers of the Atlantic coast of the United States. In some regions of the north Atlantic, particularly in recent years in Canada, the United Kingdom, Ireland, Norway, Sweden and the United States, considerable attention has been given to the maintenance and restoration of freshwater habitat and enhancement of the salmon runs by hatcheries and other semi-artificial means. Substantial progress has been made in this decade in some countries to improve salmon management. For example, an agreement between Denmark and the United States in 1972, later ratified by the International Commission for the Northwest Atlantic Fisheries (ICNAF), limited the inshore Greenland salmon catches of mixed stocks of salmon originating from various north Atlantic countries and phased out the offshore high seas salmon fisheries. These actions have given rise to renewed optimism that the Atlantic salmon resources can be maintained.

Recent decline in catch

It is interesting to note that except for the years from 1973-1976 *(Table 1)* the catches of salmon over the past dozen years remained relatively constant. However, in 1973 the catch increased over 40 percent and remained high in 1974. Subsequently, the catch dropped substantially.

This increase and subsequent decrease has occurred at a time when great concern has been expressed about the future of Atlantic salmon. But governments have not been able to control salmon fishing effectively even during this period of deep concern over their future. There seems to have been no effective effort made to prevent significant increases in catch. Consequently, 1976 showed a decline in catch to the lowest level of recent years. Thus the catches of Atlantic salmon, and unquestionably the runs of salmon, remain at a precariously low level throughout their range with few exceptions, and there is still no sign that governments are taking effective regulatory action to further control fishing.

Changes in jurisdiction

The north Atlantic countries by and large have extended their jurisdiction over fishing to 200 miles. At the same time, ICNAF is being phased out along with its safeguards preventing the further increase of the north Atlantic high seas fishery off Greenland. What effect this will have on the future conservation of Atlantic salmon remains to be seen.

While widespread changes in jurisdiction over fishery resources have occurred, intensive commercial and recreational fishing continues for salmon both in the marine and freshwater environment. At present, there are no new international arrangements to deal effectively with conservation and management of the far-ranging salmon.

The development of the salmon fisheries off Greenland in the early 1960's and the subsequent agreement between Denmark and the US is well documented by Netboy (1973) and further discussed by Buck (1977) and elsewhere. The elimination of the Greenland offshore fishery and the limitations on the inshore Greenland salmon fishery have been effective in at least preventing further development of that high seas fishery for mixed stocks of salmon.

Our report is thus far quite negative because conservation efforts in recent years have not served to adequately control the salmon catch and there is little evidence of any widespread improvement in the stocks on either side of the Atlantic. But in spite of the dismal history of Atlantic salmon conservation over the past century (only a fleeting moment in the total span of existence of this species) chances are excellent that science and technology, and the art of fisheries management have advanced to a point where it is possible, if society chooses, to restore this great resource and preserve the species for posterity. Not only is scientific and technological information available by which to improve the lot of the Atlantic salmon, but international institutions have been developed and tested to the extent that, if there is agreement among nations, effective measures can be initiated, individually and collectively, to rationally manage far-ranging species. In the north Pacific Ocean, the International North Pacific Fisheries Convention between Canada, Japan and the United States should

Table 1 Catch of Atlantic salmon (*Salmo salar*) in north Atlantic waters by north Atlantic countries (× 1,000 tonnes)

	1964	1965	1966	1967	1968	1969	1970	1971	1972	1973	1974	1975	1976
Canada	2·1	2·2	2·4	2·8	2·1	2·0	2·1	1·8	1·5	2·2	2·2	2·2	2·2
Denmark	1·7	2·0	1·7	2·0	2·3	2·0	2·2	1·8	1·6	1·7	1·9	1·8	1·6
The Faeroes	–	–	0·1	0·2	0·1	0·2	0·3	0·2	0·1	0·2	0·1	0·3	0
Greenland	1·5	0·9	1·2	1·3	1·2	1·2	1·3	1·4	1·4	1·6	1·2	1·2	1·2
Finland	0·5	0·3	0·3	0·4	0·5	0·5	0·6	0·5	0·4	0·8	0·8	0·8	0·8
Germany, West	0·3	0·2	0·2	0·2	0·2	0·2	0·2	0·2	0·1	0·1	0·1	0·1	0·1
Iceland	0·2	–	–	0·1	0·1	0·1	0·2	0·2	0·2	0·3	0·2	0·2	0·1
Ireland	1·6	1·5	1·2	1·5	1·4	1·7	1·8	1·5	1·8	1·9	2·1	2·0	1·5
Norway	1·9	1·7	1·6	1·7	1·6	1·3	1·2	1·5	1·8	2·0	1·5	1·5	1·1
Poland	0·4	0·2	0·1	0·1	0·1	0·2	0·1	0·1	0·1	0·1	0·1	0·1	0·1
Sweden	0·7	0·6	0·5	0·5	0·7	0·7	0·6	0·4	0·4	0·7	0·7	0·6	0·6
UK	2·6	2·2	2·3	2·9	2·5	2·1	2·1	1·8	2·0	4·8	3·7	1·8	1·4
USA	0	0	0	0	0	0	0	0	0	0	0	trace	trace
USSR	0·9	0·8	0·8	1·0	1·0	0·5	0·6	0·6	0·6	0·9	1·9	1·3	0·2
Total	14·4	12·6	12·4	14·7	13·8	12·7	13·3	12·0	12·0	17·3	16·5	13·9	10·9

Source: Yearbook of Fishery Statistics, FAO Rome, and International Commission for Northwest Atlantic Fisheries

be a precursor for international salmon agreements, as should the Northwest Pacific Fishery Convention between Japan and the USSR. These Conventions dealt more or less successfully with both the conservation of salmon and the allocation of the surplus among nations and users of salmon. Both Conventions dealt with high seas fishing for salmon, and it appears that both will lead to arrangements that could improve the conservation and management of Pacific salmon in the context of coastal state jurisdiction over fisheries extending to 200 miles.

On the Atlantic coast, ICNAF, the Northeast Atlantic Fisheries Commission, (NEAFC) and the International Council for the Exploration of the Seas (ICES) have played important roles in recent years in co-ordinating Atlantic salmon research efforts and, even more, in initiating efforts to allocate and rationalize fishing for Atlantic salmon throughout the north Atlantic Ocean. These Conventions are also undergoing changes since the nations of the north Atlantic have extended their fisheries jurisdiction.

The recently negotiated Convention for the northwest Atlantic, the 'Convention on Future Mutilateral Co-operation in the Northwest Atlantic Fisheries', explicitly excludes salmon from its terms. Article 1, paragraph 4, reads 'This Convention applies to all fishery resources of the Convention area, with the following exceptions: salmon, tunas and marlins, cetacean stocks managed by the International Whaling Commission or any successor organization, and sedentary species of the continental shelf, *ie* organisms which at the harvestable stage, either are immobile on or under the seabed or the subsoil.'

The fact that nations and groups of nations, such as the European Economic Community, bordering the north Atlantic Ocean have extended fisheries jurisdiction to 200 miles does not negate the need for co-operation and co-ordination among nations to conserve Atlantic salmon and equitably take into account legitimate interest of all states, those in whose waters salmon are produced as well as those in whose waters salmon migrate and feed. The extension of jurisdiction by coastal states provides coastal nations with a basis on which to regulate and control fishing for salmon within the 200-mile zone and also implies an obligation to do so. Still, as experience and research has shown in the north Pacific Ocean, salmon range widely in the ocean searching for food and favourable habitat during their period of ocean life and they are unquestionably found in waters both within and beyond the 200-mile limit and so are vulnerable to ocean fishing. Thus, the conservation of Atlantic salmon is by no means assured at present.

Because Atlantic salmon are so highly migratory, it follows that if the salmon stocks of the north Atlantic are to be conserved, there must be an effective international salmon conservation agreement. Such co-operative international arrangements are encouraged by the current Informal Composite Negotiating Text (ICNT) being considered by the Law of the Sea Conference. Article 66 of the ICNT provides a good basis for developing adequate principles for an agreement. For example, paragraph one of the Article 66 states: 'States in whose rivers anadromous stocks originate shall have the primary interest in and responsibility for such stocks'. The Article also requires the co-operation of nations where salmon from the rivers of one state migrate into or through the waters of another. Both of these principles are particularly important for an effective Atlantic salmon agreement. It must be kept in mind that the Law of the Sea Convention incorporating these concepts is not in effect and there is no assurance that it will be in the foreseeable future.

A new international agreement is suggested
In recent months a number of people in and out of government have suggested the need for a new international agreement governing fishing for salmon. Buck (1977) and John Olin (personal correspondence) among others have expressed such views. Mr Buck specifically suggests a new treaty to take the place of ICNAF. Such a treaty agreement should contain *inter alia* the following principles:

1 There must be general agreement about purposes and specific objectives among nations that produce and use Atlantic salmon. By this I mean that not only the major

north Atlantic salmon producing nations – Canada, Ireland, the United Kingdom, Norway, Sweden and possibly the USSR – must agree, but other salmon-producing nations such as France, Spain and the United States, and the user nations such as Denmark, Ireland, Scotland, England and Norway must also agree on these purposes and objectives.

The objectives of the international Commission for Atlantic Salmon (ICAS) should be to conserve and rehabilitate the Atlantic salmon runs of the north Atlantic Ocean and adjacent waters. An additional important task should be the allocation and control of the total allowable catch (TAC) of Atlantic salmon throughout its range to provide both optimum yield to the salmon-producing nations and fair and controlled access to the traditional salmon fishing nations of the north Atlantic. Also the Convention must permit protection for salmon of producing nations where those salmon migrate and intermingle with salmon from other coastal nations.

In considering the optimum yield from Atlantic salmon, the Commission should examine some of the definitions recently developed by nations (*eg* US Public Law 94-265. The Fishery Conservation and Management Act of 1976). The optimum yield must be based upon the maximum biological yield expected in any one year, modified and taking into account relevant economic and social factors. In addition, the widespread acceptance of the principle of the special interests of the coastal states with respect to anadromous species of fish means that the management of north Atlantic salmon stocks must give the nation of origin the major role in determining the total allowable catch and a favoured, dominant position in allocating it among nations. Such a position is consistent with the current text being considered by United Nations Conference on the Law of the Sea (UNCLOS) and is now incorporated in the laws and regulations governing the salmon catch of some States of the north Atlantic.

The Convention must provide that the country of origin has the primary responsibility for the stock and should in all cases be the major beneficiary of any surplus. In carrying out this concept, nations that are in the process of enhancing their stocks of Atlantic salmon – which involves rather large expenditures of funds – must be given the benefits of these investments and expenditures.

Nations intercepting those enhancing stocks of salmon, insofar as possible, must manage their fisheries so as to avoid intercepting the enhancing stocks. Without agreement on such a principle there will be little incentive for nations at the extremes of the range of migrations of Atlantic salmon such as France, Spain, the USSR, Sweden, Canada, and the United States to continue their outlays of funds for enhancement. The enhancing nation must benefit from its efforts. Enhancement in this context means the sum total of those actions by governments that lead not merely to maintaining the stocks of salmon at their current level but to increasing the abundance of salmon.

2 The area of the north Atlantic and the nations interested in Atlantic salmon must be identitfied. The area should include the waters of the north Atlantic Ocean as far south as those waters adjacent to the United States in the western north Atlantic and as far south as Spain and Portugal in the eastern north Atlantic. The Baltic and Barents Sea in the eastern north Atlantic might be included as would the Davis Strait region of the northwest Atlantic. The Convention area should be divided into logical regions which correspond to the ocean migration patterns of the various stocks of salmon at sea. Panels established within the Commission would correspond to those regions.

3 The membership of the Commission should include all those nations producing or using Atlantic salmon in the north Atlantic Ocean.

4 The functions of the Commission should be to:
  (a) provide for an international institutional framework for the nations of the north Atlantic Ocean within which regional policies and programmes can be developed and carried out to conserve the salmon stocks of the north Atlantic Ocean and provide for the rational allocation and

control of the harvest;

(b) encourage and co-ordinate the rehabilitation and enhancement of Atlantic salmon throughout its range;

(c) establish a standing committee for research and statistics. Many of the Atlantic nations belong to and work with ICES. This excellent organization has done so much to co-ordinate salmon research and the collection of statistics in past years. That work should continue. Still, the special programmes of rehabilitation and enhancement begun by some nations require especially close contact between administrators and scientists. The Research and Statistics Committee should include in addition to biologists and oceanographers, resource-oriented economists, other social scientists, and ecologists to provide the broad background needed to consider all factors involved in achieving the optimum yield from the stocks.

(d) recommend to governments conservation measures for Atlantic salmon based upon the principles discussed in the previous paragraphs and the results of extensive scientific research. Conservation measures must be co-ordinated by the Commission and applied throughout the area and such measures should lead to regulations which will control the catch made by each member nation. The Commission, based upon established criteria, must allocate the total allowable catch for any one season among the member nations. Obviously, this must be done stock by stock and must give full consideration to the special rights of the producing country. The interceptions of salmon bound for one country migrating through the fishing waters of another must be minimized. It would be anticipated that the salmon management plans for any one year would be drafted by the producing state and would be reviewed within the appropriate panel of the Commission before reaching the Commission for final approval.

(e) member nations should be bound by salmon management plans adopted by the Commission and accepted by a majority vote, providing the producing state is in agreement with the plan adopted by the Commission.

(f) all salmon fishing beyond the 12 miles limit in the north Atlantic ocean should be prohibited. This is consistent with Article 66 of the current ICNT of UNCLOS.

(g) national programmes for the rehabilitation and enhancement of salmon stocks should be presented to the Commission through the appropriate panels in order to provide for maximum co-ordination and consideration of the plans for improvement of Atlantic salmon stocks. Member nations should take into account special programmes of salmon-producing states which are designed to rehabilitate and enhance salmon stocks. Such programmes are now being undertaken by many countries.

(h) Not only should the Commission review the national salmon management plans each year, but it should also review the results after the close of the salmon season, in order to measure the effectiveness of the management plans. Such a review will be most helpful in correcting inadequacies in the individual country plans, but in addition, successful programmes and techniques can be more effectively transferred to other producing nations by such a review.

Other provisions *eg* allowing for appropriate financial and staff support for the Commission, must also be included in any such Convention, and appropriate means must be included to ensure the co-operation of the United Nations specialized agencies such as the Food and Agricultural Organization (FAO), the Intergovernmental Oceanographic Commission (IOC) of UNESCO, as well as the ICES. Provisions for international enforcement must be included where necessary in the Convention and the control and enforcement provisions of each nation should be reviewed annually.

We have learned from broad and bitter experience that no international conservation and management plan, particularly one as complex as the one proposed, can succeed if member nations do not adequately control the activities of their fishermen. The success of the programme will depend not only on co-operation and an adequate institutional framework, but also upon adequate scientific research, accurate monitoring of management programmes, and regulation and enforcement of fishing

activities throughout the north Atlantic where salmon
migrate, including the interior waters of each country.

The Commission should encourage and initiate regular
symposia such as this one. Private salmon conservation
groups such as the Atlantic Salmon Research Trust Limited
(ASRT) and the International Atlantic Salmon Foundation
(IASF) should be encouraged by governments to participate in the work of the Commission. An official advisory
committee to the Commission should be established. The
advisory committee should review the salmon management
plans of each country and the results and reports of the
research and statistics committee as well as other information available to them. They should then report indepen-
dently to the Commission before the adoption of management plans by the Commission and its member countries.

Conclusion

As was stated earlier in this paper, the outlook for Atlantic
salmon is not bright. The fresh water habitat of the salmon,
if improving at all, is improving in very few places. Fishing
effort on Atlantic salmon in most areas appears to remain
too high. The international institutions in the north Atlantic which in the past have attempted to foster conservation
of Atlantic salmon, have by and large been eliminated or
made ineffective by recent actions extending jurisdiction of
north Atlantic nations to 200 miles. If concerted action is
not taken by the nations of the north Atlantic, one can
predict the further decline of the salmon resources in most,
if not all, countries.

On the other hand, the extension of jurisdiction by
coastal states provides an opportunity and in fact, an obligation for those states to conserve the fishery resources within
their jurisdiction. By establishing an International Convention for Atlantic Salmon, salmon producing and using
nations of the world can develop rational, co-ordinated
conservation plans. They can co-operate in the rehabilitation and enhancement programmes for salmon. Lastly,
such a convention can provide for the maximum opportunity to rehabilitate, enhance and rationally manage Atlantic

salmon so that all nations, particularly the salmon producing ones, can be assured of achieving a fair return for their
efforts. Science, technology, and an appropriate institutional framework are available by which to accomplish these
goals. The future of the Atlantic salmon depends upon
concerted international action in the immediate future.
One can only conclude that the prudent course is to begin
such action now.

References

BUCK, R A. An American Point of View. *The Field*, 13 October 2 pp.
1977

CARTER, W. *The Greenland and High Seas Atlantic Salmon Fishery.* The 1970
1970   International Atlantic Salmon Foundation.

ELLIS, D V. Pacific Salmon: Management for People. Derek V Ellis.
1977   *Western Geographical Series,* Vol 13, Department of Geography,
        University of Victoria, Victoria, BC. 320 pp.

NETBOY, A. *The Salmon: Their Fight for Survival.* Houghton Mifflin Com-
1973   pany Boston. 613 pp.

UNITED NATIONS. Informal Composite Negotiating Text. *Third Law of*
1977   *the Sea 1977 Conference,* A/Conf 62/WP 10/Corr 2, 20, July 1977.
        198 pp.

US CONGRESS *The Fishery Conservation and Management Act*, Public Law
1976   94–265, 94th Congress, H R 200, 13 April, 31 pp.

3 International law and the United Nations Law of the Sea Conference in relation to Atlantic salmon

A J Aglen, member of the United Kingdom delegation to the UN Law of the Sea Conference

Introduction

The third United Nations Conference on the Law of the Sea recently concluded an extension of its seventh session in New York. But unfortunately we are still some way off establishing a Convention prescribing a new Law of the Sea and cannot yet tell what it will say about salmon. Meanwhile, a number of States have taken the law into their own hands by establishing 200 mile fishery limits within which they claim exclusive jurisdiction over living resources. There have thus been considerable changes in the situation. International law in relation to fisheries is still in a state of flux and one can only speculate on how it will eventually develop.

Although this paper is mainly about Atlantic salmon I shall have to say a little about Pacific salmon, because any new general law of the sea will have to cover Pacific as well as Atlantic salmon and the circumstances relating to the former differ in some respects from those affecting the latter and have an important bearing on the proposals under discussion.

Feeding grounds

It is perhaps a little surprising that in the first half of this century international law seemed to have very little impact on Atlantic salmon (except possibly in the Baltic) although of course it was well known that salmon spent much of their life at sea and put on most of their weight there. Indeed, it was well known that there was a very large loss of salmon at sea, generally reckoned at about 98 percent – that is to say for every 100 smolts going to sea only two would return as adult fish either as grilse weighing perhaps 4½ to 5½ pounds after one winter at sea or as large salmon averaging from 10 to 11 pounds after two or more winters at sea. More recent research has shown that in some cases the rate of return may be 10 percent or more; but still the loss at sea is very high. Very little, however, seems to have been known about the movements of salmon at sea and where their feeding grounds were. Salmon were undoubtedly caught at sea but probably in small numbers because, being generally pelagic, they did not lend themselves to capture by trawls and other gear then in use. Information was scarce in any case because it was generally thought unlucky for trawler-men to speak about salmon. At any rate I do not remember the possibility that salmon might be caught at sea by our own or foreign fishermen giving rise to any concern in this country though it was beginning to be a very live question in relation to other fish found in the sea. The late W J M Menzies hazarded the theory that Scottish salmon might go as far as the west coast of Greenland.

This remained just a theory until in 1956 a salmon was caught off west Greenland that had been tagged as a smolt in the Blackwater in Ross-shire. This discovery did not create much of a stir at the time but did so a few years later when it became known that the catch of Atlantic salmon off the west coast of Greenland had risen sharply from under 100 tons in 1959 to over 1,500 tons in 1964. By then it had been established by further captures of tagged salmon that salmon from both sides of the Atlantic were present in the Greenland fishery and that, as the fish were approaching their second winter at sea, they were likely to be large salmon, not grilse, if they returned to their native rivers. There was considerable alarm in the salmon lobbies of salmon producing countries on both sides of the Atlantic stemming from the fear that unless the Greenland catches were curbed the stock of Atlantic salmon represented by the fish returning to spawn would be greatly reduced, apart altogether from its effect on home water catches. Urgent representations were made in Copenhagen, but Denmark put up a strong resistance, arguing that it was by no means clear that the catch off Greenland had any effect on stocks or home water catches; it might, they said, be part of the very large annual loss at sea already mentioned. So the question was brought before the International Commission for the Northwest Atlantic Fisheries (ICNAF), the body responsible for conservation off west Greenland. At the same time ICNAF joined in 1965 with the International Council for the Exploration of the Sea (ICES) in setting up a joint working party of scientists to elucidate the facts. This working party has since established limits within which a given catch off west Greenland may be expected to affect total stocks and total home water catches in the north Atlantic salmon producing countries.

Closed areas

After four or five years – in 1969 – ICNAF reached an agreement by the necessary two-thirds majority on a recommendation to governments that after 1 January 1972 there should be a ban on fishing for Atlantic salmon in the sea outside national fishery limits (which were then not more than 12 miles). At the same time it endorsed an agreement with Denmark limiting the total annual catch of salmon off west Greenland. The recommended ban was not accepted by some member countries including Denmark and did not become effective. In the following years ICNAF recommended that the catch, or fleet employed in securing it, should be stabilised at the 1969 level and finally put forward again the proposed ban. This time it became effective from the beginning of 1976. On the eastern side of the Atlantic the Northeast Atlantic Fisheries Commission (NEAFC) took similar action. It too recommended in 1969 a ban outside national fishery limits but this did not become effective. After recommending a closed area round the British Isles and closed areas and a closed season to regulate the established fishery outside Norwegian limits, NEAFC repeated its recommended ban as from 1 January 1976 but this never became fully effective.

So the position reached under the auspices of the two international conservation commissions was that international law in relation to Atlantic salmon had been changed. With some exceptions, fishing for salmon outside national fishery limits was generally prohibited throughout the north Atlantic, and limitations had been imposed on the Greenland fishery and the fishery off the Norwegian coast. This was only moderately satisfactory but would have been acceptable if it had slotted into a new and more comprehensive law evolved by the United Nations Law of the Sea Conference. But things haven't worked out that way. A new law has yet to be achieved and in the meanwhile extension of limits to 200 miles by most coastal states in the north Atlantic is bringing about the demise of the two international commissions and the regulations made under them. ICNAF is giving place to Northwest Atlantic Fisheries Organisation (NAFO) whose constitution, however, does not covern salmon; and NEAFC seems to be dying slowly with no prospect of a successor. This adds a new element of urgency to the evolution of a new law.

Third Law of the Sea Conference.
All this occurred under what might be called the old regime. Then came the third UN Law of the Sea Conference. It started formally at the end of 1973 with a short procedural session followed in 1974 by a ten week session in Caracas at which substantive work started. But the Conference had been preceded by a long period of preliminary discussion. It was in 1967 that the General Assembly decided that the question of holding a conference on the general law of the sea should be studied and the task was given to a preparatory committee already considering problems concerning the exploitation of minerals on and under the sea bed. This preparatory committee – generally known as the Sea Bed Committee – had its remit and membership enlarged and over a period of six years did much useful work. It did not attempt to draft a new law but it opened up the numerous ramifications of the subject and its report persuaded the General Assembly that there were grounds for hoping that a conference, if convened, would be successful.

I will not attempt any detailed examination of the motives

and aspirations of those countries which thought a general conference would be beneficial; but I think it is germane to look at some of the considerations that bear more directly on fisheries. One of the main motivations for the Conference was certainly the radical notion that the resources of the oceans were the common heritage of mankind and ought to be managed and exploited in such a way that all mankind, but particularly the developing world, could share in them. To this end, limits of national jurisdiction should be kept narrow and freedom of fishing on the high seas beyond should give place to internationally regulated operations under which the wealth of the seas could be more fairly shared thereby bringing to an end what some regarded as the ravages of powerful distant water fleets. On the other hand, there were undoubtedly some countries which saw a conference as a means of preserving the *status quo* with narrow territorial and fishery limits and continued freedom of fishing beyond. There were yet others which had quite different notions. Several Latin American countries had claimed in the early 50's, and since maintained, limits of 200 miles for fisheries and other resources and in the run-up to the Conference this idea was propagated in a series of regional meetings in central America and elsewhere. By the time the Caracas session of the Conference started in 1974 it was clear that there was very wide support for the idea of 200 mile zones in which the coastal state would have complete control over living and other resources. I avoid saying overwhelming support for there was, and still is, a number of countries, the so-called landlocked and geographically disadvantaged states which have not accepted the rights of such wide exclusive zones. It was clear nevertheless that a 200 mile exclusive economic zone would be an essential component of any convention commanding majority support.

Outside the Conference the idea gained ground quickly and in the following years most countries in the north Atlantic with worthwhile offshore fish stocks had intimated their intention of declaring 200 mile limits without waiting for the outcome of the Conference. The United Kingdom along with the rest of the EEC joined in, more or less in self-defence, since it was pretty clear that we were likely to lose fishing opportunities off other countries and that otherwise excluded countries would concentrate on the waters round our coasts.

Meanwhile, in the Conference, texts were beginning to take shape. At Caracas a document was produced setting out draft articles reflecting the main trends of opinion on each item – sometimes two diametrically opposed in content, sometimes more than two. After discussions in Geneva the following year a single informal negotiating text was produced as a basis for further discussion. This text, the SNT, was considered in New York in 1976 and a revised version, the RSNT, was produced. This in turn was considered in 1977 after which a third text, the Informal Composite Negotiating Text (ICNT), was produced. This text incorporated amendments in the earlier texts and brought together into one document the three parts into which earlier drafts had been divided. This ICNT has been the basis of discussion at the seventh session this year. It has 303 articles, divided into sixteen parts, plus seven annexes.

Exclusive economic zones
the latest text, the ICNT, they are Articles 61 to 73. The main provisions, Articles 61 and 62, give the coastal state more than 200 miles from the base lines from which the breadth of the territorial sea is measured. The articles dealing with fisheries in the EEZ have undergone little change in the three editions of the texts except in numbering and in the latest text, the ICNT, they are Articles 61 to 73. The main provisions, Articles 61 and 62, give the coastal state complete control over the living resources in its EEZ, responsibility for conservation and management including the fixing of the allowable catch, and also responsibility for determining its own catching capacity coupled with an obligation to promote optimum utilization and to grant to other countries access to any surplus of the allowable catch over its own catching capacity. Where stocks occur in more than one zone or move seasonally from one zone to another the coastal states concerned are required to consult together on conservation and allowable catches: and there

is a similar obligation on the coastal state to consult other states interested when stocks move from their EEZ in the high seas beyond. These basic provisions are very favourable to coastal states for most species of sea fish; for example, where a state has sufficient catching capacity it can reserve the whole of the allowable catch to itself. By themselves, however, these provisions are not good for species like salmon which are peculiar in two respects: (a) because they are very dependent for their welfare and success on the coastal state in whose waters they breed, the state of origin, and (b) because of their habit of migrating over long distances into or through the EEZ of other coastal states. It was felt that it would not be sufficient in such circumstances to rely on the general obligation on coastal states to consult and that some special provision would be needed. In a general convention it would not be appropriate to have special provisions relating to one group such as salmon – let alone Atlantic salmon – and the successive texts I have mentioned have all included an article dealing with anadromous stocks, fish which breed in fresh water and migrate to sea. There is a number of such species but as far as I know the migratory habits of most of them do not give rise to the problems presented by salmon. In effect, therefore, the Article in question is designed to deal only with salmon. Below is the Article as it appears as number 66 in the ICNT.

Article 66 Anadromous stocks
1. States in whose rivers anadromous stocks originate shall have the primary interest in and responsibility for such stocks.
2. The State of origin of anadromous stocks shall ensure their conservation by the establishment of appropriate regulatory measures for fishing in all waters landwards of the outer limit of its exclusive economic zone and for fishing provided for in sub-paragraph 3. The State of origin may, after consultation with other States referred to in paragraphs 3 and 4 fishing these stocks, establish total allowable catches for stocks originating in its rivers.
3. (a) Fisheries for anadromous stocks shall be conduc-

ted only in the waters landwards of the outer limits of exclusive economic zones, except in cases where this provision would result in economic dislocation for a State other than the State of origin.

(b) The State of origin shall co-operate in minimizing economic dislocation in such other States fishing these stocks, taking into account the normal catch and the mode of operation of such States, and all the areas in which such fishing has occurred.

(c) States referred to in sub-paragraph (b), participating by agreement with the State of origin in measures to renew anadromous stocks, particularly by expenditures for that purpose, shall be given special consideration by the State of origin in the harvesting of stocks originating in its rivers.

(d) Enforcement of regulations regarding anadromous stocks beyond the exclusive economic zone shall be by agreement between the State of origin and the other States concerned.

4. In cases where anadromous stocks migrate into or through the waters landwards of the outer limits of the exclusive economic zone of a State other than the State of origin, such State shall co-operate with the State of origin, with regard to the conservation and management of such stocks.

5. The State of origin of anadromous stocks and other States fishing these stocks shall make arrangements for the implementation of the provisions of this article, where appropriate, through regional organizations.'

Pacific salmon

This Article looks rather involved and it has given rise to some difficulty mainly because of the position in the Pacific and I should therefore say a little about the situation in that ocean. There are five main species of Pacific salmon. Some of the species are good sporting fish – though I believe inferior to Atlantic salmon – and most of them produce very large spawning runs, exploitation of which provides the raw materials for canneries and other plants. Canada,

USA, and the USSR are the main producers, or states of origin, of the salmon though Japan produces increasing quantities from fish farms. All four Countries are large catchers and share the total catch which runs into hundreds of thousands of tonnes (compared with a total of between 12,000 and 15,000 tonnes for Atlantic salmon), as the following figures from the FAO Year Book of Statistics show:

Table 1 Pacific salmon catch (tonnes)

	1971	1972	1973	1974	1975
Northwest Pacific (FAO statistical area 61[1])					
Japan	132,900	117,400	131,900	129,536	162,138
USSR	82,300	33,430	76,700	48,000	103,044
	215,200	150,830	208,600	177,536	265,182
Northeast Pacific (FAO statistical area 67[2])					
Canada	63,200	76,700	86,300	63,395	36,355
USA	147,900	103,800	95,100	87,055	89,723
	211,100	180,500	181,400	150,450	126,078
Total, north Pacific	426,300	331,330	390,000	327,986	391,260
Atlantic salmon – Total	12,000	12,300	14,900	14,572	14,113

[1]excluding relatively small quantities caught in internal waters
[2]excluding small quantities caught in internal waters and statistical area 77

As will be seen the Japanese are usually the largest catchers of Pacific salmon and all four Countries have kept to their own side of the Pacific. You may wonder why this is so in the case of Japan with its large mobile fleet. The explanation is that under the principle of abstention embodied in the International North Pacific Fisheries Convention they have not fished east of 175°W longitude (which roughly divides the north Pacific in half). In the northeast Pacific there are very large concentrations of salmon returning to Alaskan or Canadian rivers. These concentrations, well outside former national fishery limits and even beyond the new 200 mile limits, would have been vulnerable to the highly efficient Japanese long line fleet had they been able to fish there. As it was the Japanese catch has come mainly from salmon of USSR origin though doubtless they have also caught fish of Canadian or American origin which migrate, presumably in less dense shoals, across the meridian of 175°W. The catching of the salmon of Soviet origin has been regulated by bilateral agreements between Japan and the USSR.

Main purposes of Article 66

Now I will turn to Article 66 again. In considering it you must remember two important points. First that this Article is supplementary to Articles 61 and 62 which give the coastal state wide powers over all living resources in its EEZ including any salmon that happen to be there. Second that only some 15 states among the 150 participating in the Conference are directly involved in salmon either as producers or catchers; there would be little hope of securing a two-thirds majority in favour of a salmon article unless the fifteen countries found it acceptable.

Paragraph 1 of Article 66 gives the states in which salmon spawn the primary interest in and responsibility for stocks originating in their rivers. Many would have preferred this to go further and give the state of origin complete and exclusive responsibility; but in cases where salmon migrate into the EEZ of other states – as UK salmon do – this would have been in sharp conflict with the exclusive powers of the coastal state of that EEZ and in any case would have been quite unacceptable to Denmark. For the same reason paragraph 2 gives the state of origin the duty of ensuring the conservation of the stocks not over the whole range of migration of the stock but only in its own waters and for fishing permitted under paragraph 3(b). This must however be read with paragraph 4 which enjoins the coastal state of an EEZ into which salmon migrate to co-operate with the state of origin with regard to conservation and management. Paragraph 2 goes on to give the state of origin power to fix a total allowable catch for salmon originating in its rivers but only after consultation with other states fishing these stocks.

Paragraph 3 is perhaps the nub of the Article. Sub-paragraph (a) in effect prohibits fishing for salmon in the sea outside the limits of EEZ except where this would result in economic dislocation for a state other than the state of origin. The thought behind this is of course, that if a state has not been fishing in an area it would not be able to start doing so because the prohibition could hardly cause economic dislocation: on the other hand where a state has been fishing in an area now outside EEZ it might continue to do so subject to the later sub-paragraphs which imply that they will do so in agreement with the state of origin and having regard among other things to their previous fishing record.

In this very brief résumé I have tried to direct attention to the main provisions of the draft Article. You may well think that it is far from satisfactory from the point of view of salmon producing countries. I agree that from their point of view it would have been better simply to provide that salmon may not be caught outside the EEZ of their State of origin, giving that State the sole responsibility for their conservation and management and the sole right of exploitation. But that would not have been acceptable to all the countries interested in salmon and therefore unlikely to fulfil the requirements mentioned earlier for acceptance by the Conference. A compromise was accordingly necessary and article 66 was aimed at securing this.

Amendments to draft Article 66
The Article in the form reproduced has survived two revisions of the negotiating texts with only minor drafting amendments. It was acceptable to most salmon producing countries and to Japan and Denmark. But the USSR was never very happy about it as regards the Pacific and felt that, whereas it seemed to give adequate protection to Canada and the USA, it did not sufficiently protect Soviet interests. In 1976 they put forward a series of amendments which seemed to us ill-conceived, and considerable effort was devoted to trying to find alternative wording acceptable to the USSR and to all the others. After about a dozen informal meetings during the 1977 and 1978 sessions agreement was eventually reached on two amendments to the draft Article as follows:

In paragraph 2, second sentence, insert 'referred to in

paragraphs 3 and 4' before 'fishing these stocks'; and in paragraphs 3 (a) add a second sentence reading 'With respect to such fishing beyond the outer limits of the exclusive economic zone states concerned shall maintain consultations with a view to achieving agreement on terms and conditions of such fishing giving the due regard to the conservation requirements and needs of the State of origin in respect of these stocks'.

These amendments were duly reported to the appropriate committee of the Conference whose chairman reported them to Plenary as having been agreed. Unexpectedly, however, objections were raised by Belgium for reasons quite unconnected with salmon. So the article as amended cannot yet be regarded as in the bag.

Uncertainties

Nor for that matter is a convention with or without an Article 66. I do not want to give the impression that nothing has been achieved by the Conference. On the contrary, a lot of useful work has been done, but to bring it to fruition several hard nuts have to be cracked. And here I must depart from descriptive fact and resort to some speculation and I hope that in doing so I shall not be too confusing. There are several uncertainties. One is whether an accommodation can be reached on the regime of the sea bed between the developing world which wants control and the industrialized world which has the know-how for exploitation. The extended seventh session concentrated largely on this question but it is not yet resolved. If this hurdle cannot be surmounted there must be a prospect of no new convention or a convention which is not comprehensive either in adherents or content.

A comprehensive convention or one dealing with the non sea bed issues might well include something like the fisheries articles in the ICNT, but that may be dependent on an accommodation being reached with the landlocked and geographically disadvantaged states. Much time has been spent on this issue without so far settling it. I would think, however, that Article 66 dealing with anadromous stocks would survive unless it falls victim to some quirk of international politics.

There is, however, another uncertainty so far as the United Kingdom and other members of the EEC are concerned. As you will know most aspects of fisheries are now within the competence of the European Community and not of member states. It follows that the obligations laid on coastal states and the responsibilities conferred by a new convention in relation to fisheries do not appertain to the member states but to the Community and then only if the Community is a party to the Convention. A clause has been put forward to secure this but so far it has not been discussed. Apart from this potential snag there is further uncertainty arising from the development of the Community's competence in fisheries which may involve it taking a larger interest in salmon. The permitted take in Greenland waters is already a matter for the Community rather than member states. The Community in fact has already made a fisheries agreement with Canada which in relation to salmon borrows both from the draft Article 66 of the ICNT and from the ICNAF regulations. Both parties agree that salmon should not be caught beyond the limits of national fisheries jurisdiction and on the limitation of the catch in west Greenland waters – 1,190 tonnes for 1978 and 1979. This factor might appear to make Article 66 less relevant to the United Kingdom because Greenland is in the EEC and the Community therefore has jurisdiction over our salmon in Greenland waters; but it will still be of some relevance since our salmon mix with Canadian and American salmon in Greeland waters. Moreover they may go into The Faeroes EEZ and The Faeroes are not yet in the Community.

Against this background I cannot, unhappily, be at all definite about the future: but I think there are grounds for not being unduly worried. Either there will be a new convention covering fisheries to which the Community and its member states are parties, or there will not, for the reasons I have mentioned or some other. Either way, however, I think 200 mile fishery zones are here to stay though their legal status and the precise regime within them may depend to some extent on the outcome of the Law of the Sea

Conference. If there is an applicable convention my guess is that it will contain something like the draft Article 66; in the Atlantic that would confine fishing for salmon to the 200 mile zones and so conservation and management of the catch outside our shores would be a matter for the Community and other countries concerned. If there is no convention the position might conceivably not be very different, at least for Atlantic salmon or perhaps I should say UK salmon. For my hunch is that the 200 mile zones in the north Atlantic cover such a significant part of it that there would be little likelihood of sizeable fisheries for salmon – or at least UK salmon – developing outside them; if so, management would again be a matter for the Community and other States concerned. But I confess that I am not sure about salmon of Canadian, American and possibly Norwegian origin; and the position in the Pacific would be quite difficult.

I do not underestimate the difficulties involved in multi-national discussions either inside or outside the EEC to fix the permitted catch of salmon off Greenland or elsewhere. But that in essence is the situation we have lived with for nearly ten years and our stocks and catches have survived. I hope history will not prove me too optimistic.

4 Discussion

*R A Buck (Restoration of Atlantic Salmon in America, Inc)
opened the discussion as follows*

No fisheries problem is more difficult politically than that of salmon, which travel through the territorial seas and fisheries jurisdictions of States other than the State of origin. National and regional considerations of self-interest conflict, causing severe social and economic disruptions. Thus, the most urgent problems affecting management today are political rather than ones of science. It is in this political arena, then, that *Salmo salar's* struggle for survival must be engaged – and now.

We have comprehensive understanding of contemporary problems of interception and exploitation of Atlantic salmon in the ocean. Present regimes are ineffectual and incapable of protecting the species. We must define and activate a relevant and urgent programme of change – new directions, new dimensions, new disciplines.

Implementation of the principle of 'river harvest' calls for just such a programme of change. The concept of limiting the harvest of Atlantic salmon to river areas is not new. Proper management techniques require that harvesting of salmon takes place only at the mouths of streams or in the streams themselves. Only in this fashion can adequate stocks be maintained for each particular river run.

The objective of river harvest is to minimize international and regional interception and exploitation. Atlantic salmon would be taken, either by commercial nets or by angling, only at the mouths of rivers or in the rivers themselves. River harvest offers the best means of control of escapement for spawning.

River harvest would relieve tensions between nations over fisheries, because it permits passage of migrating Atlantic salmon to home waters. It would be a permanent solution to the long standing, and previously condoned, practice of one nation intercepting another nation's stocks. Endorsement by Atlantic salmon producing nations of the principle of river harvest will not come easily. Many salmon fisheries, whether drift netting or with fixed engines on headlands, are traditional, inherited from generation to generation. It will be argued that to relocate and limit netting to river areas only would require relocation of families, or elimination from the fishery.

Implementation of this discipline also involves economic considerations, and must be undertaken only on a long-term phasing-out basis, with just compensation to those adversely affected. The cost of such rescue missions will be relatively small compared with the long-term economic benefits. Certainly, the single most important contribution to come out of this Symposium would be a dedication to an early and steady conversion to river harvest.

The campaign for river harvest is already under way. It is endorsed by the leading salmon organizations but many more conservation groups must be added, on both sides of the Atlantic. Specifically, we should not only endorse the principle, but also formally register our request with our own governments for action to implement it now. And, in order to be effective, we have to generate a ground swell of public opinion, education and action.

The role of government here is also clear. Wide-ranging species like the Atlantic salmon, which migrate through the fisheries zones of coastal states other than the state of origin, require the same types of special international regimes that have been set up for the tunas and the whales.

Yet Atlantic salmon are not only trans-national, but often multi-national, in some cases visiting the waters of five nations. These interchanges, and the fact that different races intermingle off Greenland, are reason enough for joint action by all nations. The immediate objective of governments therefore has to be the negotiation of a multi-lateral treaty, between the salmon producing nations and

nations interested in harvesting the species. Under the
organization set up by such a convention, an Atlantic Salmon Commission would adopt proposals for joint action by
signatory nations with respect to conservation, recreational
management and optimum utilization.

It is not expected that the Commission would propose an
immediate cessation of all netting other than riverine netting. A first priority, however, should be a proposal calling
for the long-term phasing out of coastal and drift netting.
Such a proposal could include reasonable quotas, during
the phase-out towards river harvest, for the taking of Atlantic salmon along headlands and in ocean areas where drift
netting has been traditional.

Here then, under a multilateral treaty, governmental
agencies and conservation organizations, working
together, will have undertaken a committment to river harvest – the programme of change so desperately needed if
Salmo salar is to mean anything of importance to future
generations.

*G H F Chaldecott (Chairman of Local Fishery Recreation and
Amenity Advisory Committee, Welsh Water Authority)* said that
whatever may be the justification for Sir Richard's satisfactory picture of salmon runs in Scotland the situation in
southwest Wales can only be described as bad. The problem
is complex and there is no single ill. He hopes to discover
solutions to some of the problems during the Symposium.

*D J Iremonger (Fisheries Manager, Northumbrian Water
Authority)* said that he was the person in charge of the
Northumberland drift net fishery who claimed that the
fishery was well under control. Licences are limited and
permanent sea patrols are carried out by the Authority.
Northumberland fishermen caught about 40,000 fish
compared with 400,000 in Scotland. Drift net fishing in the
North Sea out to the six mile limit will not be stopped unless
statistics show it was imperilling the runs of salmon. This is
not the case, so Mr Iremonger recommended that we concentrate on better controls by sea patrols, *etc* with more
emphasis on enforcement in all areas. There are good
relations with the commercial fishermen who are basically

conservation minded and conscious of their responsibilities.

Lord Home took the view that the Law of the Sea Conference brought out the worst in everyone but welcomed Mr
Aglen's comments on the suggested special international
convention for the Atlantic salmon.

A J Aglen in reply to Lord Home stressed the importance
of having a widely supported convention within the terms
of Article 66 of the Law of the Sea, rather than one which
covered only the 15 or so nations concerned with Atlantic
salmon. If action is to be effective it should be within the
framework of the Law of the Sea.

*Dr E C Egidius (Institute of Marine Research, Bergen, Nor-
way)* pointed out that Norwegian salmon fishing organizations were not represented at the Symposium and said that
the questions raised were somewhat outside her field. In
Norway difficulties arise because the salmon comes within
the jurisdiction of two Government departments; that concerned with the sea fisheries and that with the inland
fisheries. Until these problems are resolved, Norway might
find difficulty entering into international obligations on the
lines suggested. Legal drift netting and illegal fishing of
salmon is highly controversial in Norway today and arguments between drift netters and river owners as to who is
solely responsible for the decline in the salmon fisheries
have been intense.

D L McKernan commenting on D J Iremonger's remarks,
said that control should be exercised over the whole path of
the salmon. He was less attracted to a total ban on drift net
salmon fishing than to a sensible degree of co-operation
between all parties concerned. Conservationists now have
the tools to do much better than in the past.

L Stewart (Salmon and Trout Association) asked how could
international control be enforced and would there be an
international agreement to prohibit the sale of salmon.

Sir Richard in reply stated it was difficult even to control
salmon sales within certain national limits, the ingenuity of
the poacher being unbelievable. A total ban on the sale of
salmon being extremely unlikely at present.

R O M Williams (Salmon and Trout Association) questioned

Mr Iremonger's statement of strict control on the North-umberland drift net fishery for three reasons. The existence of this legal fishery gives rise to a complaint of unfair treatment by Scottish illegal driftnetters, it provided Scottish drift netters with legal cover for disposing of illegally caught fish, and drift netting is a dangerous method of taking salmon, causing injury and disease to the many which escape from the nets.

J Power (Department of Fisheries and Forestry, Ireland) said that references made to the escalation of drift net fishing in Irish waters may have given the impression that the responsible fishery authority was unconcerned and inactive in regard to the problem. This is not so. The Irish salmon fisheries are tightly controlled and regulated. The difficulties have arisen from illegal fishing rather than from official policies. As to illegal fishing, the Boards of Conservators and the Department of Fisheries and Forestry were doing their utmost to stamp out all illegal fishing practices.

A W May (Department of Fisheries and Environment of Canada) added that there appears to be some misconception about the Canadian commercial fisheries. For the past six years there have been no drift nets in Canada; however, there is a possibility of limited reintroduction. At the moment, 6,000 fishermen are licensed to fish with set nets and salmon are taken incidentally in nets fished for other species. The total commercial catch approximates four million lbs. Entry to the commercial fishery has been frozen for some years. Since Canadian salmon fisheries are scattered over hundreds of miles of coastline, in hundreds of communities, and since very few commercial fishermen operate in rivers and estuaries, the Canadian authorities are likely to have difficulty in accepting a concept which would restrict fishing.

Sir Richard then posed a question to Dr May asking whether there were no drift nets off the Canadian coast. Dr May replied that all the nets were set nets.

Y Harache (Centre Océanologique de Bretagne) said that drift nets are not feasible off the French coast so they are not a problem at present.

J D Kelsall (North West Water Authority) noted that Dr

Stewart referred in general terms to the problem of enforcement in relation to international agreements, conventions, *etc*. Further, Sir Richard had mentioned the success story of the phasing out of the high-seas fishery in the Davis Strait. With particular local reference to that achievement, Mr Kelsall asked if Sir Richard could say whether there is any physical enforcement presence in that large remote Arctic area to ensure that this particular agreement is being properly honoured?

Sir Richard then replied that he did not know how the regulations in question were enforced.

G H F Chaldecott (Welsh Water Authority) pointed out that the saving of kelts is important for the future stocks of rivers and that it has been little understood. On the subject of rivers in Greenland he wished to know if they could be developed for salmon. (He was informed that there were few rivers in Greenland and that they held negligible stocks of salmon. There was no prospect of serious development.)

D Lank (Atlantic Salmon Association) said that there may be no drift net fishing for salmon in Canada but that large numbers are taken in cod and sea nets generally which have the same effect. He claimed that internal squabbling between various government agencies, anachronistic privilege and abuse by defenders of native people's rights are the politics of salmon. Bad as they are in themselves, they become horrific when coupled with man's apparently innate refusal to heed the biological warning signs until the brink has been reached. Without co-operation of all groups on national levels, and without a decided change in public attitudes, international agreements in whatever form they take will remain little more than an exercise in conscience salving.

1 Commercial fishing – the netsman's view

W Hardy, Fisheries Organization Society Limited

Introduction

In England and Wales all of Her Majesty's subjects have the right to take fish from tidal waters; all kinds of fish except the royal fish – the sturgeon.

There are, however, exceptions. A large number of privately owned fisheries exist in tidal waters, established before Magna Carta, and several fisheries have the right to take all kinds of fish, including the Royal fish. These fisheries are found in most of the Water Authority areas in England and Wales and can be bought or sold as freehold or leasehold properties.

Fishing for salmon and trout with nets and other instruments is controlled by bye-laws which spell out the duration of the annual close season, weekly close period, dimensions and specifications of nets and instruments, and the method under which they operate. Nets and other instruments are, of course, also subject to licence duty.

Fisheries acts

Much ignorance and misunderstanding surrounds the use of fixed engines for the taking of salmon and migratory trout. However, section 11 of the 1923 Salmon and Freshwater Fisheries Act clearly lays down their lawful usage. Section 6 of the 1975 Act is not so clear. The omission of the words 'Salmon and Migratory Trout' give a wrong impression but the Act itself must surely be self explanatory. Fixed engines used for the taking of salmon and trout cannot be operated as a public right. They can only be operated as a private right which means in effect that members of the public cannot use fixed engines for the taking of salmon and migratory trout, and the Water Authorities cannot issue them with a licence to do so.

The Minister of Agriculture, Fisheries and Food, may, however, confirm an order made by a Water Authority to legalize a limited number of fixed nets for the taking of salmon and migratory trout for ten year periods. These orders apply to 'T' nets on the northeast coast in particular.

Water Authorities may limit the number of licences for the taking of salmon and trout with any instrument in any part of their area. By and large the limitation orders in force in every Water Authority area in England and Wales now limit the fishing effort to one third of what it was fifty years ago.

Parliament has given Water Authorities the right to control defined areas for carrying out their fisheries functions. These are spelt out in the Salmon and Freshwater Fisheries Act 1975, and cover salmon, trout, freshwater fish and eels. Water Authorities have no jurisdiction over sea fish, unless authority is given to them by the Ministry of Agriculture, Fisheries and Food.

In recent years, nets in tidal rivers, estuaries, and on the high seas have increased in numbers. For the so-called purpose of taking sea fish, no licence is required to operate such nets and no close season or weekly close time exists. Even though the nets are operating in Water Authority areas they have control only over migratory fish. Large numbers of salmon and trout are being taken illegally by sea nets and in some areas the nets operate in waters where there are little or no sea fish.

This situation must be brought under control and Water Authorities should be given *some form of jurisdiction over all species* in tidal rivers and estuaries within their defined area.

If it was right for Parliament to enact legislation to control the number of nets and other instruments for the taking of salmon and trout in rivers and estuaries in England and Wales, what is wrong in controlling similarly the nets and other instruments for the taking of sea fish?

Control of rod licences

The number of nets and other instruments which may be lawfully licensed to take salmon and migratory fish is now rigidly controlled but there is no power to control the number of rod salmon and trout licences. In some areas the number of salmon and trout anglers have reached saturation point and immediate control is necessary. At present, Water Authorities cannot refuse an applicant for a rod licence to fish for salmon and trout, irrespective of whether or not he or she has the right to fish. It is known that in many areas licences are taken out by persons for the express purpose of using them as a cloak to cover up poaching activities, some of which are carried out with some of the most horrible devices man could perfect.

Bye-laws in force in all Water Authority areas demand a true return of salmon and trout taken by licensed netsmen and rodsmen, or a nil return that no fish have been taken. During the last decade there has been one hundred percent return by the netsmen but only a thirty five percent return from the rodsmen in England and Wales, despite the fact that hundreds of letters are sent out annually reminding anglers of their obligation to comply with the bye-laws. By and large the majority of anglers refuse to co-operate. Only recently one of the Water Authorities has clearly stated that licensed netsmen and rodsmen do not send in true returns of the salmon and trout they have taken, and the Authority is therefore unable to assess the value of Fisheries.

Some riparian owners and occupiers of game fisheries are no more than stumbling blocks to Water Authority fisheries officers and their staff, who have a duty to maintain, improve and develop fisheries and find difficulty in gaining the co-operation they need. Some maintain their waters are valuable game fisheries, when, in fact, it is known that the waters hold no such potential and would be better suited for other species. It is sometimes alleged that game fisheries are heavily rated by Local Authorities, but in many cases it is established that such fisheries carry no rateable value and never have been subject to rates.

It is the duty of fishery owners and occupiers of private fisheries to remove all unauthorized persons taking fish from their waters and they may prosecute offenders under the Theft Act. River inspectors employed by Water Authorities cannot remove unauthorised people unless they are breaking the law. Riparian owners and occupiers of inland waters who live long distances from their waters cannot protect them. Poaching in the manner I have already described will escalate unless some practicable solution is achieved. Water Authorities should be given the power to investigate game fisheries, determine their suitability, and to establish ownership of them, in addition to regulating the purpose and manner in which such fisheries are operated.

The Bledisloe Committee was set up in 1957 with terms of reference to review the Salmon and Freshwater Fisheries Act 1923, the River Boards Act 1948 and to make recommendations thereon. Strong evidence was placed before the Bledisloe Committee that all non-tidal rod fishing waters should be vested in the River Boards. The committee did not share this view and recommended that such waters should remain in private ownership. They also recommended that commercial salmon fishing should continue as it was producing valuable food for the nation. It did not follow that the curtailment of netting would bring more fish to the salmon and trout angler.

With all the pressures at present on the Atlantic salmon, *ie* lawful licensed nets and illegal nets as well as the illegal taking of fish in inland waters, there has been no marked detrimental effect on the stocks in England and Wales. By and large during this season, many rivers have had the best spring salmon fishing for the past ten years.

Among all those who have an interest in this important matter, full discussion and urgent consideration should be given to controlling the illegal taking of salmon and trout.

2 The angler's viewpoint

R O M Williams, Salmon and Trout Association

Early angling experience

As an angler, I can truthfully say that fish have fascinated me throughout my life from the time when I paddled in the burn with a net to the day when I was first shown glistening rows of fresh salmon in the fish-house of one of the finest beats on the Dee. As a boy I had little opportunity to fish for salmon but had ample trout-fishing experience in the burns of the Kingdom of Fife. By the outbreak of the war, I had only caught three salmon – one on the Tay, one while trout-fishing on the Deveron and one in County Kerry. The instinctive quick strike which is habitual for the river trout-fisher is a fatal mistake when one rises a salmon to fly, and it took me until some years after the war before I learnt that one should, metaphorically, change gear when salmon-fishing and conduct affairs in the more deliberate fashion appropriate to the larger quarry. By about 1960 I was gaining opportunities of reasonable salmon-fishing, curbing my excited reactions and catching modest numbers of fish annually.

Depletion of stocks

You may remember that in 1961 and 1962 destructive drift netting spread from south of the border to rear its ugly head off our east coast and shortly thereafter ulcerative dermal necrosis (UDN) began to afflict Scottish salmon already suffering the inroads of the Greenland fishery. Of these, the angler on Scottish rivers saw only indirect evidence of netting in the reduced numbers of spring fish. But the real shock to me was the spectacle of hundreds of dead and dying fish in the Tweed during the autumns of the middle sixties. My serious salmon-fishing in Scotland therefore began at a time when post-war legislation and conservation measures were having effect and, particularly on the Dee and the North Esk, I was fishing water well stocked with salmon. Drift netting and disease radically changed that happy state of affairs, and in the later sixties it became much more difficult to catch salmon. Perseverance, which is the salmon angler's most useful attribute, became of even greater importance. One came to realise the truth of the saying that for satisfactory angling a river must hold an ample stock of healthy fish. As an old ghilly used to say: 'It's sair work if they'll no' take, but it's waur still if they're no' there'.

During this period also the pattern of salmon angling underwent considerable change, principally due to social and economic circumstances. The salmon has always been held in very high esteem both for the sport it provides and for the table, and the cost of salmon angling rapidly increased resulting from both the high price obtainable for the fish itself and the social kudos attached to the sport. In other countries where conservation measures were not operated so actively as in Scotland and industrial developments with consequent pollution grew more rapidly, salmon angling acquired an exceptional scarcity value and as a result Scotland was caught in this sporting rat race. I understand that in almost all continental countries except Norway salmon angling is either non-existent or severely limited and much the same is happening both south of the border and across the Irish Sea. Because of these trends, coupled with the weakness of British currency and the growth in fashion of salmon angling as a peculiarly rewarding sport, Scottish supply is coming under ever increasing pressure from non-Scottish demand. Added to this is the all pervading influence of inflation, and we have a situation where the cost of Scottish salmon beats, whether to rent or to purchase, has reached staggering proportions. Fortunately, for some of us, there are still proprietors who favour the angler who fishes purely for sport, and either invite rods to fish and hand in what they catch, or rent their beats without letting to the highest bidder, and even some who will lease water to angling clubs at totally uneconomic rents. In present times of penal taxation it is difficult to see how proprietors can continue these practices, and we are likely to see salmon beats fall even more into the hands of those who regard them from a purely commercial point of view, seek the highest rents obtainable and impose no restrictions on the methods of fishing or numbers of fish caught. This in turn has bred a new type of tenant who seeks to catch all he can by any means, sell his catch to cover the rent and even show a profit on the whole operation. What is essentially a sport is becoming more of a financial lottery, from which as usual the Inland Revenue and the rates-collector take their pickings.

So now in Scotland as elsewhere we face a situation where man is harrying our native salmon-stocks by every possible means, legal and illegal. On the high seas the net and line fisheries, mainly exercised by nationals whose countries have no salmon rivers of their own, seem fortunately to have been subjected to some form of control. Nearer home we have a recrudescence of the destructive drift net fishery which in the early 'sixties threatened to decimate the homing Scottish salmon. Finally, the fish run the gauntlet of the coastal nets and encounter increasing numbers of anglers, some of whom regrettably are better described as fishmongers, not to mention the gangs of poachers using nets, explosives, poison and even spearguns. In addition to these man-made threats we have nature's predators, the seals, cormorants and others and, finally, the sinister salmon disease known as UDN.

The 1978 picture
In the face of all these destructive factors it is a miracle that there are still salmon running our Scottish rivers; in fact 1978 has shown a distinct improvement in these runs against all the odds. When I am asked for some explanation for this fortunate reprieve for the salmon-angler I go back more than a century to the Scottish statutes of 1862 and 1868 and the Tweed Acts. Our far-seeing ancestors, faced

with threats which were nothing to those of today, prepared a legislative framework which has stood the test of time. In particular it set up the District Salmon Fishery Boards of Scotland by which this legislation could be administered. The essential feature of this system was the combination of fishery interest, net and rod, and it is that combination which in recent years has kept the poachers at sea in check and has operated hatcheries and cleared obstacles in the rivers. In general it has succeeded in conserving the Scottish salmon stocks. The system needs modernization but it is tragic that no government has yet implemented the recommendations of the Hunter Report which stressed the paramount value of the rod-caught salmon to the Scottish economy. However, if those of us salmon anglers lucky enough to enjoy sport in 1978 owe thanks to anyone it is to the successive members and staffs of the District Boards, the officials of the Department of Fisheries, and the responsible netsmen and fishery proprietors who have exercised forebearance and taken the long view. Dedication and moderation have characterized the management of Scottish salmon fisheries but this attitude may not continue if management was to fall into the gaping maw of bureaucracy.

Whether this year's improvement is a flash in the pan or the turning point for Scottish salmon stocks seems to depend very much on continued and improved co-operation between the established netsmen and the angling interests. Both have the same objective, the conservation and improvement of our Scottish salmon stocks, and both must eschew any temptation to make short term gains. Above all, both must maintain their vigilance against the various threats I have mentioned. I cannot see either interest on its own being able to finance the administration of salmon fisheries or persuade the government to maintain the conservation measures which have already curbed the high seas fishery and exercised increasing control over the drift nets.

As an angler my plea must be to proprietors to take an interest in their salmon asset and not to look on it merely as a useful source of income from the highest bidding tenant, whether a so-called angler out to catch enough to show a profit on his rent or a short-term netsman out to make quick money and get a semblance of legality for his poaching activities. With great respect I must say that the Crown, as owner of coastal salmon fishing in Scotland, could well set an example in these respects. The practice of the Crown Estate Commissioners in auctioning lets of netting-stations to the highest bidder can be used by the illegal netsmen to provide a legal cover for disposal of poached fish. Another outlet for such fish is the licensed Northumberland drift net fishery which appears to rely mainly on fish stocks of the Tweed and other Scottish rivers. This fishery, too, is used as an outlet for illegally caught fish. Now that politicians who appear to support the poachers have frustrated the Sale of Salmon Bill every effort should be made to stop up channels for disposal of fish taken by illegal means.

So far as the established netsmen are concerned, we must hope for continued co-operation with rod fishing interests in maintenance and improvement of salmon stocks together with moderation in exploiting situations where low river flows result in fish being concentrated at the tidal limit. At the same time, the commercial interests of the netsmen and their local employees and the big part they play in river management and control of poachers must be borne in mind, in addition to acknowledging the fact that on some rivers the proprietors own both rod and net fisheries and operate the latter for the benefit of that river's management.

The angler's contribution
Last but by no means least is the contribution which the angler should make towards salmon conservation. While consistent fishing with worm and prawn and even bait fishing may not make very serious inroads on the stocks of salmon it undoubtedly interferes substantially with the sport of other anglers using fly, particularly when beats do not comprise both banks. I would like very strongly to commend Mr Stevie Johnson's proposals contained in the July issue of the Salmon and Trout Magazine and in particular that a fly-only rule should operate on all Scottish

rivers, though I feel that on large rivers such as the Tay this
rule should apply only after 1st May. I would like to see an
end to the 'opposition' complex, whether the opposition be
the rods on the other bank or the established netsmen at the
river mouth. Above all, I would like to see a revival in the
'brotherhood of the angle', the sporting approach to salmon angling. If Scottish rivers are to remain a major
nursery of Atlantic salmon and the future generations are
to enjoy what is, to my mind, the most fascinating sport of
them all, understanding and co-operation are vital.

Current legislation
I would like to conclude with some observations on the
present statutory position relating to salmon fishing. I have
already mentioned the wise legislation in the 1860's and the
remarkable fact that this is still in operation with very little
alteration more than a century later. We also had the 1951
Act mainly designed to counter the upsurge in river poaching which took place after the last war and the 1976 Act
which did something to up-date financial penalties and to
recognize the recent growth of fish farming but otherwise
was a half-hearted attempt to give some effect to the
Hunter Committee's recommendations on trout fishing. As
I see it, the essential part of that committee's second report
was the proposal to restructure the management of fishing
for salmon, sea-trout and trout, both commercial and sporting. Less than 50 District Salmon Fishery Boards are presently operating although 106 were defined last century.
These boards function under Acts more than a century old
with inadequate finances and no jurisdiction (apart from
the Tweed) over trout fishing. Unlike almost all other civil-
ized countries possessed of game fisheries, Scotland has no
system of rod licences to finance fishery management. On
the Solway there is what can only be described as a legislative hotchpotch. Only in the murky water of pollution have
we seen some progress in the setting up of the River Purification Boards where much of the impetus has come from
anglers.
    All these problems and anachronisms were exhaustively
reviewed by Lord Hunter's committee, who recommended

a comprehensive restructuring of the management of game fisheries, a rational system of commercial trapping of salmon designed with conservation in mind, and an emphasis on the value to Scotland in human and financial terms of angling for sport. What has resulted from that report in the thirteen years since it was published? A lot of bickering among anglers and politicians about the proposed charges for rod licences (already completely out of date), a white paper from the previous Government which they could not implement and a half hearted Act from the present Government whose main object, the protection and improvement of trout fisheries, seems likely to be frustrated by the same petty bickering. Heaven alone knows what a Scottish Assembly, if it comes into being, will achieve for the preservation of our game fisheries – probably as little as has been achieved by Westminster governments since the last war. Meantime there remains the ever increasing danger that the remarkable bounty of Scotland's natural salmon rivers will be steadily destroyed by man's short sighted selfishness.

3 Illegal fishing – the Atlantic salmon 'rip-off'

J T H Fennety, Miramichi Salmon Association, Canada

Illegal Fishing

Illegal fishing of salmon, almost without exception, can be found throughout its range, and where Atlantic salmon populations are greatest the illegal fishery is heaviest.

It would be audacious of me indeed to hold myself up as an expert in the field of illegal Atlantic salmon fishing; although I am very much aware of what goes on in the name of illegal fishing in my home country I have no special claim to knowledge of illegal fishing activities in other countries. However, I have studied the overall problem in some depth. I am unable to say for certain how much of what has been said and published is true. We are reasonably sure poachers exist – that they carry on illegal activities and that they represent a very serious threat to Atlantic salmon stocks. My task, therefore, is difficult in the extreme because I am unable to produce any form of actual proof to support my claim that thousands of salmon have met untimely death at the hand or net of the illegal fishermen.

I have occasionally talked with illegal fishermen. Some have offered weak explanations for their transgressions, others have heaped scorn on all who stand in their way, whilst still others have vowed to carry on their nefarious activities until such time as it is no longer profitable for them to do so!

My target is an elusive one. Being aware of the geographic range and the multiplicity of rivers frequented by salmon, I trust you will recognize that I am dealing with an abstract of some magnitude and, therefore, cannot deal with concrete facts and figures such as you would expect from a scientific paper. Poaching is an art – not a science.

What are the major sources – or, more properly put – which illegal methods present the greatest threat? Before answering that, let me say that it is my confirmed belief that as much as 50 percent and more of all Atlantic salmon killed in very recent years were killed illegally and, being largely unreported, never appeared in the statistical data required for purposes of biological assessment of stocks in order to establish permissible future harvests!

The most serious, the most damaging, the most unconservative illegal fishery is that carried out along salmon return migration routes. The employment of various types and sizes of fishing vessels to which are attached miles of drift nets of assorted textures and dimensions will, if unchecked, bring about the total demise of salmon runs to certain rivers and very seriously impede or destroy any hope of increasing spawning populations in major river systems. This is due to greed.

The second greatest illegal fishery in terms of fish kill and stock depletion must be the so-called 'incidental catch' by assorted types of nets and traps ostensibly fishing for species other than salmon. Here again, salmon are taken in unknown and largely unreported numbers to become a further part of this unbridled greed for profit.

Illegal fishing within the home rivers represents the third largest harvest. I believe there is a widespread tendency to play down the numbers of fish taken by illegal means within the rivers themselves. I am convinced, from my personal inquiries and from the observations of others, that the illegal river kill of salmon is nearly 30 percent in some rivers which offer easy access and ideal poaching conditions. The salmon kill by means of nets, explosives, poisons, jig hooks and other assorted forms of river poaching, including unscrupulous anglers, is doubly serious.

There are perhaps other types and forms of illegal fishing for salmon but none approach in total the destruction being wrought by the methods I have previously outlined. How, you may question, can such havoc, such lawlessness, be allowed to continue? The question is a fair one and deserves an answer. Let us look at the offshore pirate who may also at times be engaged in legal fishing. At his disposal are all the sophisticated equipment of the modern electronic age – radar scanners, echo sounders, mobile radio transmitters/receivers – everything required to locate schools of fish and to warn of the whereabouts of fishery patrol vessels.

In the rivers still more sophisticated electronic devices allow the distant reporting of the movements of wardens, guardians and others. Side arms, spot lights, masks and wigs, all-terrain vehicles, high powered boats, are among the assorted paraphernalia of the poachers' trade.

Between the two extremes I have mentioned are hundreds of other illegal salmon fishermen who operate on a more modest but nevertheless efficient scale. These pirates are found off shore, on shore and in the river systems. Please note that I have not mentioned the thousands of salmon suspected of being taken illegally by legally licensed fishermen.

Illegal fishing or poaching is nothing new. It has been with us in some form or another for centuries. The ingenious methods of old have become the sophisticated methods of today. I am sorry that time will not permit a fuller review of the lengthy history of poaching.

I feel it is safe to say that the illegal fisherman or poacher has been a major factor, if not the major factor, contributing to the almost chronic instability of Atlantic salmon populations. Periodicity, or the highs and lows of salmon populations should not, I feel, be confused with the inroads of illegal fishing, although there could perhaps come a point in low salmon cycles when it would become unprofitable to poach on a major scale.

All of the points I have made are concerned solely with the illegal killing of salmon and should not be confused with over-killing of salmon by legal fishermen in the ocean waters and in the rivers.

What is the situation today? In a word – 'worse'. Worse than it has been for a number of years. Worse – because the feeding grounds of some salmon populations have been discovered. Worse – because it is now possible through electronic means to detect major congregations of salmon headed back to their home rivers. Worse – because of the employment of virtually invisible nets at sea, along the coasts, and in the estuaries and rivers. Worse – because more and more people have found that great profit can result from this low investment enterprise. Worse – because enforcement has failed to keep up with the rise in poaching. Worse – because of the weakness of law and the softness of penalties imposed on those who are caught and found guilty.

Recommendations
I would like to advance for consideration certain steps which I strongly feel should be implemented if we are ever to turn the tide in this continuing battle against illegal fishing and all of the dangers inherent in it.

First, I recommend that all those countries having significant Atlantic salmon populations should meet. Each of these countries could in its turn openly discuss its policies, and express its hopes and aspirations for a more stable and profitable fishery. Each could learn from the others of the shortcomings and frustrations which now exist and all could then work towards common goals. Only through joint action, only through the adoption of rules and regulations of similar intent and meaning can the existing chaos be resolved. After all, the number of countries is not great. Surely, as the only providers of this great anadromous species, a target of common objectives should be reasonably easy to attain. A common voice, with an openly expressed and fully united opinion, could not help being heard and listened to in all forums dedicated to species preservation, species protection and species harvesting. Recognition of the prior right of the producer state is not that far off as applied to anadromous fish. How much easier it would be in the future if the producer states were able, among other things, to be fully in charge of and empowered to make and enforce rules about the legal and illegal killing of salmon. I heartily recommend this suggestion.

If my first recommendation is too Utopian, let me challenge the Governments, both their elected and administrative arms, to clean up their act and make the positive contributions which must be made, and made quickly in order to curb rising illegal fishing and the resultant serious decline of stocks.

It should not be impossible to establish controls that would greatly reduce or, better still, eliminate illegal drift netting – this most unselective, unconservative and greedy method of fishing for salmon.

The time has come for effective restrictions to be placed on certain types of shore-based nets, often monofilament, that fish ostensibly for other species but in truth fish for salmon and kill them in large numbers as they follow the shores back to their rivers of origin.

Laxity of enforcement is one of the major reasons why the illegal killing of salmon not only continues but increases. For the most part, neither the illegal or legal fisherman has anything to fear however many fish he kills or possesses. How ridiculous to govern a resource only by the dates the season opens and closes and by the type of net and size of mesh to be employed. Other than this, the sky seems to be the limit. Does that make sense? I think not. In my opinion, all who fish for Atlantic salmon should be licensed. Every person so engaged should be obliged to adhere to the rules of a totally regulated fishery in which all aspects are covered, including quotas.

The angler or sport fisherman should be made fully aware of the authority of the state and its appointed bodies to control all aspects of the recreational fishery for salmon. Serious consideration must be given to uniform, perhaps universal, rules and regulations to govern the sport of salmon angling. Aware as I am of many of the customs which are part of angling in some countries and being aware of the high cost of salmon fishing in all countries, I nevertheless urge greater protection of all inland waters, public and private. I recommend that all who fish should be licensed and that penalties should be provided within the regulations allowing for cancellation of licences held by persons found guilty of violating fisheries laws.

Illegal sale

No review of illegal fishing for Atlantic salmon would be complete without reference to the system that supports and encourages it; namely, the market or black market which literally swallows up the ill-gotten gain of hundreds of illegal fishermen in a number of countries. There would be no systematic rape of the Atlantic salmon resource if it were not for the uninformed, unsympathetic public who all too readily provide the market. Many people are not aware that they are purchasing illegally caught salmon and this compounds the problem. Although I cannot offer an instant panacea, I recommend some steps be taken to ensure:

  a. Proper identification of legally caught salmon;
  b. That salmon be sold only by licenced vendors and
  c. That no sale be permitted of salmon taken by angling.

There is little, if anything, new in these suggestions. Several similar recommendations came out of the 1974 Conference on Illegal Atlantic Salmon Fishing.

The fact that poachers are stealing from the State – you and me – rather than from our pocket books or our homes, does not make their crime any less serious. Those who fish illegally for salmon are criminals. Purchase and possession must be considered as much a crime as stealing and selling or there can be no hope for an end to this whole unsavory matter of illegal fishing.

The greed of man increases with each passing year. That the Atlantic salmon has survived till now is a miracle; miracles run out too.

4 Discussion

D Lank (Atlantic Salmon Association) opened the discussion as follows

No matter what specific course this Symposium takes – or what spontaneous tangent it chooses to follow – there will be an underlying base of politics. I refer to politics newly created, as well as anachronistic hold-overs from ages when stupidity might have been a justifiable excuse for sowing seeds of future destruction.

In France the *Inscrits Maritimes* with their ancient rights seem to give fishermen permission to rape the dwindling salmon resource. It is then left to the *Association Nationale pour la Défense des Rivières au Saumon*, and their regional affiliates, to ensure that fish return to those rivers where Caesar's legions first saw and named *salar*. In Ireland salmon stocks have been put into jeopardy by over netting. Hydro-electric development of rivers in Norway has taken place without any regard to the need for fish passes, and in the United Kingdom salmon management only starts in the river, because there are public rights in tidal waters. Nowhere is the position worse than in Canada. There salmon have long since ceased to be defined biologically – they have become the spoils of bureaucrats and constitutional lawyers.

Add to political cowardice the human failing of refusing to believe the worst. Belatedly we find in some quarters – as witnessed by the presence of everyone here at the Symposium – an awakening concern for the future viability of a species once so numerous that Thomas Bewick wrote of Tyneside workers receiving guarantees that they would not be forced to eat salmon more than twice a week. Voices of concern are not new; they are tolerated by people who equate polite listening with positive action. In 1876, John L Rowan wrote in *The Emigrant and Sportsman in Canada,* 'It would really seem as if Nova Scotians hate the salmon, and have determined by every possible means to deny them access to their rivers.'

D T Hunt (Crown Estates Office, Edinburgh) in answer to a question, said that Crown fishings total about 350 in number, half of them being along the coast. Although the fisheries are put out to tender, all unknown applicants have their credentials checked and, if known or suspected as illegal fishermen, their offers are declined, even though they may offer the top tenders. Lettings are not made at any price. River lettings are made mainly to responsible associations or riparian owners. Forfeiture clauses are included in leases, operative if the tenants break the salmon laws. The Crown also plays its part on Scottish Fishery Boards.

Lord Thurso (Thurso District Fishery Board) said that any method of fishing which allows adequate escapement is to an extent inefficient. He considered the 'Hunter' solution too efficient and therefore too open to abuse or mishandling.

Mr Hardy commented that their putts and putchers were efficient methods of fishing.

W S Brewster (International Atlantic Salmon Foundation) said that there are differences between the US and Canadian systems whereunder fishing is controlled by national and provincial laws applicable to all rivers and the United Kingdom system whereunder local ownership sets many of the rules. Solution of salmon problems must be made to fit both conditions.

G D F Hadoke (Foyle Fisheries Commission) added that there is confusion as to our objectives in conserving the Atlantic salmon. He asked are we trying to protect inefficient anglers who are asked not to maximize the benefits of their fishery or should we try to conserve salmon to obtain the maximum benefits for the community, including the netsmen? Governments are unlikely to provide resources for salmon conservation programmes unless we can evaluate our fisheries and show the benefits which can be spread among the community at large by such a programme.

G H F Chaldecott said that only 8 out of 22 members of the Welsh Water Authority's Local Fishery Recreation and Amenity Advisory Committee are connected with fishing. Yet only the fishermen contribute finance to what is required by the Authority from this Committee generally.

G Power (University of Waterloo, Ontario, Canada) responded to the points raised by the Irish speaker by commenting on value of the Atlantic salmon to the community. He thought that at meetings such as the present there was a tendency for each individual to focus too sharply on his own specific involvements with salmon, be they angling, commercial fishing, administration or research. He said that everyone should step back and look at the broader picture. Salmon has obvious value as a living biological monitor of river water quality; water which, incidentally, we drink. It has a value to the visitor who, as part of the holiday experience, want to eat fresh salmon of the local variety. The importance of this was realized in Canada when the commercial fishing ban was imposed and salmon became a rare commodity in certain areas. Thirdly it has a value because of its fascinating life cycle and historic relations with man. We all want our descendants to have the chance to see this fish and not be forced to content themselves merely with written descriptions. Taking these and other considerations into account, it should be an easy task to convince the politicians that conservation of this species is essential.

1 Scottish salmon rivers and their future management

D H Mills, University of Edinburgh

Introduction

There are in the region of 200 salmon rivers in Scotland which contributed, for the 10 year period of 1968-1977, to an average annual commercial and rod catch of 431,378 salmon and grilse. This present level of, or any increase in, production is very much dependent on the future avail-ability and state of the spawning and nursery areas in these rivers during the ascent of returning fish.

In recent years there has been a reduction in spawning areas on some of the major river systems as a result of hydro-electric and water abstraction schemes. Hydro-electric development schemes in Scotland increased after the Second World War with the passing of the Hydro-electric Development (Scotland) Act in 1943. Since that time in the region of 25 schemes have been developed by the North of Scotland Hydro-electric Board and the South of Scotland Electricity Board. Some of them have been very extensive schemes involving the formation of reservoirs, the raising of the water levels of existing lochs and the diversion of rivers and streams by pipeline and aqueduct. Scotland's most important salmon river, the Tay and its major tributaries, the Tummel, Garry and Lyon, were the first to be harnessed for power. The development of other salmon river systems followed, including the Awe, Beauly, Conon, Garry, Moriston and Shin in the north and the Galloway Dee and Doon in the southwest. Due to impound-ing and tapping of the head-waters for these schemes, some of the rivers have lost an appreciable amount of their

Sponing

spawning and feeding areas. Fortunately, both these boards and the District Salmon Fishery Boards have put a great deal of care into looking after the welfare of salmon in these affected rivers. By the construction of fish passes and fish screens, the opening-up of previously inaccessible spawning grounds, the construction of salmon hatcheries, and the provision of compensation flows and freshets, the stocks of salmon have been satisfactorily maintained in these waters.

However, with an increase in industry and population there is an ever-growing demand for water and, according to the government publication *A Measure of Plenty* (1973), the total water consumption in Scotland is likely to double from its 1971 figure of 2,130 megalitres per day (Ml/d) to one of 4,414 Ml/d by the year 2001. This is perhaps not a lot of water when one considers the extent of Scotland's water resources. Over Scotland as a whole the average rainfall is around 1,400 mm a year. Making an allowance for evaporation and other effects, it is calculated that the total quantity of water which runs off the surface of the mainland and down our streams and rivers to the sea is some 73,000,000 Ml a year, or an average of 200,000 Ml/d. That being so, with a population of about 5.1 million the total quantity available is equivalent to about 40,000 litres per head per day. The average consumption from public supplies in 1973 was about 400 litres per head for all purposes, domestic and trade; or about one percent of the available supply. However, the rainfall varies over the year and winter storage is necessary. The development of Scotland's water resources for public supplies up to 1971 has resulted in a total of 380 reservoirs and lochs being developed and 259 river intakes being built. Since then Castlehill Reservoir on the River Devon has been completed and the large Megget scheme on a tributary of the River Tweed is under construction. On the completion of the Megget scheme and the development of neighbouring St Mary's Loch there will be six major reservoirs on the River Tweed and its tributaries, two of which result in the loss of appreciable salmon spawning areas.

water needed

Water quality

One of the effects of reduced river flow and change in flow regime as a result of water resource development has been removed with the improvement of water quality. The untiring efforts of the Scottish river purification boards, set up by the Rivers (Prevention of Pollution) (Scotland) Act 1951, have helped considerably to reduce pollution, and with an extension of their powers by the Rivers (Prevention of Pollution) (Scotland) Act, 1965, and the Control of Pollution Act, 1974, many longstanding polluting effluents have been eliminated. Unfortunately, pollution is still a problem on some existing salmon rivers and also on some rivers that, were it not for pollution, could quickly become salmon rivers. In the first category comes the River Don, which is still polluted by paper mill effluent, and in the second category are rivers in Scotland's central belt affected by iron waters from disused mines and opencast coal sites, in Fife and the Lothians in particular. Potentially viable salmon rivers such as the Leven in Fife and Carron in West Lothian are at present devoid of migratory fish, while the West Lothian Almond and Musselburgh Esk are only occasionally visited by salmon which would soon establish themselves were the iron waters to be treated and the numerous weirs removed. Although salmon are on Glasgow's heraldic coat-of-arms, because of industrial pollution it is many years since salmon have spawned in the Clyde.

Effects of afforestation

The effects of hydro-electric development, water abstraction and pollution on stocks of migratory fish are well-known and can, with effort, be alleviated. In the future, however, there are likely to be other more insidious effects on the salmon nursery areas, which, although less easily measured, are perhaps more serious. These are associated with land drainage and afforestation, for Scotland is becoming rapidly afforested, with open moorland being purchased, drained and planted by the Forestry Commission and private woodland owners. For example, it is estimated that 60 percent of the Mull of Kintyre will soon be afforested and the total afforested area in Scotland at pres-

Fig 1 A Cuthbertson drain showing effects of severe erosion only two years after ploughing. The area is east Sutherland in the river Oykel catchment.

Fig 2 Only a few yards downstream of Fig 1: severe erosion to a depth of over six feet. The eroded material is carried into a major spawning tributry of the Oykel 200 yards downstream.

ent is 0.75 million hectares, or 9.7 percent of Scotland's total land area; an afforested area of 1.6 million hectares could be achieved (Stewart, 1978). It has already been shown that the planting of conifers has seriously affected the productivity of some Scottish streams, leading to a paucity of invertebrate and fish fauna in streams flowing through mature forest with a dense tree canopy preventing sunlight encouraging algal growth and ground vegetation (Mills, 1967 and 1973 and Mills, Griffiths and Parfitt, 1978). While this effect can have direct repercussions on the value of nursery areas, the effects of rapid run-off from drainage channels can cause serious erosion (Stewart, 1963) leading to silting of spawning and nursery areas and filling in of holding pools with gravel *(Figs 1-3)*.

While drainage channels may at first prevent flooding due to a smaller surface run-off with the land being better drained, they will, during periods of heavy or continuous rain and when the surrounding land is saturated, produce flash floods resulting in serious scouring. Due to the temporary nature of these spates they are often of little value for fish ascent and do not keep the stream bedload in suspension for any length of time. So in drought years, such as have been experienced recently in Scotland, with some rivers having lower minimun flows as a result of land drainage, there is a tendency for salmon holding pools in the upper reaches of rivers to become shallower, the gravel more compacted and the stream beds more silted. This change in flow regime in afforested areas is further accentuated by water loss from the tree canopy interception of precipitation, and transpiration. Work by the Institute of Hydrology (Clarke and McCulloch, 1975) on Plynlimon in mid-Wales has shown quite conclusively that the trees intercept substantially more water than open moorland, and this could have adverse effects in long dry periods with irregular rain (Gash *et al* 1978). From work in England, it has been shown that high rainfall areas in the west of the country (which corresponds climatically to the west of Scotland) are

Fig 3   The river Cassley, east Sutherland, with a cone of gravel washed down to the mouth of the inflowing stream on the far bank. *(opp.)*

expected to have a greater interception loss than the rain-fall areas such as East Anglia. It was shown that out of a total rainfall of 2,770 mm, 790 mm were lost as interception and 310 mm as transpiration, producing a total water loss of more than twice the potential open water evaporation. It is unlikely the nursery streams can afford such water losses as these afforested areas will cause.

There is evidence that drainage in some afforested areas is reducing the pH of neighbouring waters and, in addition to low pH values from the direct effects of afforestation, there is a growing concern over the decrease in pH as a result of acid precipitation caused by sulphur dioxide carried by the wind from industrial areas. This is a phenomenon which has already had serious repercussions in salmon rivers in southern Norway (Jensen and Snekvik, 1972). Work on the effects of acid precipitation in Scotland has now started at the Freshwater Fisheries Laboratory at Pitlochry. Analyses of precipitation collected during the years 1973-1975 from various sites in Scotland were compared with results obtained ten years previously. The results showed a gradual decrease in precipitated acidity with increasing distance away from the large industrial belt around Glasgow, and an increase at individual sites from 1962 to 1975. To determine that increasing acidity could be caused by increasing sulphur dioxide dispersion the linear regression of atmospheric sulphate on free hydrogen was calculated, and the correlation was significant in most cases at the 95 percent level ($P = 0.05$). The weighted average pH values for Loch Ard, on the headwaters of the River Forth, were very similar for the period 1973 to 1975, being 4.19, 4.20 and 4.26 respectively, and the values for total acidity (precipitated) for these three years were 122, 139 and 112 micro-equivalents per square metre (Anon, 1978). Unless a salmon proprietor was aware that pH values of less than 4.5 were detrimental to young salmon, he might plant salmon ova or fry in waters with these low values to no avail.

Other threats to salmon stocks
There are a number of other activities which from time to time have threatened salmon stocks in Scotland, but these

have been of a more local nature. The recent development of the North Sea oil and gas resources has resulted in the construction of a number of pipelines through eastern Scotland which have crossed the tributaries and the main channels of rivers such as the Ugie, Don, Dee, North and South Esk, Tay, Earn and Teith. In some instances spawning and nursery areas were temporarily affected. Spraying activities, too, have caused local concern, and parts of the catchment of the rivers Helmsdale, Brora, Shin, Naver and Strathy in Sutherland and the Wick in Caithness were in an area sprayed with Fenitrothion in May, 1978, by the Forestry Commission to combat the Pine Beauty Moth *Panolis flammea* which was ravaging plantations of Lodgepole Pine *Pinus contorta*.

Predation of young and adult salmon by birds and mammals has always been of concern to Scottish salmon proprietors. The Goosander *Mergus merganser*, Red-breasted Merganser *M serrator* and Cormorant *Phalacrocorax carbo* are periodically controlled, but it is the Grey Seal *Halichoerus grypus* which is the centre of attention in this respect and present estimates show that these seals take some 5 percent of the total Scottish salmon catch. This has resulted in seal culls which are opposed by many wildlife conservation bodies and in the future it is likely that these bodies will have a greater influence on predator control policies. One mammal whose control they are unlikely to oppose, because of its depredations on bird life, is the Mink *Mustela vison*. Since 1961 there has been a dramatic spread of feral mink which have escaped from mink farms, and these animals are now known to be present in nearly all Scottish mainland counties and on some of the Islands. Cuthbert (1979) found from an analysis of mink scats from three Scottish rivers that salmon are a major food item, and predation by this animal in the future could well be serious.

Introductions of alien fish species have not always had a beneficial effect on indigenous fish stocks, and the concern shown over the possibility of the escape of a confined batch of young Coho Salmon *Oncorhynchus kisutch* into a Scottish river demonstrates the fears existing in many people's minds of the effects such an introduction might have on

Atlantic salmon stocks, so much so that the Import of Live Fish (Scotland) Act, 1978, has been passed to 'restrict in Scotland the import, keeping or release of live fish or shellfish or the live eggs or young of fish or shellfish of certain species'. Rainbow trout *Salmo gairdneri*, which can be migratory, are now being widely introduced to Scottish lochs and rivers and there are a number of records of the capture of sea-run rainbow trout in Scottish commercial salmon catches. The lack of control over the widespread stocking of Scottish waters with rainbow trout is to be deplored, as is the uncontrolled stocking of salmon rivers with brown trout due to misguided policies of trout angling clubs.

There are now over 150 salmon and trout farms in Scotland, many of them sited on salmon rivers and diverting clean water through their farm and returning to the river water contaminated with drugs, antibiotics, disease organisms, copper salts and malachite green as well as organic material. While the River Purification Boards can lay down consent standards for these discharges, as far as is known no regular check is made on dissolved substances in the farm outflows. There are also instances during drought conditions of fish farmers draining off practically the whole flow of a river, so that a section of the river between the inflow and outflow of the farm becomes virtually dry.

Management of salmon rivers

With the number of constraints on the future production of salmon it is important that the rivers are managed wisely and effectively. The Salmon Fisheries (Scotland) Acts of 1862 and 1868 set up Salmon Fishery Districts and District Boards for their administration. A Board consists of not more than three upper proprietors and three lower proprietors together with, as chairman, the proprietor having the largest annual valuation. In addition, a superintendent is usually appointed to actively manage and police the rivers in his district and is helped by a number of bailiffs who have certain powers of search and arrest which were extended under the Salmon and Freshwater Fisheries (Protection) (Scotland) Act, 1951. A total of 107 districts were established. At present only 47 of the districts have Fishery

Boards, in the remaining 60 no Boards have been constituted. The River Tweed is a special area and is administered by Tweed Commissioners. These District Boards
have only powers pertaining to migratory fish (salmon and
sea trout) and are not responsible for other freshwater fish.
Only the Tweed Commissioners have this extra control,
which was obtained through the Tweed Fisheries Act of
1969. At the beginning of the century the largest of these
districts, such as the Tay and the Spey, had a large comple-
ment of bailiffs. The Tay had in the region of 26 and the
Spey had 50. Comparable numbers today are six and five.
At the present time the whole of the River Tweed area has
only 10, and the Forth District has none. It is therefore very
evident that, however conscientious the staff, it is physically
impossible to effectively manage and police the river. At the
present time the duties of these bailiffs is almost entirely
anti-poaching, patrolling not only the estuarine and coastal
waters but also all parts of the river against increasing
attention from gangs using nets and Cymag poison. The
only other duty for which they have time is hatchery operation – the collection of fish for stripping, the maintenance
of the hatchery and the planting out of eggs and release of
the young. In the 60 districts with no boards all these duties
fall on the shoulders of individual proprietors who must
call on the overworked police to help them with poaching
incidents. The important ecological constraints discussed in
this paper are mainly overlooked, not through lack of
interest, but simply through lack of qualified staff. Any
major biological work on these rivers, outside that which is
carried out by the staffs of the River Purification Boards,
whose remit is one of pollution prevention, is done by the
staff of the Freshwater Fisheries Laboratory, Pitlochry, or
universities.

The only official published information on salmon rivers
is that produced annually by the Department of Agriculture and Fisheries for Scotland in their annual fisheries
report. This information is brief and of a general nature.
The reports of District Boards are only duplicated for
limited circulation but the River Tweed Commissioners do
publish an annual report for their members which gives a

general account of the state of the Tweed salmon fishing for the year, although individual catch figures for separate river beats or for commercial fisheries is not given. There is only one river, the Nith, for which the type of detailed information the salmon conservationist is seeking is available. This information is provided in the annual report of the River Nith Fishing Improvement Association. Fortunately, data on river quality appears in the published annual reports of the River Purification Boards.

If one is to ensure the future of Scottish salmon rivers then it is necessary to have some form of Area Board with a qualified staff as recommended by the Hunter Committee in their Second Report in 1965 (HMSO Cmnd 2691). It was planned that Area Boards would replace District Fishery Boards and that their revenue would come partly from imposing a licensing system for salmon and trout fishing as in England and Wales.

To replace the District Fishery Boards could be administratively difficult and they do serve a very useful function, and their Association of District Fishery Boards is the principal negotiating body with the Department of Agriculture and Fisheries for Scotland on salmon policies. It would be better to extend the remit of the River Purification Boards, with their existing staffs of biologists, chemists and hydrologists, to be responsible for the overall monitoring of freshwaters and their fisheries and to leave the District Fishery Boards as they are; the Inspectorate to be responsible for the policing of migratory fish rivers and to have their representatives on the new Boards to ensure that the salmon receive their share of attention. Those districts with no Boards could either be amalgamated with existing Boards or made the responsibility of the Department of Agriculture and Fisheries for Scotland. It is suggested that some such arrangement could well go a long way to ensuring the continuance of Scottish salmon stocks in the world of tomorrow.

References

ANON, *Triennial Review of Research, 1973-1975*. Freshwater Fisheries
1978 Laboratory, Pitlochry. Department of Agriculture and Fisheries
for Scotland.

CLARKE, R T & MCCULLOCH, J S G. Recent work in the comparison of
1975 effects of alternative uses (coniferous forest, upland pasture) on
water catchment behaviour. *Conference on Conservation and Land
Drainage*, Water Space Amenity Commission.

CUTHBERT, J H. Food studies of feral mink *Mustela vison* in Scotland.
1979 *Fish Mgmt* 10, 1.

GASH, J H C, OLIVER, H R, SHUTTLEWORTH, W J & STEWART J B. Eva-
1978 poration from forests. *J. Instn Water Engrs and Scientists*, 32, 2,
104–110.

JENSEN, K W & SNEKVIK, E. Low pH levels wipe out salmon and trout
1972 populations in south western Norway *Ambio* 1: 223–225.

MILLS, D H. A study of trout and young salmon populations in forest
1967 streams with a view to management. *Forestry*, 40 (1): Supplement,
85–90.

MILLS, D H. Preliminary assessment of the characteristics of spawning
1973 tributaries of the River Tweed with a view to management. *Proceedings of the International Atlantic Salmon Symposium*, 145–155.

MILLS, D H. The impact of the British Gas Corporation pipeline project
1976 on fisheries: precautions and claims. *Fish Mgmt* 7,4, 78–79

MILLS, D H., GRIFFITHS, D, & PARFITT, A. A survey of the freshwater
1978 fish fauna of the Tweed Basin. *Ann. Rept. of the River Tweed
Commissioners for 1977*.

STEWART, G G. Inter-relations between agriculture and forestry in the
1978 uplands of Scotland: A forestry view. *Scottish Forestry*, 32, 3,
153–164

STEWART, L. *Investigations into migratory fish propagation in the area of the
1963 Lancashire River Board*. 80 pp. Lancaster: Barker.

2 Ecological constraints on future salmon stocks in England and Wales

G S Harris, Welsh National Water Development Authority

The salmon resource

Notwithstanding a long history of degradation, the salmon fisheries of England and Wales still represent a resource of some importance. *Table 1* summarizes the declared salmon catch from the various sport and commercial fisheries over the last 18 years. *Table 2* gives the 1975 catch in each of 46 of the principal salmon rivers. There are, however, many other rivers, mostly small, where catches of up to 100 salmon a year are declared by anglers or commercial fishermen or both. These rivers, although individually of lesser importance, collectively represent a significant part of the total resource. In 1975 the total rod catch of salmon in England and Wales was about 26,000 compared with some 73,000 in Scotland. The commercial catch in the same year was about 90,000 in England and Wales and 957,000 in Scotland.

Table 1 Declared salmon catches in England and Wales 1960-1977

Year	Rods	Nets	Total	Year	Rods	Nets	Total
1960	21,121	45,746	66,867	1969	16,174	81,393	97,567
1961	16,056	36,427	52,483	1970	19,333	130,512	149,845
1962	24,310	53,833	78,143	1971	19,735	92,718	112,453
1963	30,054	47,548	77,602	1972	24,599	84,371	108,970
1964	28,474	52,070	80,544	1973	20,436	93,933	114,369
1965	32,162	47,748	79,910	1974	24,565	80,474	105,039
1966	35,260	56,730	91,990	1975	25,895	89,511	115,406
1967	29,608	68,103	97,711	1976	10,049	44,275	54,324
1968	16,573	51,591	68,164	1977*	17,596	75,104	92,700

Source: MAFF, London *Provisional

Management structure and functions

The principal statute controlling fisheries regulation, administration and management is now the Salmon and Freshwater Fisheries Act 1975. At a local level this Act is implemented by the ten Regional Water Authorities set up under the Water Act 1973. Okun (1977) presents the history of the water industry in England and Wales leading to the formation of the Water Authorities with their uniquely integrated multiple functions of water supply, effluent treatment and disposal, water resources planning, fisheries, water based recreation, and pollution control.

Apart from its effect of reorganising the water industry in England and Wales, the 1973 Act was significant in that it contained new and extended statutory duties and powers relevant to fisheries. The most important of these was the duty to maintain, improve and develop salmon fisheries, and other fisheries, in the respective areas of each water authority. New powers and duties relating to the conservation of flora and fauna and the development of water-based recreation, which includes sportfishing, were also incorporated into the 1973 Act.

Historical review

The history of attrition of the salmon fisheries of England and Wales has been extensively reviewed by Netboy (1968). Prior to the Industrial Revolution most rivers, with the possible exception of some in East Anglia, appear to have contained salmon. It was not until the period of increased industrialization and urbanization of the 18th and 19th centuries that the salmon resource came under serious and general pressure. By the middle of the 19th century many rivers such as the Severn, Lune, Ribble, Tyne and Tees had seriously declined while others such as the Thames and Mersey had ceased to produce salmon altogether.

By the middle of the last century the plight of the salmon was cause for popular concern. In 1860 a Royal Commission was appointed 'to enquire into the Salmon Fisheries of England and Wales'. They reported (Day, 1887) that the decrease of the salmon fisheries was consequent upon: (1) obstruction to the free passage of fish; (2) the use of fixed

Table 2 Declared salmon catches for 1975 from principal salmon rivers in England and Wales

AREA/RIVER	SALMON[1] CATCH		
	rods	nets	total
Northumbrian			
Coquet	130		
Tyne	228	45,347[2]	45,985
Yorkshire			
Esk	134	7,892[2]	8,026
Southern			
Test	1,118		
Itchen	164	360	1,642
Wessex			
Avon	600	973	1,573
Frome	274	168	442
Severn/Trent			
Severn	1,376	4,146	5,522
Southwest			
Lyn	94	110	204
Taw	264		
Torridge	207	3,363	3,834
Camel	385	255	640
Fowey	483	211	694
Lynher	177	529	706
Tamar	1,092	2,864	3,956
Tavy	110	702	812
Avon	2	238	240
Dart	132	1,221	1,353
Teign	62	2,422	2,484
Exe	109	1,600	1,709

(contd.)

AREA/RIVER	SALMON CATCH		
	rods	nets	total
Welsh			
Dee	904	2,787	3,691
Clwyd	208	1,228	1,436
Conwy	855	189	1,044
Ogwen	171	67	238
Seiont	80		
Gwyrfai	39	493	612
Llyfni	88	19	107
Dwyfawr	210	74	284
Glaslyn	86	58	144
Mawddach	580	186	766
Dyfi	664	239	903
Rheidol	102	[3]	102
Teifi	818	729	1,547
Nevern	15	183	198
Dau Cleddau	352	128	480
Taff	173	28	201
Tywi	1,587	650	2,237
Usk	498	2,040	2,538
Wye	6,796	2,347	9,143
Northwest			
Esk[4]	190		
Eden	503	1,151	1,844
Derwent	703	64	767
Leven	44	72	116
Kent	114	279	393
Lune	589	2,779	3,368
Ribble	365	633	998

[1]Includes grilse
[2]Refers to offshore net fishery
[3]No licensed nets operating
[4]To Scottish border only

engines; (3) defective regulation of fence times or close seasons; (4) illegal fishing, destruction of unseasonable fish, spawning fish, spent fish, young or fry; (5) the want of an organized system of management of the rivers and fisheries, affording the means of efficient protection against poaching and other destructive and illegal practices; (6) poisoning of waters by manufacturers, gasworks and other nuisances; (8) confusion and uncertainty of the law, and difficulty of enforcing its penalties against offenders.

Over the next 100 years much was done in an attempt to arrest the decline of the salmon, largely as a result of progressive improvements in the fisheries and, more recently, pollution control legislation. However, while some rivers such as the Wye and Ribble improved or remained relatively stable, others continued to decline, with catches on the Tyne falling from 17,000 in 1910 to nil in 1959 and the Tees, possibly once the most prolific salmon river in Britain becoming defunct as a salmon fishery in 1939.

Existing and future constraints

At this time many of the problems listed by the Royal Commission of 1860 have been dealt with and largely overcome by improved legislation and the progressive development of an effective management structure. Where problems still exist these are, to some extent, now associated with political, practical and economic factors.

England and Wales would seem to be fortunate in that many of the ecological pressures occurring elsewhere either do not occur or are only of limited local or periodic relevance. Problems associated with acid rainfall (Braekke, 1976) and pesticides (Muirhead-Thomson, 1971) are not known to occur in any general sense. Extreme temperatures (Dymond, 1963), forestry (Pennal, 1959), the growth of the commercial fish farming industry (Brown, 1978), predation, particularly by seals (Bonner, 1976), and electricity generation (Elder, 1966) may be detrimental in some restricted areas but are not regarded as extensively limiting. However, the recently revived proposals for the construction of a barrage across the Severn Estuary for generating electricity from the tides (Shaw, 1975; Department of Energy, 1978) presents alarming prospects for the future of salmon in the Wye, Severn and Esk. Disease, typically ulcerative dermal necrosis (Munro, 1970), has resulted in extensive mortalities but now seems to be a periodic local phenomenon of little long term practical consequence. Few of the past man-made barriers now exist as obstructions to the upstream passage of adult salmon as a result of the installation and improvement of fish passage facilities. Problems associated with the development of various water-based recreations, partciularly canoeing (Corbin, 1973), appear to be associated with their effect on sport fishing rather than on the fishery.

Pollution, water abstraction, land drainage and over fishing are generally claimed to be the principal areas of concern in England and Wales. These will be considered in greater detail.

Water quality
Pollution is still a serious problem in its effects on the abundance and distribution of salmon stocks in England and Wales. It appears, however, to be steadily and tangibly diminishing in its relative importance.

Implementation of the Rivers (Prevention of Pollution) Acts 1951 to 1961 combined with a heavy capital investment in effluent treatment and disposal over the last few decades has resulted in a very considerable improvement in river water quality. Indeed, the record of the water industry in England and Wales is possibly second to none in this respect. With the full enactment of Part II of the Control of Pollution Act 1974 and a projected capital investment of about £607 million over the five year period 1978-1979 to 1982-1983 by the water industry on pollution abatement programmes, further improvements should result with potentially significant, even if incidental, benefits to the salmon resource.

Table 3 summarizes the present extent of pollution, based upon a chemical classification of waters, as contained in the 1978 report *River Pollution Surveys in England and Wales updated 1975*. Over the 17 year period of the review there has been a reduction in gross pollution from 6.4 percent to 3.3 percent in rivers and from 12.4 percent to 10.5 percent in estuaries. The extent of unpolluted waters has increased from 72.9 percent to 77.6 percent in rivers and from 40.7 percent to 49.6 percent in estuaries.

Table 3 Classification of water quality in rivers and estuaries in England and Wales

	1958		1970		1975	
	km	%	km	%	km	%
Non tidal rivers						
class 1 (unpolluted)	23,500	72·9	27,370	76·2	28,037	77·6
class 2 (doubtful)	4,611	14·3	5,297	14·7	5,458	15·1
class 3 (poor)	2,058	6·4	1,724	4·8	1,449	4·0
class 4 (grossly polluted)	2,057	6·4	1,533	4·3	1,178	3·3
Total	32,226	100·0	35,924	100·0	36,122	100·0
Tidal rivers						
class 1 (unpolluted)	1,160	40·7	1,383	48·1	1,422	49·6
class 2 (doubtful)	935	32·8	675	23·4	720	25·1
class 3 (poor)	400	14·1	485	16·8	424	14·8
class 4 (grossly polluted)	355	12·4	336	11·7	301	10·5
Total	2,850	100·0	2,879	100·0	2,867	100·0

Source: '*River Pollution Surveys of England and Wales updated 1975*'

The abatement of once gross pollution in the Rheidol (Jones and Howells, 1975) and in the Tyne during the early 1960's has already enabled the restoration of locally important sport fisheries for salmon. Several once defunct salmon rivers such as the Afan, Neath, Ogmore and Ystwyth in Wales now support increasing runs of sea trout and produce the occasional rod caught salmon following a diminution in their pollution and, subject to various considerations, could well be the subject of immediate salmon rehabilitation programmes. A further reduction in pollution, chiefly in the lower and tidal reaches of other rivers, would make practical the restoration of the salmon in many other rivers, such as the Tees, Taff, Ebbw, Ely and Thames, over the next decade if, as seems probable, water quality further improves. Salmon disappeared from the Thames in about 1830. In the 1950's the lower and tidal reaches were almost fishless. Over the last 25 years an enormous effort to clean up the Thames achieved amazing success to the extent that it is now claimed to have the cleanest metropolitan estuary in the world (Black, 1977). So great has been the improvement that in 1973 the 'Thames Migratory Fish Committee' was formed to examine the possibility of reintroducing salmon and sea trout. Their report produced in 1976 concluded that, notwithstanding the problems of adequate spawning and nursery streams and passage over weirs, water quality improvements would be such that by 1980 the reintroduction of migratory fish would be possible.

Water abstraction
The adverse effects of abstraction on salmon fisheries are well known (Dill *et al*, 1975) and have long been the cause of much concern.

Total abstractions, including direct supplies to power stations, industry and agriculture, in addition to public water supplies, amount to some 7,900 million gallons per day (mgd) in England and Wales. This represents about 19 percent of residual rainfall of about 42,000 mgd. About 66 percent of abstractions is eventually returned to rivers and the nett abstractions therefore amount to about 2,600 mgd. Public water supplies of some 3,300 mgd as a whole are abstracted in roughly equal proportions: (1) from upland reservoirs and streams; (2) from rivers; (3) from ground waters. Regionally these proportions may vary. In Wales, 58 percent of supplies are from upland reservoirs and 38 percent from rivers. In the southwest 65 percent is derived from upland reservoirs and 18 percent from rivers.

Water supply strategy has now moved away from the construction of upland reservoirs with direct supply to the consumer to the increasing use of such impoundments for river regulation with the final abstraction point located downstream, often near to the estuary. By the adoption of river regulation and more recently the conjunctive use of several reservoirs in the same or other catchments, it has proved possible to optimize water yields while maintaining environmental standards by leaving water in rivers over much of their length. The Welsh Dee, with its three large upland storage reservoirs is perhaps the most comprehensively regulated river in Britain (Blezard et al, 1971). The adoption of regulation and conjunctive use on this locally important salmon fishery has enabled nett abstraction of about 15 percent to take place with no discernible effect upon past catches. In fact the river regulation now maintains a flow over almost the entire length of the river of up to 400 percent of the natural minimum flow.

Fisheries compensation, mitigation and protection schemes have long been a feature associated with water supply schemes. Some still in existence go back over 50 years. But not all schemes have resulted in damage mitigation or protection schemes being implemented, and losses to production have occurred in many areas. However, since the Salmon and Freshwater Fisheries Act 1975 now requires water authorities to 'maintain' fisheries, protection schemes such as the two-way trapping and trucking scheme associated with the Llyn Brianne-Tywi regulation scheme (Howells and Jones, 1972) and the smolt rearing programme associated with the Dee regulation scheme (Blezard et al, 1971) must figure with increased prominence in the planning, construction and operation of future water supply schemes. The Llyn Brianne-Tywi Scheme allocated 2,000 million gallons (mg) from the live storage of 13,000 mg for the release of artificial spates; the principal purpose of which is to attract salmon into the river, distribute them upstream and provide flows conducive to angling. The provision of artificial spates has been a feature of several major reservoir schemes in more recent years.

In considering the future impact of water abstraction, two facts are relevant. The first is that there has been increasing realization that money is no longer available in unlimited amounts to meet ever-increasing demands for water (Saxton, 1978). This is now leading to the evolution of a concept of manipulation of the demand for water by management control. The second is the awareness that predictions of a doubling in the rate of demand for water by the year 2001 made by the Water Resources Board during the mid 1960's were too high. Recent predictions for England and Wales now suggest that the increase may be only about 42 percent.

Greater economy in the use of water and a much smaller increased demand over the next 25 years will serve to reduce the expected increased pressures on the salmon but may replace one set of problems with another. Up until the early 1970's the future construction of barrages such as those across the Wash, the Dee estuary and the Solway Firth and Morecambe Bay (Gilson, 1966) figured large in the planning of future water supply strategy. These schemes would have presented very considerable problems in providing for the free passage of salmon adults and smolts to and from the rivers and sea. The reduced water demand combined with the high cost of these schemes makes their construction unlikely in the forseeable future – although bunded, off-stream storage in the Wash is still a possibility. Similarly, several large upland storage reservoirs originally planned may not now be built.

However, an increased demand will exist and must be met. One fear among fishery managers is that attempts will now be made to 'squeeze' a greater water yield from existing supply sources. This would imply reducing compensation flows, prescribed flows and artificial spate storage and, ultimately, less water left to flow out to sea. The result would be increased pollution in the lower reaches and estuaries of some rivers unless water quality standards were increased to compensate for a reduction in effluent dilutions.

A further and closely related problem is the expected increase in inter-catchment water transfers. The proposed new Craig Goch scheme on the upper Wye originally entailed the storage of water from four very different salmon rivers, the Rheidol, Ystwyth, Wye and Severn, in an enlarged reservoir and its eventual release into the Severn and into the Wye (and thence possibly over to the Usk) before it was abstracted into supply. Many small inter-catchment water transfers, involving only a few mgd, have occurred in the past. It is the scale and extent of future proposals that is cause for concern. Already the Kielder Scheme (Conlon, 1977) linking the Tyne, Tees and Wear has been constructed by which up to 136 mgd of Tyne water will be transferred to the Tees and Wear. Other schemes will follow.

Concern about the impact of these transfer schemes on the fisheries of the donor and receiving rivers resulted in formation of a Ministry of Agriculture, Fisheries and Food-National Water Council Joint Study Group which reported in 1976. It was concluded that there were grave risks of damage to migratory fisheries largely because of possible interference with their specific homing mechanisms.

Land drainage

Land drainage, which has a long tradition in England and Wales includes, in the context of this paper, the prevention or alleviation of freshwater or saltwater flooding to urban and agricultural areas, and the control of soil water to improve agricultural production. The problems to fisheries caused by land drainage operations are well known (Schernberger and Funk, 1973); their general effect being to reduce production and, directly or indirectly, reduce the harvest.

During the year 1978-1979 the capital expenditure by water authorities on arterial drainage and flood protection will be £18.2 million of which £7.5 million relates to the protection and improvement of agricultural land.

The rehabilitation of consequent fisheries damage has rarely been an integral part of land drainage schemes in England and Wales. Even when such work has been attempted, its efficacy in providing full and adequate restoration can usually be questioned. In the past, legal action to obtain compensation for damage caused to fisheries and fishing by land drainage works has been successfully pursued. The most recent case (Gregory, 1974) was Burgess *v* Gwynedd River Authority and resulted in £37,000 being awarded for costs and capital and amenity damage to fishing. Unfortunately, financial compensation does not repair the damage, and the loss to the resource remains.

Increased concern about the adverse impact of land drainage on the general environment resulted in the formation of a working party under the auspices of the Water Space Amenity Commission in 1976. This report, *Conservation and Drainage Guidelines,* is scheduled to appear in 1978. Although having no legal force this should help to focus attention on the general problem and the need for a new approach. The most significant factor, however, in achieving this new approach is likely to be the fact that the water authorities who carry out most of the land drainage work potentially damaging to fisheries must resolve the inherent conflict between their statutory duty to 'maintain' fisheries and the damaging effect on fisheries of unmitigated land draining schemes.

Over fishing

The Report of the Committee on Salmon and Freshwater Fisheries 1964 (the Bledisloe Report) considered, among other things, the problem of over fishing. They admitted considerable difficulty in ascertaining whether or not over fishing was occurring because of almost complete ignorance on the abundance of stocks available for exploitation and the breeding stock necessary to maintain productivity.

They pointed out that much of the evidence presented to substantiate over fishing was based on conjecture and that, notwithstanding the unreliability of the historical record, an examination of past catch statistics showed no apparent general decline in catches to indicate over fishing.

The problem of deducing trends from catch records is a very real one. It is only in the last few years that serious efforts have been made to improve the accuracy of the information derived from returns sent in by anglers and netsmen but these still only represent a fraction of the fish caught legally. Examination of the data from various sources would suggest that, allowing for seasonal fluctuations, the overall declared salmon catch in England and Wales has remained relatively stable over the years. On the Wye the catch has increased significantly over a 40 year period from about 2,500 fish in 1937 to over 8,000 fish in 1975 and it is likely that under-exploitation is occurring. Elsewhere, over-exploitation may be responsible for the decline in catches on certain rivers such as the Coquet, Lune, Exe and some others in recent years.

The pattern of exploitation over the last one hundred years has been characterized by two trends. Firstly, the demand for salmon angling has increased dramatically as shown from the following data on sales of salmon sport fishing licences in Wales: 627 in 1868, 2,132 in 1895, 2,174 in 1921, and 30,200 in 1975. In 1975 some 51,000 licences were issued in England and Wales as a whole. Secondly, there has been a substantial reduction in the licensed commercial fishing effort over the period. In Wales this has been from 509 in 1895, 263 in 1921, to 175 in 1975. The total number of commercial salmon fishing licences issued in 1975 for England and Wales was 1,025. There are now few areas in England and Wales where the number of commercial fishing instruments legally entitled to take salmon is not strictly regulated under the terms of various Net Limitation Orders.

An increase in the extent and nature of illegal fishing is a third trend causing much concern. This has resulted from the high market value for salmon – up to £4 a pound weight in the early season falling to about £2.50 during the season – combined with the difficulties of detecting, apprehending and successfully prosecuting offenders. The main problem is that any person may fish in tidal waters and in the sea for sea fish without a licence and is subject to very few restrictions. It would seem that increasing numbers of salmon are being taken under this pretext. The report *Taking Stock* (Association of River Authorities, 1974) noted that a survey of the salmon catch from one river in Devon indicated that the illegal catch of salmon by nets set adjacent to the estuary ostensibly to take sea fish represented over 35 percent of the declared legal catch by the licensed salmon nets on that river. In some areas, such as the Usk estuary, it is thought that the illegal catch may now exceed the legal catch.

Whether catch and abundance are directly related is obviously a very relevant question in applying catch statistics to management problems. But until information becomes available from other sources catch returns will continue to represent the principal means of assessing the well being of our salmon fisheries. In view of their inherent inaccuracy and the problems of accounting for illegal fishing, any assessment of the occurrence and extent of over fishing must continue to be based on arbitrary judgements.

Comment

The general prospects of increasing the abundance and distribution of salmon stocks in England and Wales are viewed with cautious optimism. Reorganization of the water industry has brought many consequential benefits. The statutory duty of the resultant water authorities to 'maintain, improve and develop fisheries' has given new meaning and impetus to future works. Both have resulted in much-needed close consultation between fisheries and other, potentially conflicting, functions.

Over fishing will continue to be the subject of emotive debate and much conjecture. There must be an increased commitment in monitoring the status, rates of exploitation and necessary spawning escapement of existing stocks if future management policies to benefit salmon are to have any meaning or real benefit. The nature and extent of the future commitment by water authorities to improving their salmon fisheries must depend to some extent on the existence of effective controls over the extent of illegal fishing and the exploitation of native stocks outside home waters.

Steady improvements in overall water quality are to be expected and should provide opportunities to restore and increase salmon stocks in a number of rivers where they are now absent or depleted. Whether this is done may depend upon political and economic rather than biological considerations.

The predicted 42 percent increase in the demand for water over the next 25 years will undoubtedly introduce new and increased problems associated with water abstractions. The satisfactory resolution of these, and other problems, will depend very much on an increase in knowledge about many aspects of the biology, behaviour and habitat requirements of the species.

The help and co-operation of colleagues within the water industry in the preparation of this paper is gratefully acknowleged. The views expressed are those of the author.

References

ASSOCIATION OF RIVER AUTHORITIES. *Taking Stock*. Association of
1974   River Authorities, London: 48 pp.
BLACK, P. The Cleaning of the Royal Thames. *Journal of the Water*
1977   *Space Amenity Commission*, London. Spring 1977: 31–34
BLEZARD, N, CRANN, H H, IREMONGER, D J & JACKSON, E; Conservation
1971   of the Environment by River Regulation. *Association of River
        Authorities Yearbook* 1970: 70–111
BONNER, W N. Stocks of Grey Seals and Common Seals in Great Bri-
1976   tain. *Natural Environment Research Council, Publication Series C*, No
        16: 16 pp.
BRAEKKE, F H (Ed). Impact of acid precipitation on forest and fresh-
1976   water ecosystems in Norway. *Research Report 6*, SNSF Project,
        Norway: 111pp.
BROWN, K. Fish Farms, a need for control. *J. of the National Water Council*,
1978   18 January 1978: 20–21.
CONLON, BOB. Kielder Water: linking the Tyne, Wear and Tees. *J. of*
1977   *the National Water Council*, 12 January 1977: 20–22.
CORBIN, F D. The canoe problem. *Salmon and Trout Magazine*, 198:
1973   109–112.
DAY, F. *British & Irish Salmonidae*. Williams & Norgate, London:
1887   p. 120.
DEPARTMENT OF ENERGY. Severn Barrage Seminar, 7 September
1978   1977. *Report of Proceedings:* written contributions HMSO, Lon-
        don: 74 pp.
DEPARTMENT OF THE ENVIRONMENT: Welsh Office. *River pollution*
1978   *surveys in England and Wales* updated 1975. HMSO, London:
        60 pp.
DILL, W A, KELLEY, D W & FRASER, J C. Water and land use de-
1975   velopment and the aquatic environment, problems and solutions.
        FAO *Fish Tech Paper*, (141): 10 pp.
DYMOND, J R. Family Salmonidae. In. *Fishes of the Western North Atlantic*.
1963   *Part 3*. Memoirs Sears Foundation for Marine Research:
        457–502.
ELDER, H Y. Biological effects of water utilization by hydro-electric

1966   schemes in relation to fisheries, with special references to Scotland. *Proc Roy Soc Edin*, B, LXIX, Pt111/1V: 246–71

GILSON, H C. The biological implications of the proposed barrages
1966   across Morecambe Bay and the Solway Firth. In *Man-made Lakes*. (Ed R H Lowe-McConnell). Academic Press, London: 129–37.

GREGORY, M. *Angling and the law*. 2nd Edition. Charles Knight, Lon-
1974   don: 199 pp.

HOWELLS, W R & JONES, A N. The River Tywi regulating reservoir
1972   and fishery protection scheme. *J Inst Fish Mgmt*,3: 5–19.

JONES, A N & HOWELLS, W R. The partial recovery of the metal pol-
1975   luted River Rheidol. In *The ecology of resource degradation and renewal*. 15th Symposium of British Ecological Society. July 1973. Chadwick, M J and Goodman, G T. John Wiley and Sons, New York: 443–59

MILLS, DEREK. *Salmon and Trout: a resource, its ecology, conserva-
1971   tion and management*. St Martins Press, New York: 351 pp.

MINISTRY OF AGRICULTURE, FISHERIES AND FOOD: National Water
1976   Council. Joint Study Group, 1976. *The Fisheries Implications of Water Transfers between Catchments*: 54 pp.

MUNRO, A L S. Ulcerative dermal necrosis, a disease of migratory
1970   salmonid fishes in the rivers of the British Isles. *Biological Conservation*, 2, (2): 129–32.

MUIRHEAD-THOMSON, R C. *Pesticides and freshwater fauna*. Academic
1971   Press, London: 248 pp.

NETBOY, ANTHONY. *The Atlantic salmon: a vanishing species?* Faber and
1968   Faber, London: 457 pp.

OKUN, D A. *Regionalization of Water Management. A revolution in
1977   England and Wales*. Applied Science Publishers Ltd, London: 377 pp.

PENNAL, J T. Effects on freshwater fisheries of forestry practices. In
1959   *The effects on freshwater fisheries of man—made activities in British Columbia. Can Fish Cult*, 25: 27–29.

Report of the Committee on Salmon and Freshwater Fisheries. HMSO, Lon-
1961   don, Cmnd 1350: 151 pp.

SAXTON, K J H. Managing UK water resources. *Journal of the National
1978   Water Council*, 19, March 1978: 15–17.

SHAW, T L. An *Environmental Appraisal of the Severn Barrage*. University
1975   of Bristol: 115 pp.

SCHERNBERGER, E & FUNK, J L (Eds). Stream channelization: a
1973   symposium. *Am Fish Soc*, NCD/AFS. Spec Publ No 2: 83 pp.

THAMES WATER AUTHORITY. *Report of the Thames Migratory Fish
1976   Committee*. Thames Water Authority, London: 40 pp.

3 Ecological constraints on future salmon stocks in the Republic of Ireland

D J Piggins, Salmon Research Trust of Ireland

The resource

There are some 13,280 km of rivers and 144,500 hectares of lakes in Ireland and all the rivers of any significance hold stocks of salmon. The total catches of salmon have equalled or surpassed those of Scotland or Norway and over 95 percent of this catch is taken by commercial methods. Drift netting at sea in public fisheries accounts for over 75 percent of the catch and about half of the estuarine catch is taken in public fisheries. Official catch statistics are not yet available for 1976 and 1977 but the catch for 1975 was about $4\frac{1}{2}$ million pounds weight, valued at £2$\frac{1}{2}$ million. It has been estimated that the catch for 1976 was some 30 percent less than that for 1975, with a further reduction of 10 percent for 1977.

The official rod catch may be underestimated because in 1970 an independent survey by the Economics and Social Research Institute estimated the rod catch to be 9 percent of the total, compared with the official figure of 3.9 percent. Overall, it has been estimated that expenditure by anglers in 1970 constituted 42 percent of the gross output of the salmon fishing industry, the balance being the value of the commercial catch. Drift netting for salmon has considerable socio-economic value for numbers of low-income families along the north, west and south coasts but the current increase in this fishing method has caused a decline in the livelihoods of estuarine and river fishermen.

Historical review

A decline in spring fish stocks began in the late 1930's and accelerated from 1961 onwards, with a concomitant increase in the numbers and average weight of the grilse. This is a continuing cyclical phenomenon, since at the turn of the century, grilse were plentiful and salmon were scarce. This cyclical reduction in salmon stocks was exaggerated by the Greenland fishery and ulcerative dermal necrosis (UDN) from 1964 onwards but these factors did not initiate the downward trend. Commercial fishing for salmon in April and May has been uneconomic of late years in many areas but there were encouraging signs of an upturn in salmon numbers during 1978.

A number of rivers in Ireland were recognized in 1975 as having much depleted stocks due to problems such as pollution, hydroelectric development, UDN, over fishing and the cyclical decline noted above. All recent evidence points to a decline in both salmon and grilse stocks, as escapements into fresh water, although the total commercial catch did not begin to decline until 1976. Rod catches have fallen, despite increased angling effort, in terms of licences issued. Both the catch of estuarine drift nets and the numbers of fish passing through counters on some thirteen river systems have also shown a general decline, whilst as noted earlier, the drift net catch fell by over a third from 1975 to 1977. A further drop in the commercial catch would appear to have occured in 1978.

Current constraints
Pollution
The level of pollution of inland waters of Ireland is not yet serious and it has been calculated that only some 4 percent of the 12,000 km of main river channels could be classified in 'doubtful' or 'bad' condition. Most of the domestic wastes are discharged to estuarine or coastal waters but the industrial discharges occur mainly on inland waters and are in excess of the combined agricultural and domestic discharges.

Domestic water use and therefore waste discharge has increased markedly over the past twenty years with the spread of urbanization and sewered wastes, allied with new rural housing and septic tank discharges. Agricultural sources of pollution are also increasing, with the development of intensive rearing operations and silage-making. The industrial pollution load is derived largely from the older factories associated with agricultural produce. There have been isolated instances of toxic pollution, particularly by heavy metals in the vicinity of mining operations, and low levels of BHC, DDE and DDT have been detected in national surveys of aquatic organisms. Peat silt pollution is a peculiarly Irish problem, arising from large-scale development of peat bogs for domestic and power-generation fuel.

The high level of potential water resources in Ireland will allow some leeway in protecting the aquatic environment against increasing pollution loads but there is no room for complacency. A large proportion of small Irish towns and villages still discharge untreated or part-treated sewage to watercourses and many of the older industries have totally unsatisfactory waste treatment plants. The lack of effective controlling legislation resulted in serious eutrophication of some large lakes by discharge of slurry from intensive pig-rearing units from 1971 onwards.

The legislative position has improved with the introduction of the 1977 Local Government (Water Pollution) Act, with provisions for adoption of water quality criteria and standards, water quality management plans on a river catchment basis and water quality control authorities. The local authorities are at present the licensing bodies for waste discharges but an anomalous situation exists in that these local authorities themselves discharge effluents (from sewage works) which are not subject to licences.

Abstraction
Although the annual *per capita* run-off of water in Ireland is some five times that of most European countries, domestic, agricultural and industrial use is increasing rapidly. The use of the water resource has proceeded somewhat haphazardly, probably as a result of a general conviction that water is at all times plentiful. Recent dry summers have effectively demonstrated that direct abstraction from rivers or small lakes without additional impounded storage was

quite inadequate for present levels of abstraction.

Considerable use is made of ground water supplies in Ireland and it was estimated in 1974 that there were 60,000 bore-hole supplies to farms alone and that some 5,000 new wells were being sunk every year. *Per capita* consumption is increasing rapidly and is estimated to reach 500 litres per day by the turn of the century.

The need for planned use and management of Irish water resources, including their recreational use, has led the appropriate authorities to engage in a programme aimed at establishing an accurate and extensive data base in this respect. Much of the present and proposed abstraction is 'totally consumptive' in that the resulting wastes are discharged to estuaries or the sea, thus reducing nursery areas for young fish as well as the water available for upstream migration of adults. There are no proposals at present, for inter-river transfers or estuarine barrages.

Power generation

There are five hydroelectric power schemes in operation on salmon rivers in Ireland, these being the Shannon, Lee, Erne, Liffey and Clady/Crolly. The Electricity Supply Board operates salmon smolt rearing stations on the Shannon at Parteen and on the Lee at Carrigadrohid. Eggs, fry and parr are also available from these stations for restocking the other rivers.

The rearing station at Parteen came into operation in 1960 and quickly expanded to an annual production of some 200,000 smolts. The restocking programme had begun to show significant results by the late 1960's but the advent of UDN, combined with increased legal and illegal netting effort, caused a marked decline in the runs of salmon and grilse. This is evident from the counts of fish at Thomond Weir (Limerick) which, whilst not complete, do give a good indication of the levels of stocks:

5 year average :	1963-1967	17,291
5 year average :	1968-1972	15,649
5 year average :	1973-1977	9,912
Provisional count :	1978	2,127

Prior to 1976, the reared fish component (derived from reared smolts) at Thomond Weir did not exceed 12 percent, but this has increased to 20 percent in 1978, indicating a progressive attrition of wild fish numbers, resulting from reduced spawning escapements.

The smolt rearing station on the Lee was brought into operation in 1971, following a disastrous decline in the stocks following impoundment. The counts of salmon at Inniscarra dam fell from 914 in 1965 to only 37 in 1972 but had increased again to 419 in 1976, when virtually all the fish had been derived from the annual production of 150,000 1+ smolts. These reared fish also support a very considerable local and coastal netting effort.

It is worth noting that of 7,657 salmon examined from drift net catches brought into Galway from 19 June to 20 July, 1978, 7.73 percent was fin-clipped and could be expected to have been derived from the reared smolt production at Parteen and Carrigadrohid.

Of the other rivers affected by hydro-electric impoundments, the counts of fish have fallen heavily on the Erne and Clady/Crolly systems but have improved somewhat on the Liffey from 1976. The decline has been aggravated by UDN but is due largely to uncontrolled exploitation of estuarine and coastal stocks.

Whilst there is evidence of reduced salmon stocks in Irish rivers affected by hydro-electric schemes, it is only fair to state that the Electricity Supply Board has made very considerable efforts to maintain and improve the stocks and that without such efforts, the effects of UDN and over-exploitation would have been much more severe.

The collapse of the Lee salmon stocks, however, provides a nice illustration of the effects of an altered environment, where the impoundments provided optimal conditions for pike and trout predators, large areas of salmon nursery ground were drowned and smolts were delayed and damaged at the turbines.

Arterial drainage

A number of extensive arterial drainage schemes have been carried out in Ireland over the past thirty years, where the responsible authority (The Commissioners of Public Works) were exempted from the provisions of the Fisheries Acts by the 1945 Arterial Drainage Act. The deleterious effects are the usual, including destruction of spawning beds, the canalization of watercourses lined with unsightly spoil heaps, the abolition of holding pools and the blanketing effect of the silt load. The drainage authority has claimed that there is no evidence of long-term damage and that some salmon angling has been improved.

Salmon rearing stations have been established, with State aid, to undertake restocking of the Corrib and Boyne systems, following arterial drainage works. On the Boyne, arterial drainage has been held responsible *inter alia* for the decline in the commercial catch of this river from an average of 20,000 salmon per annum to only some 2,000 fish in 1977.

The continuing and expensive maintenance requirements of these schemes is a further disturbing feature and it is fair to say that there are grave doubts as to their efficiency when subjected to cost/benefit analysis.

The Inland Fisheries Commission (1975) recommended that arterial drainage operations should not enjoy exemption from the requirements of the Fisheries Acts and that there should be statutory obligations for joint control of future drainage works between drainage and fishery authorities, as well as consultation with fishery interests.

Exploitation
The current over-exploitation of Irish grilse stocks undoubtedly represents the most serious constraint on their future. There is evidence that the grilse stocks increased markedly from 1962 onwards and this stimulated an increased drift netting effort, in conjunction with a grant-aided programme for larger boats, capable of carrying up to six times the legal length of net, as well as increased depth of net. These nets are now made of light durable synthetic material and may be used with considerable success during daylight hours, as well as by night.

The larger boats are also capable of fishing further from the coast (possibly exploiting 'non-native' stocks), in much rougher sea conditions and for longer periods at sea than the traditional 'currachs'.

The number of drift net licences increased steadily from 363 in 1962 to 1,156 in 1972 and has remained at approximately that level in succeeding years. Some areas of the west coast were banned to drift netting until 1972 but since then have contributed a significant proportion of the increased drift net catch. Numbers of licences have been restricted since 1974 and apparent anomalies in the issue of licences to certain areas has contributed to the considerable increase in illegal nets, including set nets, just out from the shore. The control of these types of illegal netting has proved beyond the resources of the local Boards of Conservators, whose effective jurisdiction may be said to end at the shoreline. In 1978, ships of the Irish Navy were employed for the first time, in the enforcement of drift netting regulations. The success of this procedure was limited by logistic difficulties.

With the technological advances referred to above, the drift net catch increased from 21 percent of the total in 1962 to 72 percent in 1974, with concomitant decreases in the proportions of the draft net and rod catches. It has been apparent, since 1975, that the catch per unit effort of drift nets has declined, although official statistics have not yet been published. This decline has been noted for other methods of capture (rods, river nets and traps) over a longer period and substantiates the overall reduction in escapements that is apparent from the returns of the thirteen fish counters on Irish rivers. In addition, the quality of the escapement has been impaired, in that draft net catches were shown to comprise the smaller fish, with an average weight difference (and therefore, fecundity values) of about 450g (1 lb) between these fish and the heavier fish from drift net samples. It is also noticeable that the proportion of net-marked fish in the escapements has increased markedly, ranging from over 25 percent to over 50 percent during the height of the drift netting season, predisposing them to disease attacks.

The trapping systems on the Burrishoole Fishery in Co Mayo, operated by the Salmon Research Trust of Ireland are capable of counting upstream and downstream runs with a high degree of accuracy. Complete counts are available from 1970 onwards and they confirm that production in fresh water (and therefore, environmental quality) has remained uniform but that survival rates in the sea are undergoing progressive attrition.

Knowing the average size and sex ratio of the spawning escapement, it is possible to calculate the approximate egg deposition value each year and from this the survival to the smolt stage, two years later. (Smolt age composition is 5 percent x1+, 90 percent x2+ and 5 percent x3+.) The results obtained are expressed in the following table as a range between maximum and minimum values, using different parameters for sex ratios and fecundity values.

(Note that the 1975 brood year class produced the smolts of 1978). The figures for survival from smolt to adult are included in *Table 1* for comparison where the figure for 1970 is based on the 1969 smolt count which was only accurate to within limits of 12–14,000.

Table 1 percent survival from smolt to adult stage

Brood year class	% survival rates, ova to smolt	% survival rates, smolt to adult
1970	*0·44 - 0·63*	*9·5 - 11·0*
1971	*0·72 - 0·89*	*5·5*
1972	*0·39 - 0·57*	*11·0*
1973	*0·47 - 0·54*	*12·7*
1974	*0·40 - 0·45*	*8·7*
1975	*0·51 - 0·61*	*9·8*
1976	N/A	*6·3*
1977	N/A	*4·4*
1978	N/A	*5·5**

*estimated value

The figure of 5.5 percent survival from smolt to adult in 1971 probably represents an isolated occurrence, the reasons for which are not known, but the general downward trend of the past five years is significant when related to the escalating drift net catches. The slight improvement in the survival rate for 1978 (based on an estimate, August, 1978) is also interesting, in that the grilse run was poor due to the decreased smolt run in 1977. Many of the legal drift nets fared so badly in the summer of 1978 that they had ceased operations by mid-July, allowing a slightly better escapement of later-running grilse.

When the adult returns from 1974 onwards are correlated with spawning escapements from 1970 onwards, a range of values for the survival to grilse from grilse female spawner can be derived. In order to maintain a self-sustaining population, each grilse female spawner should produce about two adult offspring, but since 1976 these values have shown a disquieting downward trend:

Table 2 survival rate to grilse

Adult return year	Survival rate to grilse, per grilse female (min/max)
1974	*1·48 - 2·06*
1975	*2·83 - 3·29*
1976	*0·97 - 1·39*
1977	*0·80 - 0·89*
1978	*0·90 - 1·00**

*estimated value

This progressive attrition of stocks must give cause for grave concern since we have no knowledge, as yet, of the level to which the wild spawning escapement can fall before reaching 'the point of no return'.

Future development

Virtually none of the ecological restraints discussed above pose a serious, immediate threat to the future of Irish salmon stocks, except that of over-exploitation. Restocking policies will have to be maintained or expanded on rivers affected by hydroelectric schemes, existing legislation concerning pollution can be effective with some amendments and further legislation is required in respect of a national water resources policy and arterial drainage.

The proposed establishment of an Inland Fishery Authority with Regional Boards will provide wider powers for the management of fisheries and control of exploitation. The Bill is expected to come before Irish Parliament in the 1978-1979 session but has not yet been published, so it is impossible to comment on the measures proposed. However, past experience would indicate that restrictions on licence numbers, size of boat, length and depth of net and weekly close seasons are virtually unenforceable. It is possible that only a complete ban on drift netting (with compensation payments) will be effective but the risk of illegal drift netting continuing would still exist, with sale of catch through contacts with the legal market. A more drastic measure, in some respects, would be to shorten the season for all forms of commercial fishing and conserve the salmon stocks by removing the market base. Perhaps the first and most difficult hurdle will be to convince the population as a whole that salmon stocks are endangered and that tough conservation measures are necessary – not to maintain stocks for gentlemen's fishing – but to conserve a very valuable national resource.

References

Annual Reports, Salmon Research Trust of Ireland.
1970–77

DOWNEY, W K & URD, G N, (Eds). *Lake Pollution, Eutrophication Control.*
1977   Stationery Office, Dublin.

McCUMMISKEY, L M. *Water Resources in Ireland.* Dublin. The Institu-
1973   tion of Civil Engineers of Ireland.

Report of the Economics and Social Research Institute, Paper No 75. *The*
1971   *Irish Anglers.*

Report of the Inland Fisheries Commission, Stationery Office, Dublin.
1975

TONER, P F & O'SULLIVAN, A J. *Water Pollution in Ireland.* National
1977   Science Council, Dublin.

TWOMEY, E. Personal Communication.
1978

4 Issues and promises for Atlantic salmon management in Canada.

J A Ritter and T R Porter, Department of Fisheries and Environment of Canada. Y Côté and B Tetreault, Ministère du Tourisme de la Chasse et de la Pêche, Canada

Introduction

The anadromous Atlantic salmon, *Salmo salar*, is distributed throughout Atlantic Canada from Ungava Bay in northern Quebec south to the Canada-United States border (*Fig 1*). Historically, anadromous Atlantic salmon populated tributaries of the Saint Lawrence River downstream of Lake Ontario. Both landlocked and anadromous forms of the species are reported to have inhabited Lake Ontario and its tributaries (Parsons, 1973) until their disappearance approximately 80 years ago. Alterations to the aquatic habitat and excessive fishing were the apparent reasons for their demise. Similarly, within the past 200 years the range of the anadromous Atlantic salmon in the Saint Lawrence River has been reduced to the Ouelle River, situated 100 km downstream from Quebec City. Presently there are more than 350 main rivers in Canada which contain significant populations of Atlantic salmon, and at least 200 other lesser rivers which support small populations. The annual production potential of Canadian waters presently producing Atlantic salmon is roughly 1.4 million adult fish. Current production from these waters exceeds 1.0 million adult salmon. Cultured stocks account for less than 5 percent of Canada's salmon production.

Commercial and recreational fishermen are the principal users of Canada's Atlantic salmon resource. Canadian commercial fishermen generally harvest more that 2,000 tonnes (600,000 salmon) annually (*Fig 2*) while recreational fishermen catch approximately 100,000 adult salmon

annually (*Fig 3*). The number of licensed commercial salmon fishermen in eastern Canada is approximately 6,900,
whereas recreational salmon fishermen number nearly
70,000. Most of the commercial harvest is made in fixed gill
nets and trap nets, situated along the open coast. Recreational fishing is principally confined to the rivers and

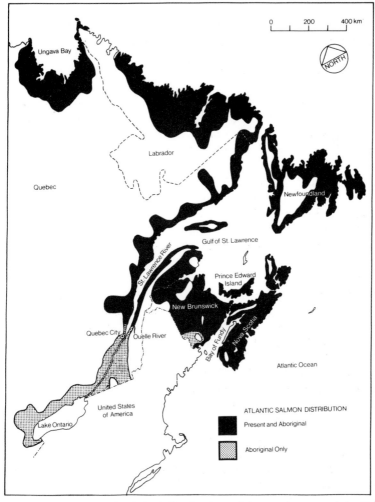

Fig 1   Present and aboriginal distribution of the anadromous Atlantic
salmon in Canada.

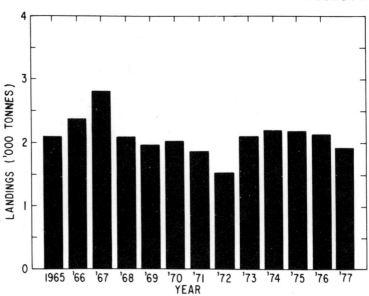

Fig 2 Commercial fisheries landings of Atlantic salmon in Canada, 1965–77.

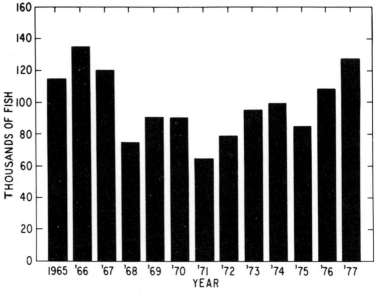

Fig 3 Recreational fisheries catches of Atlantic salmon in Canada, 1965–77.

restricted to fly fishing. An early spring sport fishery on kelts is permitted in parts of New Brunswick. The catch from this fishery represents about 25 percent of this Province's recreational catch and 8 percent of the total sport catch of Atlantic salmon in Canada.

Legislative responsibility for Canada's Atlantic salmon resource lies with the federal government. Management of the stocks is a federal responsibility in four of the Atlantic Provinces and a provincial responsibility in the Province of Quebec. The management goal, common to both Quebec and Canadian governments, is to optimize and sustain the socio-economic benefits that can be derived from the salmon resource. Both governments have a common interest in seeing that the main benefits are distributed among the residents of the province in which the resource is produced. Management of the salmon resource is being achieved through a resolution of conflicting socio-economic and biological considerations. The Atlantic salmon resource in Canada relies on a shrinking freshwater habitat attributable to industrial, municipal and agricultural activities. Proposed hydro-electric development is the main threat to the salmon of Labrador and of the Province of Quebec. Hydro officials of the Province of Newfoundland identify Labrador's potential for hydro-electric power at roughly 9,000 megawatts to be generated from 19 rivers of which 14 have or could support Atlantic salmon. Hydro-Quebec estimates that untapped hydro potential in Quebec is approximately 25,000 megawatts. (*La politique québécoise de l'énergie, assurer l'avenir*, Direction Générale de l'Energie, Gouvernement du Québec 1978, 95 pp. *Rapport sur le potential hydraulique non aménagé du Québec*, Direction Projects de Centrales, Service avant-projects, Hydro-Québec 1976, 29 pp.) Some of the Quebec salmon rivers that could be affected by hydro-electric development schemes being considered include the Romaine, Saint Jean, Moisie, Natashquan and a number of systems that drain into Ungava Bay.

The main purposes of management programmes for Canada's Atlantic salmon are to improve the biological data base, to rebuild depleted stocks, and to protect the freshwater and marine habitats. While measures taken to protect the habitats are 'preventive', initiatives aimed at rebuilding the stocks are 'reactionary'. Although restrictions imposed on users of the resource are contributing to the strengthening of weakened stocks, such restrictions appear to be necessary more and more often as a result of growing demand for Canada's declining salmon stocks. Recognition of this, of conflicts developing between user groups, and of government's concern about the costs of managing the resource, stimulated an extensive review of the social, economic and biological aspects of Canada's Atlantic salmon. The purpose of the 'Atlantic Salmon Review' is to provide the basic background information required to develop a new management plan for the species in Canada. The plan will be developed with inputs from federal and provincial agencies and interested sectors of the public.

This paper presents a synopsis of the major issues confronting managers of Canada's Atlantic salmon and a brief description of the opportunities and strategies for enhancing the resource. Conservation and utilization are discussed and the opportunities and strategies described are preliminary to feasibility studies and detailed planning exercises required prior to implementing a large scale enhancement programme for Atlantic salmon in eastern Canada.

Resource conservation and utilization
The authorized users of Canada's Atlantic salmon resources are commercial fishermen, recreational fishermen and native people. With the exception of the Greenlanders fishing along and off their coast, the commercial fishermen are Canadian and fish in national waters. Both residents and non-residents participate in the recreational fisheries and are licensed by the provincial governments. The native people are North American Indians and Inuit to whom special permits have been issued granting them permission to harvest salmon for food.

Canada's resource allocation policy for the salmon gives priority to stock conservation. Those native people, who have secured recognition of their traditional claims to fish salmon for food on the basis of reasonable need, are given priority over other user groups which fish for salmon in or near the river along which they reside. Their claims are held secondary to the basic requirements for sustaining production. That part of the resource which is surplus to the first two requirements is allocated to commercial and recreational fishermen, the other two authorized users of the resource. The priority for allocation within and between these latter two user groups has been based on socio-economic considerations.

West Greenland fishery

Canada and the United Kingdom are the principal producers of the salmon harvested at Greenland (May, 1973). The fishery that developed along and off the west coast of Greenland grew from an initial 60 tonnes in 1960 to a record level of 2,689 tonnes in 1971. Roughly three-quarters of the fish taken in this fishery are female, and almost all are one sea-winter salmon that would mature initially as multi sea-winter salmon (Parrish, 1973). In Canada, the multi sea-winter salmon are the foundation of the commercial fisheries and the chief source of eggs for the spawning grounds.

The proportion of salmon at West Greenland that are of North American origin has been estimated, using scale characteristics, to range from 32 percent to 46 percent during the years 1969-1974. (W H Lear, Fisheries and Environment of Canada, Saint John's, Newfoundland. Personal communication.) If we assume an average value, which is 40 percent and a harvest of the 1,190 tonne quota for the fishery, 476 tonnes of North American salmon would be taken annually at West Greenland. It is estimated that the fishery at West Greenland when harvesting its full quota of salmon will cause an annual loss to Canadian fisheries and spawning escapements of almost 500 tonnes or more than 100,000 multi sea-winter salmon. This loss equals about one-quarter the annual harvest of Canada's commercial salmon fisheries.

The long term effects of the Greenland fishery on stock recruitment has been reviewed by Paloheimo and Elson (1974) for salmon of the Miramichi River, New Brunswick. Their conclusion from an analysis of catch and stock recruitment data and the results of smolt marking studies was that the Greenland fishery contributed to the all time low commercial catches and recruitment of young that were observed in the Miramichi system during the early 1970's. This conclusion, although derived from data for the Miramichi River salmon, is presumed to be valid for other Canadian salmon stocks whose catch records have shown similar trends.

Although the harvest of salmon of Canadian origin at West Greenland is presently limited by the 1,190 tonne quota for salmon originating from all nations and by the established fishing pattern, the International Commission for the Northwest Atlantic Fisheries (ICNAF) agreement by which the fishery has been controlled may expire at the end of this year. An agreement between the European Economic Community (EEC) and Canada to limit the harvest to 1,190 tonnes for the 1979 fishery appears possible but beyond that the harvest strategy is questionable. Should a new agreement be established which allowed for a higher quota or moving the fishery southward and/or farther off shore of the Greenland coast, increased catches of salmon originating from Canada could be expected. Considering that the demand for the salmon in home waters exceeds our present production, Canada would not favour changes in the fishery that would result in increased losses of salmon of Canadian origin at West Greenland.

Canada's mixed stock fisheries

Most of the Canadian commercial salmon fisheries have become established along the major migration routes and harvest an intermingling of salmon from different stocks. Salmon of a particular stock that contribute to these fisheries do not follow a coasting pattern *en masse* but instead are widely distributed in time and space in individual fisheries and among the many fisheries. The mixed stock fisheries are generally located away from the rivers in which the stocks are produced. Many of the fishermen participating in them derive a major share of their gross income from salmon fishing.

Practically all of Canada's Atlantic salmon commercial

fisheries have received widespread public attention because of the mixed composition of the stocks they harvest. User groups on or near the rivers producing the salmon oppose restrictions placed on them to rebuild stocks while fishermen more distant from the rivers receive lesser cutbacks. The increasing demands placed on the resource have created conflicting views among the users as to whether fishermen on or near the river have greater entitlement to the resource than fishermen distant from the river. In the context of tradition and livelihood necessity, participants in the mixed stock fisheries have been entitled to a share of the resource as have those users on and near the rivers from which the salmon originated.

Recently, the commercial salmon fisheries along the coasts of Newfoundland and Labrador have been the prime targets of interest because their catches, which collectively account for more than three-quarters of Canada's commercial salmon harvest, comprise salmon from a mixture of stocks originating from all parts of eastern North America. The attention that these fisheries received was amplified in the early 1970's when restrictions were imposed on commercial and recreational salmon fishermen of the other provinces in which salmon stocks had declined to dangerously low levels. In this context, a working group was established in 1975 to review the biological information pertaining to the interception of salmon of non-local origin by the commercial fisheries in Newfoundland-Labrador. The working group estimated that 25 percent of the Newfoundland-Labrador commercial catch in the late 1960's and early 1970's was comprised of salmon originating from rivers in Quebec, New Brunswick and Nova Scotia. The prime interest of the working group has been to develop a series of regulatory options which could be used to minimize the catch of stocks of non-Newfoundland and non-Labrador origin while causing the least possible interference with the harvest of Newfoundland and Labrador stocks. The various options developed were based on biological considerations.

Regulatory controls to rebuild stocks have generally been imposed on fisheries situated on or near a river so as to ensure that only the intended stocks are affected. Restriction of mixed stock fisheries to achieve the same effect within a particular stock could result in over-escapements of spawners to other rivers. To effectively restrict mixed stock fisheries for conservation or re-allocation requires a thorough knowledge of both the fisheries and the biology of the stocks they harvest. This knowledge is being derived through ongoing programmes and review processes such as the Atlantic Salmon Review.

Regulating commercial and recreational fisheries
Most Canadian salmon stocks are harvested by both commercial and recreational fisheries. Generally, entry to commercial fisheries is limited and the fishing effort controlled by season and the amount of gear. Recreational fisheries, although not restricted with respect to entry, are controlled by season, gear type and bag limit. In New Brunswick and the Province of Quebec angling on some rivers is restricted by private ownership of angling rights or lease of the waters, or by provincial ownership and control of the waters. Restricted access on selected provincial waters has ensured quality angling in those areas.

Commercial fisheries restrictions have generally been more severe than controls imposed on recreational fisheries. An example of this is the management programme implemented in 1972 to rebuild stocks of the major salmon rivers in New Brunswick and in the Gaspé area of the Province of Quebec. The fishing ban imposed under this programme has prevented commercial fishing for salmon in these areas for the past seven years. The ban encompasses 460 licensed fishermen who, although annually compensated for not fishing are now eager to recommence fishing. The recreational fishermen were restricted at the same time by season adjustments in some areas and by a reduction in the bag limit to two fish in both New Brunswick and the Province of Quebec. In spite of these restrictions their catches have increased substantially and thus they have extracted some of the benefits from the ban on commercial fisheries. Full recovery of the stocks in the major rivers affected by the ban is projected for the early to mid 1980's. Peak production levels will not be attained at the same time in all systems because of differences in the depleted state of the stocks.

The recreational and commercial fishermen are authorized users of the resource and as such have been entitled to a share of the available harvest. Restrictions imposed on recreational and commercial fishermen have generally been for conservation rather than for re-allocation to other user groups. Canadian and Quebec governments maintain a common position that the resource is to be shared by the recreational and commercial fishermen and that allocations are to be based on maximizing the socio-economic benefits that can be derived from the salmon.

Native food fisheries
Interest in utilizing the Atlantic salmon has developed among Indian bands situated in Atlantic Canada as recently as the mid-1970's. This new interest in the salmon resource coincides with widespread movement across North America of native people (Indians and Inuit) pursuing their aboriginal claims to lands and resources. Increases in the abundance of Atlantic salmon in the major river systems of New Brunswick and the Province of Quebec, occurring with the closure of their commercial fisheries in 1972, were local stimuli to the movement in these areas.

In Atlantic Canada, the native groups are located in Nova Scotia, New Brunswick, Labrador and the Province of Quebec. A few Indian bands in New Brunswick and the Province of Quebec and all native groups in Labrador are authorized to harvest the salmon under food fishery permits. The agreements under the food fishery permits, signed between governments and the band councils, have been designed primarily to rationalize native exploitation and protect the salmon stocks. Since governments are responsible for the well-being of the salmon resource, conservation has been given priority over native claims. The agreements authorize limited salmon fishing for food purposes only, in specific areas on or adjacent to the reservation. A major and universal condition of the agreements was a total restriction on sale or barter of salmon by the native people. Signed agreements have generally specified quotas, fishing zones, seasons, types of gear and numbers and lengths of nets. Following the signing of initial agreements in Atlantic Canada, other Indian bands located along major salmon rivers have expressed interest in negotiating similar arrangements.

Major breaches in the terms of existing agreements between governments and some Indian bands have been encountered. Market prices for Atlantic salmon have been high and the native people are attempting to reinforce their claims to the fisheries. Reports of infractions include fishing at periods other than stated and agreed upon, significantly exceeding the quotas established as band food requirements and openly selling Atlantic salmon. The establishment of food requirements of native communities has been a problem as has the procurement of accurate catch and effort statistics for the food fisheries. Attempts to include native participation in the tabulation of statistics have not been successful. Efforts by governments to maintain regulations have led to confrontations and to escalation of Indian demands.

Although aboriginal claims by native people to fish and wildlife resources have yet to be resolved, progress is being made towards the development of settlements. Through the existing agreements a dialogue has been established between governments and the native people. Government conservation officers are now known and tolerated on most reservations.

Salmon by-catch

Many of the inshore fisheries throughout eastern Canada have been harvesting the Atlantic salmon in other species gear. The magnitude of this 'by-catch' varies considerably with location and gear type; an individual fisherman's annual catch could range from a few fish to several hundred. Salmon by-catches most often occur in inshore fishing gear used to catch herring, mackerel, cod, gaspareau and shad. The salmon by-catch of non-licensed salmon fishermen is sold locally and only an estimate is recorded in catch statistics, whereas salmon by-catch of licensed salmon fishermen is generally recorded in salmon catch statistics. Indications are that much of the salmon by-catch is made in gear 'purposefully' set to catch salmon.

Accurate estimates of the levels of by-catch, although few in number, indicate that its magnitude is significant in certain areas. In a study of 1976 salmon landings for the Province of Newfoundland and Labrador it was estimated that approximately 29 percent of salmon landings in Newfoundland and three percent of the Labrador landings were made in gear not licensed for salmon. (D Reddin, Fisheries and Environment of Canada, Saint John's, Newfoundland. Personal communication.) The by-catch in 1976 is estimated to equal 380,250 kg or 19 percent of the Province's commercial salmon catch. Herring and mackerel gill nets and cod traps accounted for 60 percent and 33 percent of the by-catch respectively.

In the Province of Quebec the by-catch of salmon has been most evident in the Gaspé area since 1972 when the commercial salmon fishery was closed. Catch records indicate that the by-catch in the Gaspé area has increased to 17,600 kg in 1977 or approximately one-third the 1971 catch by licensed salmon fishermen. This increase has coincided with government incentives to support an inshore cod fishery, primarily utilizing monofilament nets. Indications are that salmon by-catch in the Gaspé area is significantly higher than that shown in official catch records.

Although no comparable estimates are available for by-catches in and about New Brunswick river systems closed to commercial salmon fishing, catch statistics indicate that salmon by-catches in these areas have also increased. Based on reported catches the majority of New Brunswick's 1976 by-catches were made in herring and mackerel gill nets (37 percent), mackerel drift nets (31 percent) and groundfish gill nets (25 percent). Excluding the mackerel drift nets, this same gear accounted for Nova Scotia's salmon by-catch almost equals the catch reported that year for licensed salmon gear in Nova Scotia, (79,069 kg).

By-catches account for between 20 percent and 30 percent of the total Atlantic salmon harvest by Canada's commercial fisheries. Indications are that by-catches are increasing in many areas, a situation requiring the implementation of management strategies to curb losses of salmon. By-catches made in gear purposefully set to catch salmon will, in most instances, be more easily controlled through regulation than by-catches made incidental to catches of other species for which gear is set. In Newfoundland, recent adjustments to the season for mackerel and herring fixed net fisheries have reduced by-catches of salmon. Elsewhere and in Newfoundland, programmes are ongoing to provide improved catch statistics and understanding of those fisheries for other species that harvest salmon as by-catch. Solutions to by-catch problems will be developed from the information derived from these programmes.

Illegal fishing
Illegal fishing for salmon exists in both marine and inland waters. It predominates in the areas of high production and along rivers that are readily accessible.Although jigging or snagging accounts for a high percentage of the illegal fishing violations and is a serious problem in the smaller rivers, it does not have as great an impact on the salmon resources as illegal netting in both coastal waters and the larger rivers. Despite the general knowledge that the illegal harvest of salmon is substantial in certain areas, quantification of losses and determination of its impact on the resource have been difficult.

The increase in the illegal harvest of salmon is coincidental with decreases in the availability of legally caught salmon. This was noted to occur in New Brunswick and the Gaspé area of Quebec, following the implementation of the ban on commercial salmon fishing in these areas in 1972. High prices, availability of local markets, and increased abundance of salmon in the rivers are the principal incentives for the high levels of poaching in these areas. Short-term solutions to Canada's illegal fishing problems lie with our enforcement groups and court systems. Education and the development of increased community involvement in management of the Atlantic salmon resource will be key factors in the long-term solution to these problems.

Resource enhancement

A large scale Atlantic salmon enhancement programme in eastern Canada appears to be justified on the basis of demand, opportunity and feasibility. The demands of the various user groups for the salmon resource have increased beyond the present production capability. Inventories of our rivers and stocks indicate opportunities to both expand the range of the species and increase salmon production within accessible streams. Many of the technical measures that would be used in a large-scale enhancement programme are similar to those used in existing programmes. The social and economic benefits from enhancement of the stocks would be distributed throughout eastern Canada; principally to the traditional users of the resource, *ie* recreational and commercial fishermen and the native people.

Optimism as to the feasibility of Atlantic salmon enhancement is strengthened by the successes of existing programmes such as that on the La Have River in Nova Scotia in which adult salmon production by that river has more than doubled in the past six years as a result of an enhancement scheme involving fishway construction and hatchery stocking. (R Gray, Fisheries and Environment of Canada, Halifax, Nova Scotia. Personal communication.) The 1977 sport catch on this small system was 1,700 salmon, more than twice the record catch for this system prior to enhancement. Similarly, on the Exploits River, on Insular Newfoundland, adult salmon production has increased five to six times since the late 1950's as a result of enhancement activities on that river involving fishway construction, adult transfers, and fry stocking from spawning channels and deep substrate incubators. The adult salmon run to the Exploits River in 1977 after commercial harvest in the sea exceeded 8,000 fish. In the Province of Quebec, the renowned Moisie River is expected to triple its present production within the next five years as a result of a joint venture by the Government of Quebec and a private corporation in which the range of salmon is being extended 165 km through fishway construction and adult transplants.

Opportunities

The opportunities for Atlantic salmon enhancement in
eastern Canada exist as a result of the environmental constraints limiting production of this species in fresh water.
Inventories of rivers indicate a large potential for increasing salmon production through the opening and colonization of obstructed areas and re-colonization of accessible
areas lacking viable stocks. Approximately 90 percent of
the potential for enhancement lies in waters inaccessible to
salmon because of natural or man-made barriers. The
remaining 10 percent exists within waters accessible to salmon but requiring recolonization. These barren, accessible
waters include those formerly obstructed by dams or pollution, those which continue to experience industrial or
domestic pollution, those affected by severe fishing pressure over an extended interval or a combination of the
aforementioned factors.

Potential production from colonization is approximately
562,000 adult salmon that would be available annually to
Canadian fisheries and spawning escapements. Production
potential is based on estimated stream habitat potential and
assumed smolt production capabilities that range from 0.2
smolts per 100 square meters for waters in Ungava Bay area
of northern Quebec (Powers, 1969) to 3.5 smolts per 100
square metres for the more productive rivers on Insular
Newfoundland. Assumed survival rates from smolt to adult
return to Canadian fisheries and spawning escapements
generally ranged from 10 percent to 14 percent. The
waters in the province of Newfoundland and Labrador and
the Province of Quebec account for 54 percent and 27
percent of this adult salmon production potential, while
streams on Prince Edward Island, an area virtually devoid
of Atlantic salmon, have almost no potential for increase.
Full production from all waters with potential for
enhancement would increase Atlantic salmon production
in Canada above the potential of its present salmon-
producing waters by approximately 40 percent. Quebec's
increase would be 49 percent, Newfoundland and Labrador's 42 percent and the other three provinces' 22 percent.

Full production from colonization of all waters with potential for enhancement would make available, above allowances for spawning needs, 419,000 adult salmon for allocation to fisheries operating within Canadian inshore and inland waters. This represents more than 50 percent of the 1977 harvest of Atlantic salmon by Canadian fisheries. The weight of the harvestable salmon from all waters with potential for enhancement is roughly 1,500 tonnes or approximately three-quarters Canada's 1977 commercial salmon catch.

Atlantic salmon production in Canada could be further increased through the development of specialized commercial and recreational fisheries totally supported by culture. These specialized fisheries would be located so as not to interfere with production or harvest of natural-producing stocks. This strategy of sea-ranching may be used to compensate for large industrial schemes such as hydro-electric development. The creation of specialized fisheries by this strategy is technically feasible.

Pen-rearing of Atlantic salmon in the sea is a further stock enhancement strategy that is being considered in Atlantic Canada. Small-scale pilot studies carried out in coastal waters have generally had limited success because of low winter sea water temperatures and associated ice and winter storms. The success and widespread application of sea-pen culture of salmon in Atlantic Canada is dependent upon the development of technology that will permit the overwintering of fish in the sea in spite of prevailing lethal surface water temperatures. Private investment in sea-pen culture of Atlantic salmon is expected should the strategy prove to be technically and economically feasible in Canadian waters.

Techniques

The major thrust of an enhancement programme would be to extend the range of the Atlantic salmon into inaccessible areas through provision of fish passages and stocking with young salmon. The fish passage problem of any enhancement project would be resolved by removing the obstruction, or constructing a fishway, or trapping the fish at the base of the obstruction and transporting them over or around the obstruction. This latter strategy is the least preferred because of the annual costs required for operations, while obstruction removal is preferred where possible in view of past records of effectiveness and low cost. Associated with many up-stream fish passage problems, particularly at hydro-electric dams, is the requirement to develop safe downstream passage for juvenile salmon produced above obstructions.

The seed stock for colonization could range from adults, originating from nearby rivers, to cultured juveniles. The adult transfer technique is the least costly of the various seeding alternatives, and although it has been used successfully in the Newfoundland area, its application in enhancement projects is limited by the availability of sufficient genetically suited brood fish. Culture facilities would provide most of the seed stock for enhancement projects. The cultured stocks would range from unfed fry to smolts and originate from modern hatcheries, spawning channels and swim-up fry incubation boxes. The stocking strategies employed would be specific to the project and based on their appropriateness in terms of biological effectiveness, brood fish availibility, costs and time frame.

For the province of Nova Scotia, New Brunswick and Prince Edward Island, opinion favours hatcheries and the production of smolts to support proposals for salmon enhancement. This strategy is preferred because of scarcities of suitable brood fish for colonization programmes and a recognition of the opportunities to develop specialized commercial and recreational fisheries supported principally by cultured smolts. A third reason is the likelihood that government will be expected to provide preliminary support to initiatives in the private sector aimed at developing a viable aquaculture industry involving Atlantic salmon. For these three provinces a hatchery modernization scheme, involving replacement of the older inefficient stations with three new hatcheries and the upgrading of two others, would be proposed. In the Province of Newfoundland and Labrador the strategies favoured are fry stocking from deep-substrate egg incubators and adult transfers. A major fish culture facility would provide support to the egg incubators and a base for research activities. Consideration is also being given to the use of natural lakes as rearing ponds that would be stocked with fry from the deep substrate incubators. As preliminary investigations into the use of natural lakes as rearing ponds for salmon are producing encouraging results (V Peppar, Fisheries and Environment of Canada, Saint John's, Newfoundland. Personal communication), more detailed studies are proposed to determine the feasibility and practicality of widespread application of this enhancement strategy. The province of Quebec would also require some form of culture facilities to support salmon enhancement projects should they be undertaken.

Planning and time frame
The most practical time frame for implementation and evaluation of a large-scale Atlantic salmon enhancement programme for eastern Canada would be 20 years. Prior to implementation of the programme, a two or three year planning period would be required. In this planning phase, social and economic evaluations of proposed enhancement initiatives would be carried out to enable selection and priorization of projects. A programme to increase public involvement in salmon enhancement would be initiated, and the detailed biological and engineering information required for identification, costing, scheduling and implementation of specific projects would be developed.

Impact
A large-scale Atlantic salmon enhancement programme aimed at increasing salmon production throughout eastern Canada would strengthen the economic base of coastal communities, some of which have very few other sources of income. The programme would increase earning opportunities for commercial fishermen, and those employed by the support industries of fisheries. Recreational fisheries would be enhanced, thus providing increased tourist revenues, enjoyment for more anglers, and stimulation of local businesses that cater to recreational fishermen. An

Atlantic salmon enhancement programme would decrease unemployment and social assistance payments, thus partially offsetting regional disparity through resource generated income. The encouragement of public awareness, involvement, input and concern for fish resources through public forum and media coverage of salmon enhancement and conservation projects would discourage illegal fishing through overt community disapproval of such activities.

Conclusions

In spite of the encroachment by industrial and development activities on the habitat of the salmon and the depleted state of several of the stocks, optimism exists regarding the future of Canada's Atlantic salmon resource both because of recent developments and because of initiatives proposed or being considered. Governments at the federal and provincial levels have recently strengthened their legislation pertaining to the protection of the environment and the prevention of illegal fishing. The Atlantic Salmon Review, which is nearly completed, will provide the basis for developing a new management plan that will take into account the heightened demands for salmon. Should salmon enhancement prove to be worthwhile and desirable, more Atlantic salmon would become available for allocation to the various users of the resource.

Acknowledgements

We wish to acknowledge that much of the material presented in this paper was taken from task force reports of the Atlantic Salmon Review or provided by members working on the Review. We are particularly grateful to them and others who provided information and/or advice on the various topics dealt with in this paper. The manuscript was critically reviewed by Drs A W May, G Moisan and J H C Pippy and Messrs R E Cutting, N E MacEachern, J D Pratt and G E Turner.

References

MAY, A W. *Distribution and migrations of salmon in the northwest*
1973 *Atlantic*. International Atlantic Salmon Foundation, Special Pub. Series, Vol 4 (1): 373–82.

PALOHEIMO, J E & ELSON, P F. Reduction of Atlantic salmon *(Salmo*
1974 *salar)* catches in Canada attributed to the Greenland fishery. *J Fish Res Bd Canada* 31: 1467–80.

PARRISH, B B. *A review of the work of the ICES/ICNAF Joint Working*
1973 *Party on North Atlantic salmon*. International Atlantic Salmon Foundation, Special Pub. Series, Vol 4 (1): 383–96.

PARSONS, J W. *History of salmon in the Great Lakes, 1850-1970*. United
1973 States Department of the Interior, Fish and Wildlife Service, Bureau of Sport Fisheries and Wildlife. Technical Paper 68, 79 pp.

POWERS, G. *The salmon of Ungava Bay*. Arctic Institute of North
1969 America, No 22: 7–72.

5 Present status of the Atlantic salmon stocks in France and environmental constraints on their extension

A R Brunet, Conseil Superieur de la Pêche, Paris

Introduction

The river basins frequented by Atlantic salmon, from the south to the north, are the Adour (Gave d'Oloron and Nive), Nivelle, Loire (Allier) and approximately 25 small coastal rivers in Brittany (mainly), Normandy and Picardy. Unfortunately, these salmon stocks are in danger of extinction. For example, the annual number of salmon taken in the Adour (Gave d'Oloron basin) from 1972 to 1977 showed a reduction from 600 to 200 (66 percent) for angling and 2,000 to 100 (95 percent) for net fishing. These figures must give rise to alarm. The main causes for the reduction appear to be ulcerative dermal necrosis (UDN) disease (which appeared in the early seventies), and increased captures at Greenland.

By a decision of 30 June, 1975 the Interdepartmental Committee for Nature and the Environment decided to take action to safeguard and develop the salmon stocks. A salmon programme to extend over five years (1976 to 1980) was established. It was necessary to modify the existing fishing regulations so as to permit a greater number of fish into the rivers either to spawn naturally or provide stock for hatcheries where ova would be reared, some to the smolt stage.

Fishing regulation and enforcement

Regulation

In the Allier the opening date for fishing has been progressively changed from 20 January to 12 March. Sanctuaries, extending over 20 to 32 kms, out of a total length of 400 kms, have been established.

These measures now appear insufficient, and suggestions have been made in France that there should be a total ban on salmon fishing for several years.

Enforcement
Twenty water bailiffs in regional mobile squads control salmon fishing in fresh water. Salmon fishermen in France number about 3,000. Their numbers have decreased steadily since 1972, but not as fast as the decline in catches. On the other hand the numbers of other types of fishermen is 1,000 times greater and they are increasing year by year.

Technical programme
This can be summarised under five headings:

Stock evaluation and population dynamics
By means of counters installed in fish passes in the lower stretches of rivers and the tagging of smolts, information is collected. Control stations already exist on some of the coastal rivers in Brittany. The runs of adult fish are incompletely recorded but those of smolts are more accurate.

Broadly, the smolt runs in the Allier-Loire Rivers were estimated to be 25,000 in 1975, 40,000 in 1946 and 50,000 in 1977.

Creation of rearing stations
The aims were: (1) Re–introduction of salmon into denuded rivers and (2) Development of existing stocks, the second aim being given priority.

Salmon were re-introduced into the good biological quality waters of rivers which had runs until recent years. An experimental phase of releasing smolts and checking on the return of adults was deemed to be important before starting a programme of providing hatcheries, fish passes *etc*.

A programme on these lines, to extend over three years, was started on the Dordogone River in 1977. Any returning adults being checked at the first impassable dam in the Bergerac area. The ova used for this experiment were obtained partly from the Allier and partly from Scotland.

Development of existing stocks

In rivers still having salmon, the progeny of native spawners are released in their original river. Regional hatcheries, managed by the Conseil Supérieur de la Pêche, the fishing district federations or research laboratories, have already been established and others are planned in the Torpt and Ell in Normandy, Augerolles in Auvergne, and Navarreux in Béarn. Extensive rearing (mainly in Brittany and the Basque country) will supplement these hatcheries and advantage will also be taken of the highly productive watercress ponds. Genetic and sanitary control will also be enforced in privately owned hatcheries.

The fish ecology laboratory of the National Institute for Agronomic Research (INRA) which is concerned, *inter alia*, with salmon research, operates an experimental hatchery and nursery streams on the St. Pée-sur-Nivelle in the Basque country.

Details of the individual programmes were given:

Jacques Dumas, INRA St. Pée-sur-Nivelle

Until recently the River Nivelle possessed only a residual population of about 20 adult Atlantic salmon. In 1977, a sample of 52 adults from this river showed that this population was being restored and that hatchery-reared salmon contributed 58 percent of the total.

Smolts were released in the spring of 1976 from the INRA experimental station in St. Pée-sur-Nivelle. They received a double mark; cold-brand plus adipose fin clip. First returns of adults of hatchery reared fish gave information on the appearance and retention of the cold-branded scars. Of the fin clipped salmon 76 percent bore a readable mark 19 to 20 months after branding.

Grilse made up the bulk of the sample (91 percent of wild fish and all those of hatchery origin). 'Hatchery grilse' were obtained from ova imported from the River Thurso (Scotland); the re-capture rate in the river of hatchery reared salmon released as two-year-old smolts was 12 times greater than that of one-year-old smolts (1.42 percent compared with 0.12 percent).

Both wild and hatchery-reared grilse of the River Nivelle had one of the best growth rates in the Atlantic basin, averaging 67.7 cm in length. Sex-ratios of 1.5 to 1.7:1 in favour of females are very high for grilse.

Releases of hatchery-reared smolts of remote origin (2,000 km) have given a good start to the process of rehabilitation of the Nivelle salmon stock.

Finally, plans are being made for the construction of fish ladders on three dams to open up the Upper Nivelle basin to spawning adults.

P Davaine and E Beall, INRA St. Pée-sur-Nivelle
Since 1975, INRA has attempted to introduce Atlantic salmon into the Kerquelen Islands, a 6,000 km archipelago in the South Indian Ocean (49°S, 71°E).

Batches of 50,000 to 100,000 ova of Danish or Scottish (Polly River) origin packed in ice in insulated polystyrene boxes took 10 days to 30 day by air and sea before reaching the Islands. Upon arrival in the middle of the summer, eyed eggs were incubated in a small hatchery until the yolk sac was absorbed. Surviving fry (50 to 80 percent) were then released in two lake systems which had easy access to the sea and rivers with suitable spawning grounds.

Population inventories were made by electrofishing in representative sections of the streams. Survival after one year was very good (up to 90 percent in some sections) and the growth rate was fair (average length 10 cm one year after release). Smoltification occurs mostly at two or three years old, sometimes at four.

A few pre-grilse were captured in 1978 at the mouth of the river, and the first adults are expected in 1979.

Other laboratories, such as that at Rennes, are also involved in salmon research within the framework of the five year programme. These studies are essentially aimed at practical results. Significant results have already been obtained.

Passage of fish over dams
Fish passes, or Borland type fish lifts are required for many

works under construction or scheduled for erection. On any waters having migratory salmon the contractor is responsible for the erection of the necessary passage for fish. Subsidies may be available where adequate safeguards for the passage of fish are provided.

Faced with the strong demand for hydro-electric harnessing of rivers, it is often difficult to provide adequately for the salmon. It is, however, significant that in the Adour basin the administration has opposed the erection of new dams in those sections of the river frequented by salmon.

Existing works: Where the existing works have no proper facilities for the passage of fish the body concerned is approached with a view to provision of fish passes *etc.* The Government may make a financial contribution but usually the work done must be such as not to interfere with working of the plant associated with the obstruction.

Attempts are being made to build fish passes on coastal streams in Brittany and the Basque-Béarn region. Because of the shortness of the rivers and the small number of dams, chances of success are good. In the case of long rivers such as the Loire the capture of adults below the lowest dam and transferring them to the upstream spawning grounds would appear to be the most practical solution.

Environment improvement

Particularly in the spawning reaches improvement of spawning grounds has been undertaken by clearing tree stumps and cutting back growths on the banks. In Brittany and Normandy long stretches of rivers have been cleaned in this way, with the financial assistance of interested organizations.

Anti-pollution measures: Where pollution appears to be a danger to salmon stocks, finance may be available, in connection with the salmon programme, to combat the difficulty.

Y Harache and P Proutet
The Centre Océanologique de Bretagne (CNEXO) has,

since 1972, undertaken studies of the salmon stocks in the rivers of Finisterre, mainly the Aulne and Elorn, with a view to the estimation of stock size, characteristics based upon scale reading, evaluation of water quality, together with restocking experiments and rearing in sea cages of both Atlantic and coho salmon.

Four nursery streams of the Elorn and Aulne Rivers were restocked with ova and unfed fry of Scottish (Tay) origin and the results evaluated. Nine recaptures were made in 1977 and 1978 in nursery streams from these stockings with foreign fish, the river and sea ages and sizes being identical with those of local stock. A small hatchery producing 10,000 smolts was operated in conjunction with the local association.

Bi-weekly sampling for water quality of the Elorn River was undertaken at 13 stations in fresh water and a complementary programme was undertaken by another research ream of the Centre Unité Littoral as regards the Rade de Brest, including the Elorn estuary.

Advantage was taken of the coho salmon sea cage rearing experiments to conduct a similar experiment with smolts of the Atlantic salmon which were introduced into the sea pens in June 1976. Survival was low due to bacterial infection but the fish reached sexual maturity in December 1977 producing 15,000 ova. The fry were small and further mortalities occurred. Further experiments are in progress.

Conclusions

Actions taken for the protection of salmon are necessarily long term, five years elapsing before the effects of any measures can be assessed. However, there are some encouraging signs of improvements. These are:

(1) UDN has regressed since 1975,
(2) Overall pollution levels appear to be improving and
(3) There have been increases in smolt runs in the Allier-Loire rivers. Reports indicate they have doubled from 1975 (25,000) to 1977 (50,000).

The majority of these smolts were hatchery reared.

Tests carried out by INRA on the Nivelle river with ova of Scottish origin showed that out of 50 recaptured adults, 58 percent were derived from the hatchery to which they returned.

Sea trout (fario and rainbow) are produced naturally in many French coastal rivers, where they appear to be abundant. Ova of Polish origin have been planted systematically in Normandy and less systematically with fario and rainbow trout from Danish imported eggs.

An environmental improvement for salmon will benefit also sea trout. In France, where angling has a long tradition, sea trout interest many fishermen, even in the Mediterranean streams where these fish have started to appear. Sea trout also do not face the hazards of a long sea travel and the harmful fishery off Greenland, as do salmon.

6 Planning as related to the restoration of Atlantic salmon in New England

W Stolte, United States Fish and Wildlife Service

Introduction

A co-ordinated plan for the restoration of Atlantic salmon in New England has become a necessity. There remains today much confusion regarding the restoration programme at the Federal, State and private levels. Competition for funds and hatchery fish exists between programmes, and it has become increasingly difficult for the United States Fish and Wildlife Service to develop realistic objectives and programme priorities.

Therefore a major thrust of the United States Fish and Wildlife Service is the development of a co-ordinated Federal State restoration plan for New England. A number of Federal restoration plans have been written in the past. None was ever implemented because they failed to obtain input from the State participants during their development.

This planning operation has been under way for 19 months. The plan will have three components addressing: (1) the Connecticut River, (2) the Merrimack River and (3) selected rivers in Maine. Although the three components are themselves unique, they will encompass similar philosophies and deal with a number of similar problems.

Philosophies

The philosophies of the participating agencies had to be incorporated in order for the Atlantic Salmon Plan to be a viable working document. These philosophies have been defined in two principal ways:

1. The development and maintenance of a salmon population entirely from hatchery production in order to provide specific levels of sport harvest.
2. The development and maintenance of a salmon population with the principal objective of optimizing the wild smolt production.

Their importance lies in two areas. (1) hatchery needs, and (2) management programmes.

The first definition requires total reliance on the hatchery and generates a management programme that addresses only the sport fishery. Supply and demand become the pivotal considerations. Although hatchery production needs based on specific adult population levels can be reasonably estimated for many of our rivers, the actual adult needs are unknown. This makes the justification of various hatchery production programmes difficult.

Management programmes, although narrower in scope than those that would be needed relative to the second definition, would not be without their problems. Sport fishing exploitation rates in the United States vary from less than 10 percent to approximately 25 percent of an adult population (Meister, 1978; personal communication). How the salmon manager will cope with the potential excess of adult salmon is both important and difficult. The traditional concept of Atlantic salmon fishing may very well be in jeopardy.

The second definition, in reality, will also require a reliance on the hatchery. The development and maintenance of a spawning population will require hatchery supplementation in most cases. However, hatchery programme needs can be estimated based on specific wild fish deficiencies. Justification would be more easily established than in the previous situation.

Management programmes, designed to protect a required number of spawners, would be challenging in view of the existing fisheries programmes and the major clientele supporting the participating agencies.

A combination of the two definitions will be necessary in the Atlantic Salmon Plan. The United States Fish and Wildlife Service believes quite strongly that restoration should be a recovery operation. This relates specifically to the second definition. We also realize that sport fishing will be important. However, it should be provided only by salmon not needed for spawning.

Major problems

There are four basic areas that present immediate problems to each of the three restoration programmes: (1) brood stock development, (2) fish passage, (3) hydroelectric facilities, and (4) resident freshwater fisheries.

A lack of suitable stocks from which eggs could be obtained continually plagues the Connecticut and Merrimack Rivers' programmes. This problem is obviously not as critical in Maine.

Fish passage may have to be considered at, possibly, 100 obstructions.

Downstream migrant losses at approximately 64 hydroelectric facilities will have to be considered. It has been estimated that up to 51 percent of the smolt population leaving the Merrimack River may be lost before reaching the marine environment (Rizzo, 1977; personal communication). The need to rehabilitate old dams, not now producing power, increases with our energy needs; therefore this problem may very well become magnified.

Our major rivers, such as the Penobscot, Merrimack, and Connecticut Rivers, have a diverse freshwater fish fauna. The Penobscot River has at least 38 species, the Merrimack River, 46, and the Connecticut River, 60 species (Scarola, 1973; Wightman, 1973 and 1971; Bridges *et al*, 1969; Whitworth *et al*, 1968; Cutting, 1963; and Bailey *et al*, 1939). Potential salmon predators such as chain pickerel *Esox niger* (Lesueur), small mouth bass *Micropterus dolomieui* (Lacepede), and the American eel *Anguilla rostrata* (Lesueur), *etc* abound in much of our waters. There are also areas having wild populations of rainbow trout *Salmo gairdneri* (Richardson), brown trout *Salmo trutta* (Linnaeus), and brook trout *Salvelinus fontinalis* (Mitchill) supporting significant sport fisheries. Additional areas support intensive sport fisheries for trout using put-and-take programmes. Whether or not a successful restoration of Atlantic salmon will have a significant impact on these fisheries, or *vice versa*, is unknown.

A fifth factor peculiar to the Connecticut River is the important commercial fishery for American shad *Alosa sapidissima* (Wilson). This fishery operates in the lower 100 kilometres of the river during April, May and June and harvests approximately 15 percent of the shad entering the Connecticut River (Jones *et al*, 1976). The potential impact that this fishery will have on the salmon restoration programme is unknown.

Strategic plan for the restoration of Atlantic salmon to the Merrimack River – a model

I would like now to focus attention on the restoration plan itself. The Merrimack River salmon plan is given as an example as it is nearly completed and is serving as a guide in the development of the restoration plans for the Connecticut River and selected rivers in Maine.

The goal

Our first priority was to develop a goal that would encompass the philosophies of the various co-operating agencies. The following goal statement reflects both recovery and sport fishery programmes:

'To restore the Atlantic salmon resource to a level of optimal utilization of the existing habitat in the Merrimack River Basin for public benefit.'

The recovery programme

The recovery approach necessitated that we address the following four questions: (1) What could the habitat be expected to produce relative to wild smolts? (2) How many smolts could be expected to reach the marine environment? (3) What marine survival could be expected? (4) What would be the size of the spawning escapement needed to produce the expected wild smolt production?

The basis for our speculation on these questions came from salmon studies being conducted in the Merrimack River, the Connecticut River, selected rivers in Maine, and scientific publications. Aside from current studies, we relied heavily on data regarding salmon in the Penobscot River.

There are two reasons we relied on the Penobscot River data for comparative purposes: (1) both the Merrimack River and the Penobscot River are similar biologically and physically, and (2) the salmon being released into the Merrimack River are primarily of Penobscot River origin.

From field surveys the salmon nursery habitat was quantified. Only the Pemigewasset River system, the principal tributary of the Merrimack River, offered acceptable salmon habitat. Production estimates for the Pemigewasset River and its tributaries range from 2.0 to 3.25 smolts per 100 square-metre unit; the average being 2.6. It was concluded that 86,000 smolts could be produced annually.

We then estimated that only 43,000 smolts would actually reach the Merrimack River estuary. This figure was based entirely on the expected losses (4.0-15.5 percent) at each of seven hydro-electric dams. Some of us feel that these estimates are excessively high. However, the estimated total loss may be more accurate than we think since downstream migrant losses due to predators have not been assessed.

Of the 43,000 smolts that are expected to reach the ocean, we anticipate that only three percent, or roughly 1,300 salmon, will return to enter the mouth of the Merrimack River.

We have speculated further that a spawning population of at least 1,700 salmon will be required in the Pemigewasset River. As most of us had anticipated, a wild run of salmon in the Merrimack River could not sustain itself without hatchery supplementation.

The sport fishery
Since the spawning population will have to be maintained through hatchery supplementation, it is obvious that any sport fishery will increase our hatchery production needs. We have calculated that to produce one adult in excess of the spawning population will require the release of 200 smolts. However, the actual size of the hatchery programme cannot be realistically estimated since it will depend on the magnitude of the sport fishery that develops.

Areas of concern

The plan then addressed those areas that concerned the participating resource agencies. Our most pressing problem deals with providing access to the Pemigewasset River for returning salmon. There are presently seven hydroelectric dams; one flood control structure; three low-head dams; and one natural barrier that will prevent salmon from reaching the spawning grounds.

Additional areas that were discussed are:

The reliability of our estimates

Water quality (present and projected)

Minimum river flows (no water management policy exists today)

Water diversions

Resident fisheries

Incidental harvest of salmon (inshore coastal waters and river)

Salmon poaching

Projected development within the basin

Management of Atlantic salmon within the basin

Objectives

We then turned our attention to developing the long-range objectives of the restoration plan. There were two:

(1) Develop and maintain a run of Atlantic salmon in the Merrimack River such that 2,000 fish will be available for spawning in the Pemigewasset River system within 15 years.

(2) Provide 1,000 adults in excess of the spawning population for a sport fishery within 15 years.

Three broad strategies dealing with obtaining sufficient numbers of smolts, providing access to the Pemigewasset River for returning salmon, and providing for the management of the resource were necessary in order to achieve the above objectives.

Each of these strategies can be considered in a number of ways – what we call achievement alternatives. In fact, 22 alternatives were generated.

The tedious job of analysing these alternatives was complicated by the inter-dependency of the alternatives themselves. However, the analysis did provide us with a range of egg, fry, smolt, and brood stock requirements as related to expected impacts at hydro-electric facilities and the method of providing adult access to the Pemigewasset River.

Obviously this was important since the entire programme would be a hatchery product until successful natural reproduction was achieved. Throughout the analysis we have made the assumption that hatchery smolts would not survive as well as their wild counterparts and have estimated an adult return rate of one percent.

With an estimated range in hatchery smolt requirements of between 425,000 and 865,000 fish annually and the fact that the current egg supply was not sufficient to meet even the minimum smolt level, we asked the Merrimack River Policy Committee for guidance. Decisions at the administrative level provided the direction necessary for a continuation of the effort. They are shown, very briefly, in *Figs 1 and 2*.

(1) A trapping and transportation programme beginning at the lower-most dam on the Merrimack River would be implemented initially. This would eliminate the need to build 11 fish passage facilities while at the same time reduce the overall smolt requirement. A fish lift at the lower-most dam is expected to be in operation by 1982.

(2) Downstream migrant protection facilities would not be considered initially.

(3) A management plan for Atlantic salmon would be formulated by the three participating State agencies.

(4) Studies would be undertaken to reduce the speculation within the plan. Data collected will enable us to revise the plan when necessary and if need be, redefine the objectives.

(5) A brood stock development programme capable of providing 1.2 million eggs annually would be initiated.

Summary

Admittedly the Atlantic salmon restoration effort on the Merrimack River or, for that matter, in New England as a

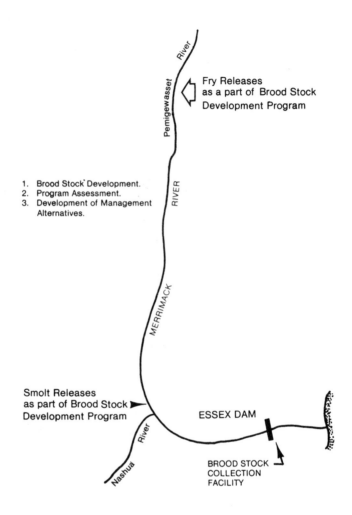

Fig 1   Merrimack river salmon restoration plan – phase I.

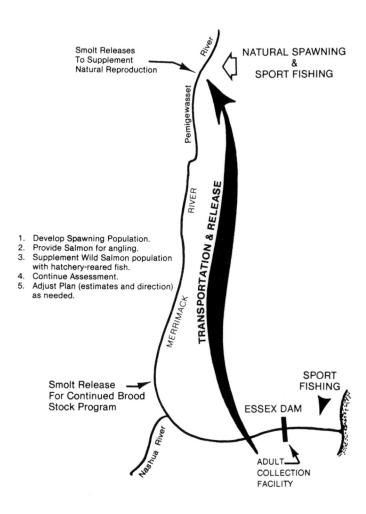

Fig 2 Merrimack river salmon restoration plan – phase II.

whole, is a relatively small programme regarding expected adult salmon population sizes. However, we believe that our expectations and current direction are much more realistic than they were in the past, and that they will meet our needs.

We also realize that we must be continually aware that the Atlantic salmon is but a single species – a species that will place specific demands on a water resource – demands that will be only one segment of the existing and projected uses.

Finally, the adult returns to New England Rivers in 1978, most notably the Connecticut River, have given the total restoration effort an important and needed degree of success. Potential consumers of the resource and, more importantly, the very large number of non-consuming users, are providing the support we will need in the months and years ahead. We are proceeding not only with cautious optimism but with renewed enthusiasm.

References

BAILEY, J R & OLIVER, J A. The fishes of the Connecticut River
1939   watershed. In. *Biological Survey of the Connecticut River Watershed.*
         New Hampshire Fish and Game Dept. Survey Report No 4.
         Concord, NH pp 150–89.

BRIDGES, C & OATIS, P. *Merrimack River anadromous fish restoration study.*
1969   Annual progress report. Federal Aid project, AFS-7, Segment 1.
         MA Div Fish and Wildlife. Boston, MA. 84 pp.

CUTTING, R E. *Penobscot River salmon restoration.* Maine Atlantic Sea-Run
1963   Salmon Commission. Bangor, ME. 162 pp.

JONES, A & MINTA, P & CRECCO, V. A review of American shad studies
1976   in the Connecticut River. In *Proceedings of a Workshop on American
         Shad.* USFWS, Newton Corner, MA and NMFS, Gloucester, MA.
         pp 135–62.

KNIGHT, E, MARANCIK, G, GREENWOOD, C & KIMBALL, C. Performance
1977   of three year classes of Atlantic salmon in the Merrimack River
         system. *Progress Report, Fishery Resources. USFWS.* Laconia, NH.
         15 pp.

SCAROLA, F. *Freshwater fishes of New Hampshire.* Special publication, New
1973   Hampshire Fish and Game Dept. Concord, NH 131 pp.

WHITWORTH, R, BERRIEN, L & KELLER, W T. *Freshwater fishes of Con-*
1968   *necticut.* State Geological and Natural History Survey of Connec-
         ticut, Bulletin 101. Storrs, CT. 134 pp.

WIGHTMAN, P. *Anadromous fish restoration in the Merrimack River.* Annual
1973   progress report. Federal-Aid project, AFS-10, Segment 3. New
        Hampshire Fish and Game Depot. Concord, NH. 31 pp.
1971   *Merrimack River thermal study.* New Hampshire Fish and
        Game Dept. Report. Concord, NH. 183 pp.

7 Discussion

*B B Parrish, (Marine Laboratory, Aberdeen) opened the
discussion as follows*

The excellent papers presented in this session have provided a great deal of interesting and pertinent information on a number of important issues concerning the impact of ecological factors on the productivity of salmon stocks, and the quantities available for exploitation, whether by commercial or sports fishermen. In opening the discussion I will confine myself to just two items, which I think are of considerable importance in the formulation of future management plans for Atlantic salmon.

The first issue, which was dealt with briefly by Dr Mills in his paper, concerns the impact of natural predators, other than man, on salmon stocks. It is known that salmon are preyed upon by a number of bird and mammal species during their freshwater and marine life-history phases, and there is substantial evidence that this predation reaches quite high levels in some areas. My question to the panel of speakers is, therefore, should predator control form an integral component of future management plans, aimed at increasing the quantities of salmon available for exploitation by man and if so what criteria and yardsticks should be used in its formulation?

The second issue is one which has not been mentioned specifically in any of the papers, although one of our speakers, Mr Stolte, and a number of distinguished members of the audience are very well qualified to express views on it. It concerns the ecological risks to the Atlantic salmon of the introduction, either deliberately or accidentally, of non-indigenous species of fish. Perhaps especially other salmonid species. My question to the Panel is: what is the right policy to adopt with respect to such introductions in the context of a management plan for Atlantic salmon?

Dr Mills, answering Mr Parrish's question regarding predators, said that mergansers, goosanders and cormorants are not protected in Scotland. Mink are serious predators of salmon, competing with the otter.

Dr Piggins added that there was a case for predator control when rearing smolt but that in some cases one has to live with predators.

Y Harache (Centre Océanologique de Bretagne), who acted on the panel, said he agreed with Dr Piggins but in his view more research should be done as regards certain predators.

W S Brewster (International Atlantic Salmon Foundation) said that salmon returning to the Connecticut River recently were heavily infested by copepods and furunculosis and there was very heavy mortality in the fish in this river.

P F Elson (St Andrews, N B Canada) commented on predator control in salmon streams, specifically with reference to mergansers *Mergus merganser,* (goosander in Europe). In a study of several years duration in Canada, smolt output from an experimental stream was increased by about four times to 4-6 smolts per 100 yards of river bottom by restricting merganser incidence to an average annual rate of about one bird/10 miles of river 10 yards wide. Natural abundance had been much greater at one brood every 2-4 miles on a 25 yard wide stream throughout summer plus heavy periodic invasions of flying birds in spring, autumn and winter. Natural predators have been reduced by trapping of such furbearers as mink, otters and racoons, and feathered predators such as hawks, eagles and owls have been greatly reduced by widespread use of DDT in recent decades. There are still many Canadian rivers where mergansers severely limit smolt output, but the speaker had not seen indications of sufficient abundance to warrant control in his limited travels on European rivers.

I A Duncan Miller (Scottish Landowners Federation) queried Dr Mills' suggestion that the functions of the Scottish District Fishery Boards be included in those of the River Purification Boards. He preferred the joint interest of net and rod fishing solely concerned with salmon, rather than submerging those interests among many others with political overtones. Although few in number, river bailiffs now use modern technology, but by far the greatest ill-effect on salmon in unpolluted Scottish water is drift netting. He enquired whether any of the panel could indicate the major factor affecting salmon in each of the countries for which they speak.

Dr Mills replied referring to the fact that only about 40 District Fishery Boards had been established out of over 100 possibilities. District Boards publish reports only for limited circulation, only the Tweed Board publishing a proper report. There is also the fact that fish, other than salmon, are not covered by District Boards. His opinion was that such Boards could not cope with the present situation and it would be better if the Boards were combined.

Dr Harris said that in his opinion abstraction was the most serious problem in Wales.

Dr Piggins thought that in Ireland the most serious problem was drift netting at sea.

Dr Egidius thought that in Norway the most pressing problem was air-pollution by industry in other parts of Europe.

P Dolan (*Department of Fisheries and Forestry, Ireland*), in referring to Dr Piggins' remarks, pointed out that, as regards arterial drainage, a pre-drainage survey of all matters relative to fisheries in a drainage catchment is carried out. Using this survey a restocking programme is drawn up together with a rehabilitation scheme for spawning and nursery grounds, holding pools and angling stretches. The cost of these programmes is borne by the Arterial Drainage Division of the Office of Public Works. As regards lake impoundment, a pre-impoundment survey is made, and records of flow patterns in the outflowing river are taken. Schemes are then drawn up to retain the traditional flow pattern in the river and lake. Augmentation of drought flows also is sometimes possible. Fish passes, *etc* are provided where needed.

R A Buck (*Restoration of Atlantic Salmon in America, Inc*), said that there are many reasons why plantings of coho

salmon will inhibit Atlantic salmon. One of the most important is that cohos may feed in the same region as Atlantic
salmon. Sports fishermen, during the fall runs of cohos in
estuaries and rivers, will also take migrating Atlantic salmon, with spoons, other lures and flies. This presents an
almost impossible regulatory problem for wardens seeking
to protect Atlantic salmon on their spawning runs. Cohos,
unlike Atlantic salmon, die after spawning and it will be
claimed that the resource should not be wasted. But in
taking cohos, the whole run of Atlantic salmon could also be
decimated.

Y Harache (*Centre Océanologique de Bretagne*) said that coho
salmon have been introduced into France both by private
firms and CNEXO, a governmental agency for marine
aquaculture, as they appeared to be an interesting alternative for marine rearing in the particular environmental
conditions in France. Casual losses and a major escape did
occur in recent years. Fish escaping from the net pens were
mostly recaptured in the vicinity of the pens and seemed to
show a sedentary behaviour. There are indications that if
they returned to the rivers they did so in November and
December with the winter rains and, as no counting stations
were operating on the rivers, they were not seen nor was
angling and commercial fishing carried on at that time. A
major escape from a private freshwater hatchery in Normandy led to 32 recaptures of mature cohos and some
juveniles were found later. However, there is no example of
an established population of an exotic species outside its
natural range of reproduction without massive and regular
introductions of large numbers of smolts. Under these
conditions it appears improbable that escapes from net
pens will lead to an established durable population able to
compete with Atlantic salmon. The risk seems very limited
but, of course, exists to some extent. Pathological risks
appear more dangerous as complete security is very rarely
matched by biological monitoring even if, as in this case,
much care is taken regarding sanitary control of the
imported eggs. Coho salmon have also been introduced
into Spain for similar purposes.

S P L Johnson (*Jedburgh, Scotland*) said that Scotland is fortunate with its stocks of Atlantic salmon so it would be a great mistake to introduce Pacific salmon into the country.

J D Kelsall (*North West Water Authority*) said that barbel were introduced into the River Severn, where a population explosion began around 1964 in the middle reaches of the river. Co-incident with this the rod catches of salmon over these reaches declined drastically, though runs of salmon continued to pass through these reaches and were caught above and below them. No proof exists that the increase in the numbers of barbel were responsible for the decline in salmon catches but the coincidence is highly suggestive.

Dr E C Egidius (*Institute of Marine Research, Bergen, Norway*) (who kindly consented to answer questions relating to Norway) said that far too little is known about the role of disease and parasites in wild fish population. It is known that epizootics occur in these populations and that all kinds of stress is a very important factor in disease outbreaks.

As regards sea-ranching, which will be started in Norway, the fish will be given every protection available through vaccination. The Norwegians have also considered the possibility of acclimatizing the smolts and bringing them past the barrier of predators in their coastal waters.

In Norway there is the problem of a steady decrease in pH in the lakes and rivers in the south of the country and also to some degree on the west coast, due to air pollution from the heavy industrial areas on the continent and Great Britain.

Over fishing of salmon, usually blamed on drift netting, is also a problem. At present, Norway has no legislation regarding drift netting but legislation on the subject is expected to pass through the Parliament during the winter session with effect from 1 May, 1979. According to the proposed legislation, drift netting will be allowed only under licence. Such licences will be obtainable by professional fishermen and farmers who have been registered as drift netters in the previous three years.

M J Parry (*Severn Trent Water Authority*) asked Mr Ritter what financial appraisal have his enhancement schemes received.

Mr Ritter replied that there are two options for restoring salmon stocks where over-exploited, namely (1) Restrict catches or (2) Enhance the resource. Both of these have a cost factor. Mr Ritter expects 415,000 extra salmon from his enhancement programme.

Dr Parry asked if appraisal had been given to his options and, if so, how?

Mr Ritter replied that their schemes were carefully examined as to whether they were desirable and worthwhile. A cost benefit analysis is made as regards the social and economic benefits. If the funds which would be needed by a scheme would be better spent in some other project, then the salmon project would be dropped.

1 Ocean ranching – general considerations

J E Thorpe, Freshwater Fisheries Laboratory, Pitlochry, Scotland

Introduction

Ocean ranching of salmon is defined as an aquaculture system in which juvenile fish are released to grow on natural foods, unprotected, in marine waters from which they are harvested at marketable size. As salmon are terminal predators their total cultivation in captivity as currently practised in several places in Europe and North America, is a biologically wasteful process, being a nett consumer rather than a producer of high grade protein. Ranching, on the other hand, has biological validity (*Fig 1*).

The total annual production of flesh by a species population depends on two characteristics, namely number of individuals and growth rate. Among salmonids the upper limitation on numbers is set by availability of spawning substrate and nursery area for the juvenile stages in rivers. This limited production capacity of rivers has been progressively reduced by human activity over almost the entire geographical range of *Salmo* and *Oncorhynchus* species through destruction of that spawning substrate and nursery ground. Activities which lead to this are gravel abstraction, canalization, gradient modification; construction of weirs and hydro-electric dams; drainage, water abstraction and diversion; domestic, agricultural and industrial pollution. In some areas, notably the Pacific, reduction of numbers has also been caused directly by over-exploitation. The limitations on growth rate of salmon at sea are unknown. Since many rivers in Europe, North America and Japan have lost their salmon populations within the last

Stock   Protection

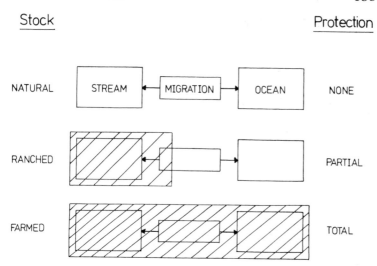

Fig 1 The relationship between natural, ranched and farmed production of salmon. Hatched areas indicate portion of life-cycle spent in captivity.

200 years, it may be safely assumed that the numbers of juveniles entering the oceans are now much fewer than formerly. Numerical limitations to ocean production are partly artificial and therefore may be compensated for, and hence the current interest in programmes of stock enhancement by both public and private organizations. This activity is a nett producer of protein to man, as the small cost in nutrients of rearing a 1-50g juvenile (depending on species) is outweighed by nutritive value of the crop of 2-10 kg adults (see below). These fish are being used as harvesters of otherwise unavailable marine protein (*Fig 2*), cropping these sources at no energy cost (Mathews *et al*, 1976) (*Table 1*) to the human exploiter, and presenting them in a package highly acceptable to the ultimate consumer. Since precise homing at maturity to the point of entry to the ocean is characteristic of this group of fishes, exploitation of an individual stock can be carried out efficiently at a fixed harvest site.

Historical development
Salmon conservation practices have developed gradually

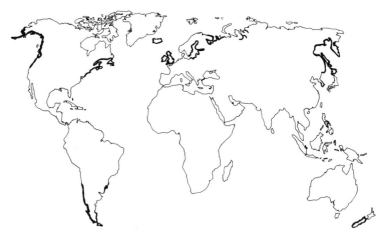

Fig 2 Coastal areas from which various species of salmonids are released in stock-enhancing and ranching programmes.

over many centuries. The one-for-the-pot-one-for-the-river systems of harvest on North American rivers probably erred heavily in favour of the river. In feudal Japan a system called 'Tanegawa No seido' operated in the 18th century, (Kobayashi, 1979), in which spawning salmon were protected in certain streams and rivers. Such protective measures through seasonal prohibition on fishing have been widespread, but it was not until the discovery of methods of artificial fertilization of salmonid eggs by Jacobi (1763) in Germany that any positive attempt was made to give assistance to the salmon to increase its numbers. At this time details of the life-history of Atlantic salmon, *Salmo salar*, were almost unknown, but Shaw (1836) demonstrated that parr were the juvenile freshwater stage by rearing such fish in ponds from known parents. This early experiment was followed up on the River Tay, Scotland, at Stormont-field, (Buist, 1866) where several thousand smolts were reared, marked and released, and adults recovered on returning to spawn. The impact of these releases on the total numbers of fish returning to the Tay system is unknown, but must have been minuscule. In North America, brook trout, *Salvelinus fontinalis*, were first spawned artificially in 1853 (MacCrimmon, 1965; Bowen,

1970) in Ohio and within a few years several hatcheries had been established in the New England states and the northeast. Atlantic salmon were first hatched artificially in North America in 1858 in Quebec (MacCrimmon, 1965), and in 1866 Samuel Wilmot constructed a hatchery at Newcastle, Ontario, to propagate them. He intended to release young salmon into Lake Ontario, and harvest them at marketable size from his private fishery reserve. The Canadian government forbade this as a private venture, but funded it as a public one. Wilmot built a 'reception room' – a covered trap on a by-pass channel through which all returning salmon were diverted – as part of his facilities. Thus the first salmon ranching enterprise was born, although it was to augment the wild stock rather than to exploit a captive run. Ultimately Newcastle produced over one million young salmon annually, until environmental deterioration destroyed the Lake Ontario salmon population. Government-run hatcheries were built elsewhere in eastern North America at this time, to restore salmon stocks to their former abundance. At the end of the century, on the Pacific coast and in Japan, there was an awareness that the growing commercial fishing industry might threaten the existence of *Oncorhynchus* stocks. In 1900, the US Government passed a law requiring salmon canneries to operate hatcheries, later giving tax incentives to those propagating 10 fry for every adult harvested (McNeil, 1979a). The hatcheries were built and thousands of millions of fry were released. As these were mostly sockeye (*O nerka*) and coho (*O kisutch*), which both require extensive periods of rearing in freshwater before release to sea, the law had been complied with but the programme was a monumental waste. More government

Table 1 (*from Mathews et al, 1976*). Energy efficiency ratios of animal protein-producing systems in the USA.

System	Ratio (%)
Grain-fed beef	10
Pen-reared salmon	13
Trawl-caught bottom fish	16
Ranched salmon	25
Grass-fed beef	35
Eggs	40
Grass-fed milk	100

hatcheries were built and operated until the 1930's, by which time most private ones were uneconomic and had closed.

The harnessing of major salmon rivers for power generation led to a resurgence of interest in artifical propagation of salmon, and focused attention more clearly on the biological requirements of these fish. This in turn led to improvements in hatchery equipment and husbandry, giving better output, and more encouraging results in adult returns. The need for good results was nowhere more important than in Sweden (Carlin, 1968), whose rivers had provided the major spawning and nursery grounds for much of the Baltic stock of Atlantic salmon. Swedish power companies were required by law to consider the losses to fisheries when assessing the gains of an engineering project. Power dams rapidly converted most rivers into chains of reservoirs, reducing nursery areas so much that planting of fry would serve no useful purpose. Therefore rearing techniques had to be developed to produce viable smolts which would survive to maintain the traditional coastal and open Baltic fishery. Similar developments for similar reasons, have taken place elsewhere in Europe, USSR, North America and Japan.

Those in North America and Japan have been more varied, primarily because the fish reared, *Oncorhynchus* species, *Salmo salar* and *Salmo gairdneri*, differ in their individual requirements. The knowledge gained through these rearing studies has enabled the hatcheries to improve their efficiency (biological and economic) to the point where they are now contributing substantially to the maintenance of commercial fisheries (*Table 2*). The catch from Japanese hatchery production amounts to eight million fish per year, that is about 28,000 tonnes. These data, and those of McNeil (1979a), show that artificial propagation at present contributes 20-30 percent of the world catch of Pacific salmon, that is 50-75,000 tonnes per year.

These contributions come from schemes designed to enhance, for common exploitation, the present reduced wild production of salmon species. But the technology so developed can also be applied in a more precise way to the maintenance of discrete stocks for exploitation on return home to the propagator's premises. This, too, is now a viable system, being practised for profit in both the Atlantic and Pacific oceans. Many problems remain to be solved in biological, management, economic and legal areas, in all of which improvements are required.

Problem areas
Biological
General: Detailed knowledge of the biology of an animal gives leads to ways in which it may be manipulated for human benefit. Real improvements in hatchery equipment and practice are consequent on advances in knowledge of ecology, behaviour and physiology of the freshwater stages of salmon (see McNeil and Bailey, 1975; Thorpe, 1979; Thorpe and Wankowski, 1979). Both Piggins (1979) and Isaksson (1979) have found that returns of their hatchery fish are poorer than those of comparably sized wild Atlantic salmon smolts migrating at the same time. The recovery ratios were: Ireland – 3.6 wild : 1 hatchery, Iceland – 2.8 wild : 1 hatchery. There is therefore room for improvement of the product. Knowledge of the marine phase of salmon life histories is still sparse, particularly for Atlantic salmon. For example, gross oceanic movement patterns have been plotted for some *Oncorhynchus* spp, but similar data is lacking for *S salar*. The ecology and behaviour of post-smolts of all salmons is a 'black box' area, which must hold clues to environmental influences over growth and maturation rates, both subjects of considerable importance to the rancher. The ecological role of salmon at sea is little understood. Only rough guesses can be made of the original number of juvenile fish which entered the oceans. The

Table 2 Contribution of hatchery production to commercial fisheries for salmon

Country	Species	Fishery	% of catch	Authority
Sweden	*Salmo salar*	Baltic	25	Carlin 1968
Ireland	*Salmo salar*	R. Shannon	20	Piggins 1979
		Burrishoole R.	40	Piggins 1979
		R. Lee	c.100	Piggins 1979
Japan	*O. keta*	Japan	80	Kobayashi 1979

carrying capacity of the seas for salmon is unknown, and therefore with increasing enhancement and ranching activity a close watch will be needed for signs that this may have been exceeded.

Genetic

Protected rearing permits a much improved survival of fish through their first vulnerable months of life. It thus promotes the survival of genetic combinations which might in the wild have been eliminated as unfit early in life. Furthermore, when such fish are released, the contribution of a few individual parental types to the progeny generation is exaggerated, and thus the maintenance of genetic diversity and range of adaptability in that stock is endangered. To this risk is added another. Hatchery stocks can tolerate much higher exploitation rates than natural stocks, in the sense of retaining genetic identity. Therefore enhancement and ranching programmes require precise methods of exploitation to ensure minimal damage to the genetic diversity of recipient wild stocks.

Homing

The key feature of salmon biology which makes ranching these animals feasible is their homing precision. The maturing fish aggregate themselves about the mouth of their natal river and within that river, and thus require no searching, driving or aggregation by their hunters. The homing mechanism has been shown to include environmental and genetic components. Coho salmon (*O kisutch*) and rainbow trout (*S gairdneri*) have the capacity to distinguish specific chemical compounds present in water at exceedingly high dilutions (Cooper and Hasler, 1976). More importantly, they use that capacity in distinguishing the home stream from other waters (Scholz *et al*, 1976). In experiments with hatchery fish the timing of imprinting with artificial chemical cues has been shown to be quite critical, implying that wild fish acquire home orientational information at a precise period of out-migration as smolts.

Migration

Models of homing based on sequential acquisition of environmental cues during outward migration, and the replaying of this sequence in reverse, have been proposed (Harden Jones, 1968). Such a mechanism may operate when the fish is in a confined 'linear' environment, such as a river, but recent Canadian evidence suggests that other mechanisms must operate at sea (Turner and Ritter, personal communication.) Atlantic salmon smolts tagged on emigration through the Miramichi estuary, New Brunswick, show several patterns of subsequent movement. One of these takes the fish all the way around Newfoundland, so that on return to the Miramichi the adults have not retraced any part of their outward journey. An innate orientation mechanism would account for such a movement better as the acquisition of sequential cues cannot. Taguchi (1957) noted that populations of chum (*O keta*) and sockeye (*O nerka*) were displaced seasonally in the same direction as north Pacific water masses. Mathisen and Gudjonsson (1978) have suggested that some Atlantic salmon become entrained in oceanic eddies near Iceland. Such eddy circuits would be completed in 225 days, so that a smolt entering the eddy from southwest Iceland in late summer would be returned to the proximity of its home river early in the following summer, just prior to the time at which maturing adults enter the river (Isaksson, 1979). Thus oceanic migration may be primarily a passive process, only requiring active navigation at critical points, such as the final identification of the home river. This model makes energetic sense, in that the fish is then required to expend minimal effort in swimming against currents. The question remains as to what induces the fish to make the effort at all. Godin *et al* (1974) have shown experimentally that thyroxine treatment reduced rheotactic behaviour in 15cm juvenile Atlantic salmon in July and August. Thus a change in hormonal status similar to that occurring in fish of this size normally in spring at downstream migration as smolts, induces behaviour facilitating such migration by altering *inter alia* their responses to currents. It is hypothesized here that further changes in hormonal status associated with sexual

maturation, induce the reverse process, increasing rheotactic responses preparatory to upstream migration. This
would aid escape from entrainment in an eddy, and permit
active entry into areas of estuarine influence. Since Pacific
salmon from the USSR, Japan and North America intermingle on feeding grounds, as do Atlantic salmon from
Canada and northwest Europe, such a migration model can
only be valid if the mechanisms of active orientation are
triggered differently in these stocks, ensuring their segregation in appropriately different directions. This implies
differences in developmental timing, and in pituitary
response to external stimuli, that is innate differences
under genetic control. It seems likely that such differences
occur within Atlantic salmon stocks (Simpson and Thorpe,
1976). At the finer level, segregation from common feeding
grounds by salmon from different parts of Europe or
Canada, and within those stocks of populations from different rivers, again requires differences in response resulting in fish arriving in the appropriate coastal area at the
appropriate time for upstream migration.

    Thus whereas local environmental cues at departure
from a river mouth or release device are decisive in re-
aggregating adults at return, innate characteristics of those
stocks are likely to determine the 'coarse' homing of that
population. Therefore stocks used for ranching should be
derived from local genetic material.

Management
It also follows from this argument that if adult salmon only
become segregated into discrete river stocks on entry to
those rivers, exploitation on a stock basis can only be prose-
cuted in rivers. Such a recommendation was made for
exploitation of Atlantic salmon in Scotland (1965) by a
government committee which saw the need for development of more rational systems of salmon management.
Currently, this restriction would be impractical in areas
where extensive high-seas fisheries exist (north Pacific, Baltic), but is a goal to keep in view. Over-exploitation of wild
stocks as a result of increased fishing following enhancement and ranching (see above, and Lannan (1979), McNeil

(1979a)) could be avoided by using this management system together with artificial imprinting of hatchery stocks to permit their decoying as adults into separate harvesting devices (Scholz *et al*, 1976). Wild and ranched stocks would then be managed separately, and risks of over-exploitation and reduction of genetic diversity minimized.

Economic

Management on a river stock basis would also protect economic investment, since maximal benefit from the returning fish would accrue to the propagator. Such schemes using Atlantic salmon function profitably in Iceland (Isaksson, 1979), where fishing for salmon at sea was made illegal in 1932. Returns of adults, as a percentage of smolts released, have averaged 9.4 percent since 1972. These fish are chiefly grilse, averaging 2.5kg, and giving a harvest of about 8kg/kg of smolts released. At the experimental trap facility at Furnace, Co Mayo, Ireland, returns of 2.4 percent and a harvest of 1.8kg/kg smolts released looks less promising (Piggins, 1979). However, recoveries of Irish hatchery fish in their off-shore drift net fishery are 4.5 times those in their rivers. Were salmon not exploited at sea the return rates at the Furnace trap might then be in excess of 13 percent, a harvest of 10kg/kg smolts released. At this level Irish salmon ranching would also be profitable, (although not currently permitted). Releases of experimental batches of Atlantic salmon reared at the Almondbank unit, Scotland, have shown return rates of up to 8 percent as grilse, averaging 3.5kg. This represents a minimal potential harvest of 6kg/kg smolts released, as it was achieved through the traditional discontinuous seine-net fishery operating on the R Tay for five and a half days out of seven, and only seven months of the year. Also, this level of return was attained despite illegal drift netting off the Scottish east coast.

Some enhancement and ranching programmes are funded by governments for social rather than profit motives. In North America two types of enterprise are recognized, profit centres and cost centres (McNeil, 1979b). The former are commercially based ranching ventures, usually privately financed, designed to be profitable and compete with the rest of the salmon trade. The latter produce fish to compensate for depleted wild stocks, and to augment those where recreational demand exceeds supply from wild recruitment. Taxes on commercial and recreational fisheries finance these cost centres.

Legal
In areas such as the United Kingdom and Ireland, no substantial improvements in practice, and no real advances in private salmon ranching, can be expected until a more favourable legal framework is devised to protect these enterprises. Essential legal changes would include:
  proscription of all salmon fisheries at sea;
  legalization of trap fisheries;
  legalization of ranching harvests during close seasons for wild-stock fisheries;
  definition of ownership of salmon released from hatcheries.

Conclusions
Ranching of Atlantic salmon is a biologically meaningful form of cropping protein resources from distant marine areas at minimal energy cost. The technology exists to mount such enterprises, and while there is much scope for improvement in production techniques and product quality, present methods can be profitable. Caution is necessary in choosing genetic material for ranching, and in harvesting on a stock basis, to minimize impact on valuable wild populations. Stock-unit managment requires a readjustment of traditional methods, and a new legal foundation to make it workable.

References

ANONYMOUS.*Scottish Salmon and Trout Fisheries*. Dept of Agr and Fisheries 1965   for Scotland Cmnd 2691. HMSO Edinburgh.
BOWEN, J T. A history of fish culture as related to the development of

1970   fishery programs. *In* A Century of Fisheries in North America, N
        G Benson (Ed). *Amer Fish Soc Spec Publ* 7.71–93. Washington.
BUIST, R. *The Stormontfield piscicultural experiments*, 1853–66. Edin-
1866   burgh. 32 pp.
CARLIN, B. *Salmon conservation in Sweden*. At Salm Ass Ann Confer-
1968   ence. Montreal.
COOPER, J C & HASLER, A D. Electrophysiological studies of mor-
1976   pholine–imprinted coho salmon *(Oncorhynchus kisutch)* and rain-
        bow trout *(Salmo gairdneri). J Fish Res Bd Canada* 33: 688–94.
GODIN, J G, DILL, P A & DRURY, D E. Effects of thyroid hormones on
1974   behaviour of yearling Atlantic salmon *(Salmo salar). J Fish Res Bd
        Canada* 31: 1787–90.
HARDEN JONES, F R. *Fish Migration*. Arnold, London.
1968
ISAKSSON, A. Salmon Ranching in Iceland. In *Salmon Ranching*, Thorpe,
1979   J E (Ed). Academic Press, London.
JACOBI, S L. On the breeding of trout by impregnation of the ova. *Han-
1763   nover Mag*. 1765 No 62.
JACOBI, S L. Method of breeding fish to advantage. *Hannover Mag*. 1763
1763   no 23.
KOBAYASHI, T. Salmon propagation in Japan. In *Salmon Ranching*, J E
1979   Thorpe (Ed). Academic Press, London.
LANNAN, J E. Salmon ranching in Oregon. In *Salmon Ranching*, J E
1979   Thorpe (Ed). Academic Press, London.
MACCRIMMON, H R. The beginning of salmon culture in Canada. *Can
1965   Geog J* 71 (3): 96–103.
MCNEIL, W J. Salmon ranching in Alaska. In *Salmon Ranching*, J E
1979a   Thorpe (Ed). Academic Press, London.
MCNEIL, W J. Legal aspects of ocean ranching in the Pacific. In *Salmon
1979b   Ranching*, J E Thorpe (Ed). Academic Press, London.
MCNEIL, W J & BAILEY, J E. Salmon Ranchers Manual. N W Fisheries
1975   Centre, Processed Report July 1975. Auke Bay, Alaska. vi &
        95 pp.
MATHEWS, S B, MOCK, J B, WILLSON, K & SENN, H. Energy efficiency of
1976   Pacific salmon aquaculture. *Progve Fish Cult* 38(2): 102–6.
MATHISEN, O A & GUDJONSSON, T. Salmon management and ocean
1978   ranching in Iceland. *J Agric Res Iceland* 10(2).
PIGGINS, D J. Sea ranching of salmon in Ireland. In *Salmon Ranching*, J E
1979   Thorpe (Ed). Academic Press, London.
SCHOLZ, A T, HORRALL, R M, COOPER, J C & HASLER, A D. Imprinting
1976   to chemical cues: the basis for home stream selection in salmon.
        Science 192: 1247–49.
SHAW, J. An account of some experiments and observations on the Parr,
1836   and on the Ova of the Salmon, proving the Parr to be the young
        of the salmon. *New Philos J* 21: 99–110. Edinburgh.
SIMPSON, T H & THORPE, J E. Growth bimodality in the Atlantic salmon.
1976   *ICES CM* 1976: M22.
TAGUCHI, K. The seasonal variation of the good fishing area of salmon

1957   and the movements of the water masses in the waters of the
       western north Pacific. II. *Bull Jap Soc Sci Fish.* 22(9): 515–21.
THORPE, J E. Rearing salmonids in freshwater. In *Fish Keeping*, A D
1979   Hawkins (Ed). Academic Press, London.
THORPE, J E & WANKOWSKI, J W J. Feed presentation and food particle
1979   size for juvenile Atlantic salmon *Salmo salar* L. EIFAC Sym-
       posium on Finfish Nutrition and Feed Technology, Hamburg.
       Paper E. 53.

2 Genetic variation in production traits between strains of Atlantic salmon

K Gunnes, Department of Animal Genetics and Breeding, Agricultural University of Norway

Introduction

Fish farming is a growing industry in Norway. In 1971 the production of Atlantic salmon was 100 tonnes and that of rainbow trout 540 tonnes. The production has gradually increased and in 1977 it was 2,500 tonnes of Atlantic salmon and 2,000 tonnes of rainbow trout. Output of Atlantic salmon is expected to increase further.

It is very important for the fish farmers that the fish they are dealing with give the best economic results. The fish must have good growth, slaughtering qualities, *etc*.

In 1971 the Department of Animal Genetics and Breeding at the Agricultural University of Norway started selection experiments with Atlantic salmon at the Research Station for Salmonids, Sunndalsøra and Averøy. During a four year period wild brood stock were sampled in 40 rivers or river systems. Salmon from each river are considered as a separate strain or breed. From each strain full-and half-sib families were made. During the incubation period each family of eggs was held in a separate tray, and fish resulting from them were reared in separate tanks throughout the fry and fingerling stages. At an age of 190 days after start-feeding the fish were weighed individually. When the fish had reached 10-15 grams in average weight the best 320 fish from each family were selected and marked by freeze-branding. All marked fish smoltified at one year of age, and were gradually acclimatized to sea water during a three-week period in May of the year following that in which they were hatched. They were then transferred to floating net

cages in the sea for growing to harvest size. 120 from each
family were placed at the Research Station for Salmonids,
Averøy unit. The other 200 fish were divided into four
groups and distributed to private fish farms along the Norwegian coast. In the sea period weight samples were regu-
larly taken in order to follow the mean growth rate at each
fish farm. Individual weights and lengths were taken at
slaughtering, which was done after a two-year period in the
sea. At Averøy slaughtering qualities were registered.

Although the experiments were designed to benefit farmers growing fish in the usual Norwegian way, most of the
results obtained were also relevant to the development of a
sea ranching system.

Mortality in the fresh water phase
Mortality was recorded for each family for the following
developmental periods: uneyed eggs, eyed eggs, alevins,
fry in first feeding period, fry the first nine months after
first feeding. Significant differences between strains were
found for egg, alevin and fry mortality. The heritabilities
estimated within strains were rather low, less that 0.08.
(Kanis, Refstie and Gjedrem, 1976). These estimates,
together with the high fertility per female and the relatively
low cost per egg and fry, have led to the conclusion that
these traits should not be given high priority in a selection
programme. The strain differences have, however, shown
that it is possible to improve the survival by selection. In the
future if the mortality rate should increase due to genetic
changes, we certainly must include these traits in the selection programme. The most suitable trait to work with
would then be mortality in the eyed egg stage.

Growth in the fresh water period
For growth in the fresh water period large differences between strains were found (Refstie and Steine, 1978). *Fig 1*
shows the differences expressed as deviation from the least
square mean in phenotypic standard deviation units. When
calculating genetic parameters from this material, the
heritabilities for weight and length at 190 days of age were
0.15 and 0.17, respectively.

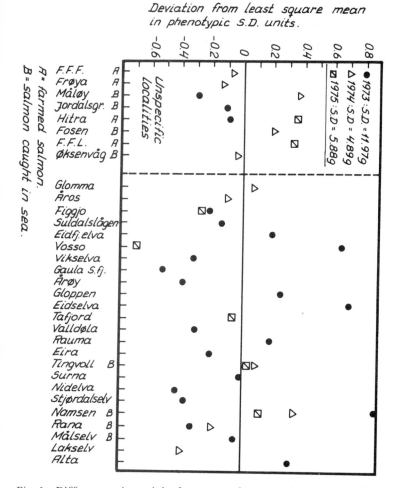

Fig 1 Differences in weight between salmon strains, measured in phenotypic standard deviation units (Refstie and Steine, 1978).

Most of the fish smoltified at one year of age. Great variation between strains was found for percentage one-year-old smolt (Refstie, Steine and Gjedrem, 1977). Smoltification depends on the size of the fish and, as shown before, there were great differences for growth rate. But the heritabilities estimated for percentage of one-year-old smolt were low. The best chance of improving this trait is by applying family selection, because phenotypic selection is only expected to give rather small progress.

Growth rate in the fresh water period, here expressed as weight at a constant age, is certainly an important trait. Progress in growth rate will lead to production of larger smolts, and a higher percentage of one-year-old smolts. We expect it will also lead to better growth in the sea water period.

Differences in resistance of salmon parr to vibrio disease
During the autumn of 1972 an infection of *Vibrio Anguillarum* occurred at the Research Station for Salmonids, Sunndalsøra. There were significant differences between strains in mortality resulting from the attack. This indicates differences in resistance against the infection.

The mortality for different strains is shown in *Table 1* and varied from one percent to 30 percent (Gjedrem and Aulstad, 1974). The heritability for this trait was estimated to be 0.11. Vibriosis is the most troublesome disease on Norwegian sea fish farms, and it is obvious that this trait should be incorporated in a selection programme. Attempts are now being made to find easy methods to measure the resistance against the disease.

Growth in the sea
The different strains and families were placed at five different fish farms along the Norwegian coast. *Fig 2* gives the growth rate in the different farms for one year-class. The other year classes gave a very similar result. As can be seen there were great differences in growth rate between fish farms. The differences were mostly due to different management and especially differences in food and feeding routines.

Great differences between strains were found for all year classes tested. *Fig 3* gives the differences for the 1973 year class. The strain variance accounted for 6.7-8.6 percent of the total phenotypic variance for weight and 5.4-9.3 percent for length at slaughtering (Gunnes and Gjedrem, 1978). These figures are of the same order as found in the fresh water period (Refstie and Steine, 1978).

Table 1 Number of salmon parr and percent dead from vibrio disease from different rivers (Gjedrem and Aulstad, 1974)

Locality (river)	No. of fish in hundreds	Percent dead of vibrio disease
1 Altaelva	124	1·05
2 Målselva**	57	1·50
5 Namsen**	110	2·09
7 Fosen**	111	1·58
12 Jordalsgrenda**	41	2·42
13 Usma*	19	4·59
14 Surna	58	8·90
16 Driva	40	1·01
18 Rauma	33	5·17
26 Gaula, Sunnfjord	150	5·98
28 Laerdalselva	42	8·08
31 Loneelva*	20	4·09
35 Etneelva	24	0·87
40 Sandvikselva	153	4·59
41 Luleå (Sweden)	58	29·71

*Grilse river
**Salmon caught in sea

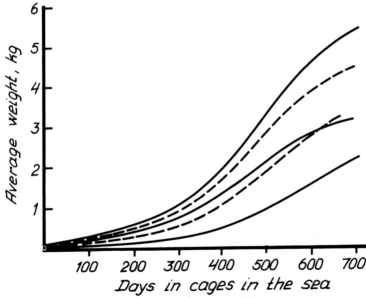

Fig 2 Growth curves of Atlantic salmon at different fish farms, year class 1973 (Gunnes and Gjedrem, 1978).

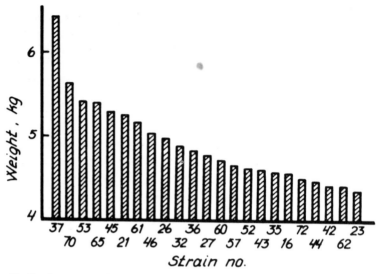

Fig 3   Average weight of slaughtering for different strains of Atlantic salmon, year class 1973.

An interesting question raised in this investigation was whether there are genotype-environment interactions, here represented by strain and fish farm. In other words, is the ranking of strains for growth performance the same at each fish farm? The result of the analysis of variance for weight is given in *Table 2*. The interaction is significant for all three year classes. However, looking at the component of variance in percentage of the total phenotypic variance the figures are rather small, 1.3-3.7 percent for weight and 1.2-3.2 percent for length at slaughtering (Gunnes and Gjedrem, 1978). Taking into account the wide range in the environmental conditions between the farms *(Fig 2)*, the interaction must be considered to be rather low and of little practical importance. It is concluded that it is not necessary to develop more than one breed of salmon for fish farming in Norway, even when the environmental conditions vary considerably. This is very important for the efficiency of salmon selection because the testing capacity will always be a limiting factor.

Heritabilities were calculated within strain and were found to be 0.31 for weight and 0.28 for length at slaughtering. The genetic correlation between weight and length was close to unity both in fresh water and sea water, (Refstie and Steine, 1978 and Gunnes and Gjedrem, 1978). It is concluded that these two traits have the same genetic background. The coefficient of variance for weight at slaughtering is about three times as large as that for length (31.7 for weight and 9.6 for length). Weight at slaughtering will be one of the most important traits in a selection programme.

Age at sexual maturation is of great importance in fish farming as well as in sea ranching. Most of our salmon become sexually mature after two and a half years in the sea, and therefore they have to be slaughtered after two years in the sea. At slaughtering after two years in the sea we recorded differences between strains in percentage immature fish. *Fig 4* gives the differences for year class 1973. If it is desirable, it is possible to select for later maturation and in that way give possibilities for production of larger fish.

The variation between strains for carcass dressing percentage was large, and it varied from 84.1 percent to 91.2 percent for the year class 1973.

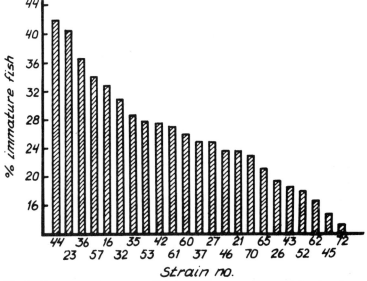

Fig 4 Percentage immature fish in different strains of Atlantic salmon, year class 1973.

Table 2 Analysis of variance for weight of salmon at slaughtering after two years in the sea. Degree of freedom (DF) and mean squares (MS) given for different year classes. (Gunnes and Gjedrem, 1978)

Source	1972		1973		1974	
	DF	MS	DF	MS	DF	MS
Between farms	4	10·9*	4	9·1**	4	162·8**
Between strains	16	101·6**	22	75·1**	8	380·3**
Interaction Farm-strain	36	25·4**	88	6·3**	21	37·4**
Error	6842	3·1	10449	2·3	23023	2·4

*p <0·05   **p <0·01

References

GJEDREM, T & AULSTAD, D. Selection experiments with salmon. I. Differ-
1974   ences in resistance to vibrio disease parr *(Salmo salar)* *Aquaculture*, 3: 51.59.

GUNNES, K & GJEDREM, T. Selection experiments with salmon. IV.
1978   Growth of Atlantic salmon during two years in the sea. *Aquaculture.* In press.

KANIS, E, REFSTIE, T & GJEDREM, T. A genetic analysis of egg, alevin and
1976   fry mortality in salmon *(Salmo salar)*, sea trout *(Salmo trutta)* and rainbow trout *(Salmo gairdneri)*. *Aquaculture*, 8: 259–68.

REFSTIE, T & STEINE, T A. Selection experiments with salmon. III.
1978   Genetic and environmental sources of variation in length and weight of Atlantic salmon in the fresh water phase. *Aquaculture*, 14: 221–34.

REFSTIE, T, STEINE, T A & GJEDREM, T. Selection experiments with
1977   salmon. II. Proportion of Atlantic salmon smoltifying at 1 year of age. *Aquaculture*, 10: 231–42.

3 The management of Atlantic salmon in floating sea pens

R Young, Unilever Research Laboratory, Aberdeen

This paper discusses the issues concerning the rearing of Atlantic salmon in floating net pens. It compares the effectiveness of the net pens with the two alternative systems, *ie* enclosures and shore based tanks. The selection of a retention system for any given species is determined by a number of factors. There are advantages and disadvantages to all three methods, both technological and economic. Different requirements, skills and business objectives are likely to lead to different solutions to similar problems, and compromise is usually the only answer.

Most of the findings below are drawn from the experience of the Unilever Company, Marine Harvest Limited, in farming fish on the west coast of Scotland and on some experimental findings of Unilever Research.

Methods for farming fish

Fish may be farmed extensively or intensively. Extensive farming is usually associated with large areas of water, a low level of stock management, low capital and operating costs, and a low yield per unit volume. It is normally practised in sluggish ponds or coastal embayments. Intensive farming is practised in small production units, with advanced stock management, high stocking densities, high feeding rates, careful selection of stocks, high capital and operating costs, but a high yield per unit volume.

Salmonids require attentive husbandry, high quality water and foodstuffs, and careful control of stocks. For these reasons they are usually farmed intensively.

There are three basic types of retention systems for intensive marine fish farming:

On-shore systems with pumped water only
Enclosures
Sea pens

NB This ignores the possibility of sea ranching.

Enclosures

The fish are enclosed in a secluded part of the sea, perhaps between an island and the shore. The two open ends are closed off either by dams or by net barriers.

In addition to the natural water circulation in the enclosure, there is likely to be a requirement for large pumps which increase this circulation.

Floating sea pens

The pen is made either by a net or by solid mesh panels suspended from a flotation collar. They can vary in size from 10m³ volume to as much as 2,000m³. They rely on the natural water movement to ensure constant replenishment of oxygen and removal of ammonia, *etc*.

Site selection

The main requirements for siting a group of floating sea pens is that there should be adequate water exchange coupled with sufficient shelter to ensure that the pens do not break up. There is almost always a basic conflict between these two factors since the best oxygen exchange is invariably found in places of maximum exposure to wind, waves, currents and tide. The secondary factors to be taken into account are:

Adequate depth of water
Good substrate
Good quality water
Good exchange
Reasonable water temperatures (8-18°C)
Shelter from the worst effects of weather
Absence of competing activities
Planning permission
Shore access and

Proximity to road and/or rail transport.

Again, several of these are in conflict. The overriding requirements for good quality water coupled with shelter from the worst exposure has resulted in most salmon sea farms in the UK being sited in the indented and sparsely populated west coast of Scotland.

Security of fish from predators

Predators have proved to be a bigger problem than expected and one that may not be recognized by those not personally involved in salmon farming. Potential or actual predators which have been identified in our salmon farms in Scotland are shags, cormorants, gulls, herons, otters, seals and humans. The relative importance of each of these is not yet known and methods of reducing the effect of them are likely to be difficult. Several urgent areas of research are revealed by this observation, *viz*

predator recognition

development of devices that will keep them away

designing of holding facilities with predator exclusion in mind.

We intend to explore these fully in the near future since losses during the sea water stages of salmon farming are extremely costly.

Health monitoring and control

Atlantic salmon reared in sea pens are exposed to a similar range of diseases as those observed in the wild. One of the advantages of farming in pens, however, is that constant observation of the fish is possible. We are continually trying to improve our techniques of health monitoring. As this improves it enables us to take prompt action. Our policy is to take the appropriate simple, safe and effective action at an early stage. Because the fish are divided into discrete units of a few thousand fish in a pen, it is possible to deal with a few selected groups without interfering with the rest of the stock. Consequently, we should never experience the same degree of debilitation that many anglers will have seen in wild salmon.

Fish counting and selection

As the farmer increases the scale of his farm, *ie* as he gets more and more fish, there is an increasing necessity for him to have an accurate count of his stock. The main reason for this is that without knowing the exact total weight of fish in a pen it is impossible to administer the correct amount of feed and there are risks of either wastage or under-feeding. In addition, to be able to prepare a suitable harvest plan, the number of fish in the pens must be known. By regular counting, fish losses can also be monitored and appropriate steps taken to eliminate them. In summary, we need to know our exact numbers of fish to achieve ideal husbandry control and so ensure production at least cost.

The requirements of a fish counting method are that it should be rapid, accurate, easily integrated into the process and should not damage the fish, *eg* through scale loss. Consequently handling of fish should be minimized.

Many methods of fish counting are available or under development, *eg* electronic sensing, hand counting, Asdic sonar and video TV.

For our requirements of counting salmon in net pens, video appears the most promising technique at the moment.

An extension of fish counting is the requirement for grading and selection. After one year in the sea, a significant number of fish may start to mature and are ready then to be harvested as grilse. They must be carefully selected without damage, from the remainder of the population which is left for another year in the sea before harvesting as salmon.

One of the main advantages which fish farming has to offer over capture fisheries is its potential ability to provide fish to suit market demands and not merely offer for sale whatever happens to be caught on a particular day. This is another important reason for being able to select certain fish from among a population. The more compartmentalized the farming system employed, the more feasible it is for this to be realized.

Feeding control

Salmon will feed actively throughout daylight hours and, if hand feeding is employed, this will require shift working or long working hours during the summer months. An alternative is to use automatic feeders.

In the early years, these proved very unreliable. There were problems of providing an adequate and reliable power source at sea and of keeping the feed dry to minimize the danger of 'bridging'. These problems have largely been solved and satisfactory automatic feeders are now available commercially. Even so, hand feeding has distinct advantages over automatic feeding. On occasions, salmon take less food than normal. The human element can detect this and consequently reduce the input. This is very important as it minimizes food wastage – an important factor in the cost of rearing Atlantic salmon. In addition, one of the first signs of stress or ill health in fish is that they go off their feed. Frequent hand feeding ensures the accompanying observations of feeding behaviour and general stock surveillance.

Design of the sea pens

When designing a sea pen suitable for rearing salmon, the engineer must pay attention to the requirements below:

Good water exchange

Minimum cost

Manageable size

Good access to the fish

Easily cleaned of fouling and

Long life

There is a very difficult compromise to make between the desire to have a strong escape-proof and weather-proof pen and the necessity to minimize the capital expenditure involved. In addition, the pens must be moored to the sea bed to prevent them from being washed on to the shore by wind and tide. This is usually done by a series of mooring ropes and anchors which must allow for the rise and fall of the tide and the flexing action of the pen caused by wave motion.

Our approach to pen design has been evolutionary. We

originally adopted a very cautious approach and built pens made of wire mesh panels which were strong and safe. These proved to very effective and durable and some are still in use today. After we had carried out a careful cost appraisal of our operation, however, it was obvious that this design was uneconomical. Over the next few years we produced a series of pens of different designs culminating in the net pen we use today.

Already now there is a variety of pens on the market which others have produced in an effort to solve the same cost/risk equation we were dealing with. As you would expect, we believe that our compromise is the best and that we have succeeded in achieving a cost effective, secure, containment for a manageable number of fish.

Comparison of three main types of fish retention

In *Table 1* are shown the three main types of fish retention systems in order of how well they solve the problems associated with each of the factors discussed above. The figures are not meant to represent any kind of absolute value and no attempt is made in the table to rank the importance of the factors.

Table 1 Comparison of the three main methods of retaining salmon in sea water

	Type of retention system		
Factors to be considered	Shore based tanks	Floating Sea pens	Coastal enclosures
Security of fish from predators and escapes	1	3	2
Health monitoring and control	1	2	3
Counting, selection and harvest	2	1	3
Site availability	2	1	3
Capital cost	3	2	1
Operating cost	3	1	2
Feeding control	1	2	3
Labour cost	3	2	1
Systems failure	3	1	2

NB The figures given are rankings, in the order 1 = best, 3 = worst, and not absolute values

Security of fish from predators and escapes
Net pens do not fare very well compared with the other two systems in coping with this problem. Obviously, it is relatively easy to ensure that no fish escape from a shore-based tank and that it is rendered secure from predators. It is possible to install a suitable fence around the perimeter of a coastal enclosure thus excluding four-legged and two-legged animals. The only point of escape from the enclosure is *via* the dam which is generally a very small proportion of the total circumference and so can be secured at a reasonable cost. The points of access to a net pen or a group of pens are very much greater by comparison. The groups are generally remote, scattered, and may not be in view from the shore base.

Health monitoring and control
In shore-based tanks, the fish are visible at all times of the year and in most weather conditions. Consequently routine observation of fish behaviour and condition is simple and effective. If any disease symptoms are detected it is relatively easy to take the appropriate action, and because the total numbers of fish are divided into a series of tanks, it is possible to be selective. Net pens provide a similar opportunity of observation and selectivity but generally at more cost and trouble. Enclosures may be poor at coping with this requirement because the fish may not be seen for several days and even then only a small proportion of them are easily visible. Moreover, the opportunity for selectivity is low.

Fish counting and selection
Fish can be selected and counted with almost equal facility in shore-based tanks and net pens. The smaller the number of fish in a unit, *ie* tank or pen, the easier this operation is to perform. Enclosures fare badly in comparison since all the fish are in the one shoal or herd. However, techniques for counting fish in enclosures are being developed in Norway and, if successful, may overcome the problem. Selective harvesting is likely to remain a formidable obstacle.

Feed control
There is not a significant difference in the ability to control feeding among the three systems. All these methods of marine farming tend to employ simple mechanical feeders which ensure a minimum of wasted food. As described earlier, we rely on the skill of the fish farmer to feed his fish by hand to ensure maximum efficiency. Norwegian farmers who favour enclosures have developed very sophisticated methods of feeding their fish and the excellent feed conversion ratios they obtain are testimony to their success.

Systems failure
Both the shore based tank type of farm and the sea enclosure rely on pumped water to ensure that a sufficient level of oxygen is always available to the fish. There is always a possibility of failure and sophisticated precautions to eliminate this danger are liable to prove expensive. It is probable that this is much more of a risk in tanks than in enclosures since fish should survive for longer periods in the enclosure, without pumps being in use, whereas in shore based systems, a few minutes under a specific set of conditions can prove fatal. Net pens sited in sea lochs rely on the natural movement of the water to provide a constant supply of oxygen.

Cost considerations
It is obvious that cost is of major importance in any attempt to assess the relative desirability of the three types of marine fish farming. We believe, however, that if we consider only the cost side, *ie* capital, labour, and operating costs, then the enclosures are an attractive alternative to the option we are pursuing.

Site selection
Site selection is probably the compelling factor in favour of net pen culture. The requirement for the shore based tank farm to be sited near sea level in an area of minimum rise and fall of tide tends to make the number of possible sites extremely limited. The special geographic requirements necessary for an enclosure are not likely to be available in

abundance outside Norway. When considering pen farms, it is clear that the fewer the number of pens on the farm, the more is the number of potential sites. Consequently there could be a considerably greater number of sites in Scotland suitable for fish farming than was originally envisaged. In addition, net pens are more adaptable to the environmental conditions and are more flexible in stock management.

4 The role of genetics in Atlantic salmon management

R L Saunders and J K Bailey, North American Salmon Research Center, St Andrews, Canada

Introduction

Although *Salmo salar* has been extensively studied for many years, comparatively little effort has been devoted to its genetic aspects. It is only within the past 10-15 years that genetic principles and their management implications have been appreciated by fishery biologists. Gardner (1976) gives an extensive review of observations showing environmental and genetic influence on sea age and maturation of Atlantic salmon. Much of the genetics work on salmon in the past 10-15 years involves surveys of natural populations and selection for traits important in fish farming. There is great variability relative to domestic animal populations and this suggests that fish will respond quickly to genetic selection. To manage our Atlantic salmon resource effectively it is necessary to amalgamate the knowledge of all scientific disciplines. The objective of this paper is to review some of the recent progress in the field of fish genetics with particular emphasis on Atlantic salmon and to indicate its relevance to any management scheme.

The stock concept

Sound management of salmon for either angling or commercial fisheries should recognize the stock concept. This allows for maximum cropping and ensures that sufficient broodstock remain to renew successive generations. A stock of salmon, as defined by Ricker (1972), refers to those individuals of a species which spawn in a particular stream and which do not interbreed with other such groups spawning in a different place or in the same place at a different time. Each salmon river has its own stock; many medium or large-sized rivers have a number of stocks, one or more in each tributary. There may be separate stocks along the main stem of a long river. The term 'run' is used to describe a stock or stocks, the members of which return at about the same time, *eg* spring, summer and fall runs of salmon. Several stocks may comprise a run. The phenomenon of homing in anadromous salmonids coupled with natural selection in response to environmental variation has resulted in the development of numerous stocks which often show obvious differences in physical, physiological and behavioural traits. Homing assures that the majority of a stock returns to its natal stream for spawning thereby maintaining a more or less discrete genetic pool. Genetic differences which develop in a stock through natural selection or genetic drift are thereby maintained and strengthened as a result of relative isolation.

Ricker (1972) compiled information concerning observed differences among Pacific salmonid populations and hereditary and environmental factors influencing them. He concluded that differences between stocks usually have both a genetic and environmental basis. Ricker estimates there are 10,000 stocks of Pacific salmonids around the rim of the north Pacific. We estimate 2,000 as a conservative number of Atlantic salmon stocks in Europe and North America. Individual stocks have developed over many generations; each is probably unique in respect to certain traits. Some traits are obvious such as morphology and life history patterns while others such as behavioural and biochemical traits are more subtle. Each stock is adapted to its particular river environment. This uniqueness of stocks means that once lost or altered, none can be replaced exactly.

History of Atlantic salmon genetics studies

Atlantic salmon biologists have only recently accepted the stock concept and its genetic basis but already the management possibilities are being realized. The late Dr Börje Carlin and his associates of the Swedish Salmon Research

Institute at Alvkarleby have considered genetic aspects in their Baltic salmon management programme. Dr David Piggins has conducted selective breeding experiments at the hatchery of the Salmon Research Trust of Ireland since the early 1960's. Drs Dag Møller and Trygve Gjedrem, and their respective colleagues, began work in the early 1970's to survey the numerous wild Atlantic salmon stocks in Norway and to determine the genetic components for many traits such as growth rate and age and size at sexual maturity. The North American Salmon Research Center (NASRC) began operation in 1974 as a result of the organizational efforts of Dr Wilfred Carter with early direction in genetics by Dr John Calaprice. Whereas the Norwegian genetics studies have been in support of salmonid aquaculture, the main emphasis at the NASRC has been on determining the genetic influence of traits important for management of wild salmon populations. The Atlantic salmon smolt rearing unit at Almondbank, Scotland has been led by Dr John Thorpe for the study of environmental and genetic aspects of Atlantic salmon production. Some of the background for the progress with Atlantic salmon genetics research was provided by the earlier selective breeding work of Donaldson and his colleagues working with Pacific salmonids at the University of Washington.

Atlantic salmon traits

A number of traits in Atlantic salmon show stock specific differences (*Table 1*). In some cases laboratory studies have been conducted to determine the relative importance of genotype and environment. For many traits the genetic influences are unknown and only speculative. Genetic effects can be partitioned and are a function of additive, dominant and epistatic action of genes (Falconer, 1964). Dominant and epistatic effects are caused by specific gene combinations and since these are disrupted at each segregation and recombination they are difficult to interpret and of little predictive value. When the expression of a trait is influenced by a large number of genes, each of which makes a small contribution to the total, the effect is genetically additive. Additive effects are not disrupted during segregation and recombination.

Most salmon genetic studies have been in selective breeding programmes for pen rearing operations and were designed to determine the additive genetic component or heritability of various economically important traits. Heritability is defined as the ratio of additive genetic variance to the total variance and is a measure of that portion of the total variability which is transmitted from parent to offspring in a predictable fashion. In other words, heritability is a measure of our ability to predict the appearance, performance or behaviour of offspring based on like characters in their parents (Simon, 1970). If there is heritability for a trait, fish can be expected to respond to selective

Table 1 Characteristics showing stock specific differences in Atlantic salmon

Characteristic	References
Fecundity	Pope *et al,* 1961; Baum and Meister, 1971
Egg size	Aulstad and Gjedrem, 1973
Survival to various life stages	Ryman, 1970; Kanis *et al,* 1976
Rate and patterns of growth	Lindroth, 1972; Naevdal *et al,* 1975; Gjedrem, 1976, Møller *et al,* 1976; Refstie *et al,* 1977; Thorpe, 1977
Precocious sexual maturity in male parr	Schiefer, 1971; Schaffer and Elson, 1975; Thorpe, 1975; Saunders and Sreedharan, 1977
Age at smolting	Refstie *et al,* 1977
Age and size at sexual maturity	Ritter, 1972 & 1975; Elson, 1973; Naevdal *et al,* 1976, 1977 & 1978; Ritter and Newbold, 1977
Seaward migration	Saunders, unpub; Gardner, 1976; Farmer *et al,* 1978; Solomon, 1978
Migratory behaviour at sea	Ritter, 1975; Jessop, 1976; Saunders, 1977
Seasonal pattern of adult return from the sea	Zarnecki, 1963; Saunders, 1967; Elson, 1973
Multiple spawning	Dymond, 1963; Ducharme, 1969; Wilkins, 1972
Resistance to disease	Gjedrem and Aulstad, 1974
Resistance to low pH	Gjedrem, 1976; Edwards and Hjeldnes, 1977
Tissue protein and enzyme specificity	Nyman, 1967; Møller, 1970; Payne *et al,* 1971; Nyman and Pippy, 1972; Wilkins, 1972; Elson, 1973

breeding for that trait, the higher the heritability the more rapid the expected response.

Fecundity, egg size, survival
Although fecundity has been observed to differ among stocks of anadromous and landlocked salmon (Pope *et al*, 1961; Baum and Meister, 1971), no detailed study has been done to show the relative genetic and environmental contributions which determine this trait. While the stock specific nature of fecundity suggests genetic influences, a significant environmental effect is also likely. There is a genetic component in egg size among Norwegian salmon stocks (Aulstad and Gjedram, 1973). Survival during incubation and in juvenile stages is influenced by genetics and has a pronounced maternal effect (Kanis *et al*, 1976). These findings apply under hatchery conditions; it is reasonable to expect that there is also a significant genetic component of survival of juvenile stages in nature. A genetic basis has been suggested for survival and adult return of hatchery reared smolts planted in the Baltic sea (Ryman, 1970). The extent of genetic-environmental interaction in these traits has not been determined.

Growth, precocious maturity, smolt age
Growth rates at various life stages are influenced by genetics (Naevdal *et al*, 1975, 1976, 1977 and 1978). The Norwegian aquaculture industry is benefiting from the findings that growth rate is moderately heritable and is selecting stocks on the basis of superior growth. Therefore, it is feasible to identify and to breed stocks selectively for improved growth; this is important to the success of pen rearing operations. Patterns of juvenile growth appear to have a strong bearing on smolt age and possibly on age and size at sexual maturity (Thorpe, 1975 and 1977). Precocious sexual maturity among male parr may have a heritable component and appears to be associated with the grilse/larger salmon phenomenon (Schiefer, 1971; Saunders and Sreedharan, 1977; Thorpe, 1975). Age at smoltification also has a significant genetic component (Refstie *et al*, 1977) which is of importance from hatchery production

efficiency and economic considerations. Smolt age probably has a bearing on overall survival and the length of sea life (Ritter, 1975).

Age and size at maturity – grilse vs larger salmon

There is evidence that age and size at sexual maturity has some genetic basis (Ritter, 1972 and 1975; Elson, 1973; Naevdal *et al*, 1976, 1977 and 1978; Gardner, 1976; Ritter and Newbold 1977). This trait is of great importance in management of natural stocks since it affects ultimate yield of returning adults as a result of size difference between grilse and larger salmon (Gardner, 1976), total natural mortality owing to time at sea (Gardner, 1976) and contributions to distant and local commercial fisheries (Saunders, 1969). Fish which mature as grilse make little or no contribution to the Greenland salmon fishery; the largest component is fish beginning their second sea winter (Saunders *et al*, 1965; Gardner, 1976). The optimum harvesting strategy for grilse versus larger salmon depends on stock specific characters including grilse/larger salmon ratio, comparative sizes, season of return and migratory patterns at sea.

One of the major problems in Norwegian aquaculture is that many salmon achieve sexual maturity after only one year of pen rearing. Choice of late maturing stocks and selection for this trait offer promise in overcoming this problem. While most grilse in Canadian rivers are small (1-3 kg), those in some Irish rivers occasionally exceed 5 kg. Perhaps it is possible through genetics research and selective breeding to develop stocks of large grilse.

Seaward migration

The parr-smolt transformation involves a number of morphological, physiological and behavioural changes which pre-adapt young salmon while still in freshwater for life in the sea (Hoar, 1976). Photoperiod is the environmental cue acting through the endocrine system to effect these changes (Saunders and Henderson, 1970; Saunders and Sreedharan, 1977). Although a number of studies have been done on physiological and behavioural aspects of smolting, we know of none on possible stock specific smolting responses to environmental influences. Timing of smolt runs in nature appears to be influenced mostly by temperature (Elson, 1973, Solomon, 1978). It is possible that there are stock specific responses to the environmental cue or cues for smolting and to those for triggering migratory behaviour.

Seaward migration of smolts occurs in the spring during the period of increasing day length, rising temperature and, usually, increased river discharge. The smolting phenomenon culminating in migration may be thought of as a 'window on the sea', open for a short time each year. If all stocks responded similarly to smolting cues and migratory triggers, it is likely that smolts would be reaching the sea over a long period. Smolts produced in headwaters of long rivers might not experience threshold temperatures for triggering migration in time to reach the lower river and estuary when environmental conditions are appropriate there. For example, if the salmon which once lived in the headwaters of the Connecticut River began their smolt migration in late May, it is likely they would have found too high temperatures in the lower river and Long Island Sound when they reached these waters in June or July. Some would find the 'window' closed. Some salmon stocks in headwater streams appear to have developed a special behaviour to get them to sea at the appropriate time. Large parr from some headwater streams move downstream in the autumn (Gardner, 1976) and may overwinter in the lower reaches. During the following spring they complete smoltification and move to the sea. Hatchery reared smolts commonly show downstream swimming or migratory behaviour in circular ponds during spring. Some stocks show this behaviour as large parr in the autumn (McAskill). We interpret downstream movements in autumn as stock specific behaviour developed to ensure timely arrival at sea the following spring. If this suggestion is borne out, there are obvious implications for choice of stocks for salmon transplant projects.

Migratory behaviour

Although differences in migratory behaviour at sea have been recognized for different Atlantic and Pacific salmonid stocks (Ricker, 1972; Jessop, 1976; Saunders, 1977), these observations are difficult to quantify and estimates of the genetic contribution to migratory behaviour are not available. If a significant contribution is found, this trait assumes great importance in any restoration or enhancement attempt requiring the establishment of salmon stocks in rivers far removed from donor rivers. It appears from tagging experiments that not all mainland North American Atlantic salmon stocks contribute to the same extent to distant fisheries in Newfoundland and Greenland. Salmon from the Penobscot, Machias and Naraguagus Rivers in Maine, and from Quebec and northern New Brunswick contribute heavily to these distant fisheries, while stocks from the Bay of Fundy contribute to a lesser extent or not at all. Salmon from one of the Bay of Fundy stocks, the Big Salmon River, are rarely if ever taken outside the Bay of Fundy (Jessop, 1976).

Seasonal return patterns

Seasonal patterns of adult return, the early-late run phenomenon, probably has a genetic basis in Atlantic salmon as it surely does in the Pacific salmonids (Ricker, 1972). Certainly, there is also a strong environmental component in the timing of spawning runs where river discharge rate and water temperature affect upstream movement of salmon. The northwest Miramichi River has early and late runs representing separate stocks which spawn and have their nursery areas in the upper and lower reaches of the river respectively. Environmental conditions were likely responsible for the development of stock specific patterns of adult return which are of undoubted survival value. Presumably, natural selection has adapted the genotypes in these stocks and reinforced the appropriate behaviour patterns. Timing of adult return affects the availability and quality of salmon and is therefore an important management consideration for both sport and commercial fisheries.

Multiple spawning

Like most salmon traits that have been studied, the degree of multiple spawning probably has some genetic basis. Stocks of Atlantic salmon show different incidences of multiple spawning (Dymond, 1963; Ducharme, 1969). Although genetic effects are likely since some rivers are known for the presence or absence of salmon spawning two or more times, the picture is not clear because commercial and angling fisheries sometimes bias any sample against the larger fish. The interval between successive spawnings varies among individuals and may also be stock specific (Went and Piggins, 1968). Although both sexes sometimes live to spawn more than once, it is more common for females to do so. This suggests an adaptation to optimize reproductive effort. The optimum strategy would favour multiple spawners which, because of their larger size, produce more eggs.

Disease resistance

Resistance to disease is of great importance because of outbreaks of epidemic scale in large monoculture operations. It is essential that fish released from hatcheries be disease free to avoid introducing diseases among wild stocks. Outbreaks of kidney disease, vibrio, infectious pancreatic necrosis, furunculosis and enteric red mouth have become alarmingly common and have wiped out some hatchery stocks or forced hatchery closure. The finding that resistance to vibrio differs among Atlantic salmon stocks (Gjedram and Aulstad, 1974) and has a significantly high heritability means that selection for resistance to this disease is promising. It remains to be learned if similar possibilities exist for selection against other diseases.

Resistance to low pH

Norwegian studies have revealed some degree of heritability for resistance to low pH in brown trout (Gjedram, 1976; Edwards and Hjeldnes, 1977) but no such studies have been reported for Atlantic salmon. Scandinavia receives acid precipitation from atmospheric circulation of sulphuric acid which results from use of fossil fuels in western Europe. Acid precipitation has resulted in intolerably low pH's in some salmon rivers. If studies show that resistance to low pH is heritable in Atlantic salmon, then selection for such resistance offers some hope of re-establishing stocks where some have been lost. New England and the Canadian Maritime Provinces face a similar threat from the projected increased use of coal to meet energy needs in the northeastern United States.

Protein specificity

Biochemical genetics studies have indicated that tissue proteins can be characterized electrophoretically and used as a basis of distinguishing salmon stocks and thereby determining the origins of fish caught at sea (Nyman, 1967; Møller, 1970; Payne et al, 1971; Nyman and Pippy, 1972; Wilkins, 1972; Elson, 1973). Stocks are separable on the basis of frequencies of genes coding for various isozymes. In addition to permitting separation of stocks, characteristic electrophoretic banding patterns can be used to detect interspecific hybrids. Isozymes can be used as genetic markers and pre-screened broodstock can be crossed so as to characterize strains where conventional tagging is impractical. This makes possible the evaluation of reproductive success of a planted stock where wild stocks already exist. If the planted fish are homozygous for a particular enzyme allele which is not found in the native stock the progeny of the planted stock will be separable from indigenous fish.

Local vs foreign stocks

Ricker's review of a number of studies involving attempts to transplant Pacific salmonids shows that adult returns are generally better for hatchery reared juveniles planted in their native than in foreign streams (Ricker, 1972). Fish from a non-native but nearby stock return more successfully than those from a distant stock. Jessop (1976) planted hatchery reared smolts of Miramichi, Restigouche and Big Salmon River parentage in the Big Salmon River. Adults of all three stocks returned to Big Salmon River but in greater numbers for native than for non-native stocks. Big Salmon River fish contributed less to distant fisheries than did Miramichi and Restigouche fish. Ritter (1975) suggests that

releases of hatchery reared smolts in foreign rivers give
fewer adult returns than releases in donor rivers. The
farther the recipient from the donor river the fewer the
adult returns. Saunders (1977) suggests that sea migration
behaviour is inherited and has developed through many
generations to take the salmon from its natal river to and
back from its feeding area(s) at sea. Introduced stocks may
suffer initially from unaccustomed predation. A corollary
of these suggestions is that migration 'programmes' of salmon stocks from widely separated rivers may involve
specific behaviour in response to environmental stimuli
such as temperature, salinity, ocean currents and predation. In support of this concept are the observations that
sockeye salmon fry from stocks which spawn in inlet and
outlet streams move downstream or upstream, respectively,
soon after emerging from their redds (Raleigh, 1967;
Foerster, 1968) to enter lakes where they live for a year or
more before going to sea. The hypothesis for inherited sea
migration behaviour in Atlantic salmon awaits further testing.

Releases of locally reared smolts of Miramichi parentage
in the Penobscot, Naraguagus and Machias Rivers in Maine
were generally unsuccessful, giving few adult returns,
mostly as grilse rather than larger salmon which are typical
of those rivers (Meister). Later attempts, using residual
stocks from the Naraguagus and Machias Rivers, to restore
a salmon run in the Penobscot were successful with the
establishment of a hatchery assisted run of mainly early
run, two sea-year salmon in that river. The donor streams
had been previously stocked with Penobscot salmon and
may have acted as refuges for the Penobscot stock which
were absent from the Penobscot for many years. This successful salmon rehabilitation project shows the value of
using local stocks.

Natural vs hatchery smolt production
Until the 1950's, it was common hatchery practice to release
fry and parr stages of salmon to supplement natural production. This was largely discontinued because it was difficult to evaluate the effectiveness of such releases. Carlin

and his colleagues (1955) developed an ingenious smolt tag and began reporting the successful procedure of planting hatchery reared smolts in the Baltic Sea. This practice evolved in Sweden where most major salmon rivers were dammed for hydro-electric power. It was legislated that power companies must compensate for lost natural salmon production. Thus began an extensive sea ranching programme through which Baltic salmon production was largely maintained through hatchery production; natural fresh water production was virtually eliminated. Hatchery reared smolts were released and broodstock was supplied through returning adults.

Salmon workers in other countries quickly seized on Carlin's techniques and largely abandoned their fry-parr planting schemes. Carlin's methods have been a valuable addition to our salmon management techniques during the last 20 years and are sure to continue as such. We suggest, however, that it is time to re-examine the comparative effectiveness of fry-parr and smolt planting from a genetic point of view. Of particular concern is the inevitable selection in a smolt rearing programme for fish which respond favourably to intensive rearing practices. Under natural conditions, perhaps 90 percent of mortality occurs during fresh water stages. If this stage is by-passed during one or more generations, the resulting stock may have reduced fitness during the critical fresh water stages even though they have demonstrated satisfactory and even improved performance at sea. Many smolt planting programmes are evaluated on the basis of first generation returns from the sea. However, the contribution to subsequent natural reproduction is not known. It is possible that fitness of indigenous stocks may be reduced through interbreeding with introduced fish. Calaprice (1969) cautions against inbreeding which has resulted from many hatchery attempts at selection for the above mentioned and other salmonid traits. He warns that 'the effect of selection and inbreeding will be to decrease genetic variance within the populations, and the latter may be expected to result in a reduction of fitness in the populations undergoing selection.' Since natural salmon populations show a wide range of phenotypic variability, it is reasonable to assume that variation confers some adaptive significance on successful populations.

If the objective, as in the Swedish smolt planting programme and in sea ranching for commercial production, is to improve survival at sea and to bypass the fresh water life stages, then such a system has merit. For supplementing and developing natural salmon production, planting fertilized eggs or fry-parr may be more appropriate than using smolts.

An alternative to complete hatchery dependence on freshwater production which is more desirable from a genetics point of view is the utilization of stream-side incubation and/or artificial spawning channels. Studies with stream-side incubation boxes in Newfoundland (Porter and Meerburg. 1977) and on artificial spawning channels with Pacific salmon (Barnes and Simpson, 1977) have shown that percentage survival from egg to swim-up fry can be greatly increased over natural production. Therefore, the same number of eggs will produce greater numbers of parr or, more importantly with respect to restoration, an equivalent number of parr can be produced with fewer eggs. Because of the passive nature of eggs and sac fry, mortalities resulting from predation and the drying up of redds because of low water conditions can be assumed to occur at random and one might expect little genetic advantage to be conferred on individuals which manage to survive these critical developmental stages. More intense selection would be expected once the fish begin active feeding and therefore adaptive genotypes will become relatively more important to reproductive success.

The first priority would be to construct broodstock collection and incubation facilities on prospective donor streams and to assess the relative effectiveness of artificial and natural incubation. Incubation facilities could then be constructed on the recipient river and the 'excess' percentage of eggs from a large number of females could be transferred to these units. This would allow natural selection to adapt the new population, at least from the swim-up fry stage, and would provide a large genetic base for the founder stock. Once the introduced fish had reached sexual maturity it would be necessary to construct adult collection facilities to provide eggs for the next generation. Any excess broodstock could be allowed upstream; hopefully those which escape the sport fishery would spawn naturally. Because these fish would have been reared in the river from the egg stage, the probability of successful adaptation and restoration should be increased and it would eventually become possible to phase out streamside incubation.

North American Salmon Research Center programme
The research programme at the North American Salmon Research Center has focused its initial genetics studies on age and size at sexual maturity and migratory behaviour at sea. Salmon from several New Brunswick stocks are hatched, reared and released as smolts at NASRC to develop quantitative data on the above and other traits. Donor rivers are chosen on the basis of contrasts in respect to various traits we wish to study. A diallel crossing scheme was used for the first four spawnings and will be replaced by a hierarchal design in 1978. Strains of salmon have been marked using fin clip combination, cold brands, modified Carlin tags and coded magnetic wire micro tags (Jefferts *et al*, 1963). The use of internally readable magnetic micro tags is planned for the near future. This will allow permanent, positive identification of several hundred families. Returning adults can be identified as to strain and family and individuals selected as broodstock.

Our programme began with the 1974 year class. Smolts from this and subsequent year classes were released from 1976 onwards. The first grilse returned in 1977. Grilse and two sea-year salmon are now returning and these will provide data leading to evaluation of the diallel crosses for a number of traits. Some of the returning adults will be used as broodstock for selective breeding experiments.

Although the programme is in its early stages, there are already findings in respect of juvenile stages of salmon and the first adult returns show interesting trends. There are both genetic and environmental components in precocious sexual maturation of male parr. Size of parr in early summer apparently affects maturation in the fall. There is marked difference in incidence of precocious males among the stocks studied and there is consistent heterosis or hybrid vigor for this trait (Saunders and Sreedharan, 1977). Growth rate differs among the stocks being reared under uniform environmental conditions. Bimodal growth patterns are evident by autumn of the first year in all of the strains being reared (Bailey and Saunders, 1978). Precocious sexual maturity, difference in juvenile growth rate and bimodal patterns of growth are thought to influence subsequent growth rates and to affect the ratio of grilse to larger salmon. Preliminary data from the first smolt releases show intriguing strains and to grilse size. Some of our grilse are in the 2.5-3.5 kg range, well above the size usually found in Canadian stocks. Whether these large grilse are the result of our breeding programme or of special environmental conditions will be learned in due course.

A new run of salmon has been established in a stream adjacent to the Salmon Center. Nearly 300 grilse and larger salmon have returned to date. This sea ranching exercise was designed to produce data on adult returns for age and size at return, sea migratory behaviour, seasonal patterns of return and other traits affecting overall performance. One early finding with the adult returns is that one of the first three pure stocks released gave many times more grilse and older salmon returns than the other two stocks. The stock showing the best performance and apparent adaptability to hatchery and sea ranching conditions is from a stock that has been hatchery reared and sea ranched for 3-4 generations at another New Brunswick hatchery. The other two stocks were taken from wild spawners. This is consistent with improved returns among other hatchery inbred lines (Piggins, 1973). We believe that our early genetics findings with juvenile and adult salmon are an indication of important contributions to be made in future Atlantic salmon management.

References

AULSTAD, D & GJEDREM, T. The egg size of salmon *(Salmo salar)* in
1973 Norwegian rivers. *Aquaculture* 2: 337–41.

BAILEY, J K & SAUNDERS, R L. *Bimodal growth trait frequency distributions in*
1978 *strains of artificially reared Atlantic salmon (Salmo salar) parr produced*
in a diallel experiment. In preparation.

BARNES, R A & SIMPSON, K S. Substrate incubators workshop. Report
1977 on current state-of-the-art. *Fish Mar Serv Tech Rept* 689: 67 p.

BAUM, E T & MEISTER, A L. Fecundity of Atlantic salmon *(Salmo salar)*
1971 from two Maine rivers. *J Fish Res Board Can* 28: 764–67.

CALAPRICE, J R. Production and genetic factors in managed salmonid
1969 populations. In *H R MacMillan Lectures in Fisheries.* Symposium
on Salmon and Trout in Streams (Ed T G Northcote). University
of British Columbia, Vancouver, BC. 377–88.

CARLIN, B.Tagging of salmon smolts in the river Lagan. *Institute for*
1955 *Freshwater Research, Annual Report* for 1954. Drottningholm,
Sweden, pp 57–74.

DUCHARME, L J A. Atlantic salmon returning for their fifth and sixth
1969 consecutive spawning trips. *J Fish Res Board Can* 26 : 1661–64.

DYMOND, J R. Family Salmonidae. In *Memoir,* Sears Foundation for
1963 Marine Research, Number 1, Part 3. New Haven, 1963. 457–502.

EDWARDS, D J & HJELDNES, S. *Growth and survival of salmonids in water of*
1977 *different pH.* SNSF-project, Norway, FR10/77, 12 p.

ELSON, P F. Predator – prey relationships between fish eating birds and
1962 Atlantic salmon. *Fish Res Board Can Bull* 133: 1–87.

ELSON, P F. Genetic polymorphism in northwest Miramichi salmon in
1973 relation to season of river ascent and age at maturation and its
implications for management of the stocks. *Int Comm Northwest Atl*
Fish Res Doc 73-76, Ser no 3028, 6 p.

FALCONER, D S. *Introduction to quantitative genetics.* Oliver and Boyd
1964 Limited, London. 365 p.

FARMER, G J, RITTER, J A & ASHFIELD, D. Seawater acclimatizaion
1978 and parr-smolt transformation of juvenile Atlantic salmon,
Salmo salar. J Fish Res Board Can 35: 93–100.

FOERSTER, R E. The Sockeye Salmon, *(Oncorhynchus nerka). Bull No*
1968 *162. Fish Res Board Can* 422 p.

GARDNER, M L. A review of factors which may influence the sea-age and
1976 maturation of Atlantic salmon *Salmo salar L. J Fish Biol 9:*
289–327.

GJEDREM, T. *Genetic variation in tolerance of brown trout to acid water.*
1976 SNSF-project, Norway, FR5/76, 11 p.

GJEDREM, T. Possibilities for genetic improvements in salmonids. *J Fish*
1976 *Res Board Can.* 33: 1094–9.

GJEDREM, T & AULSTAD, D. Selection experiments with salmon. I. Dif-
1974 ferences in reistance to vibrio disease of salmon parr *(Salmo*
salar). Aquaculture 3: 51–59.

HOAR, W S. Smolt transformation: evolution, behaviour and physiology.
1976   *J Fish Res Board Can.* 33: 1233–52.

JEFFERTS, K B, BERGMAN, P K and FISCUS, H F. A coded wire identifica-
1963   tion system for macro-organisms. *Nature* 198: 460–62.

JESSOP, B M. Distribution and timing of tag recoveries from native and
1976   non-native Atlantic salmon *(Salmo salar)* released into Big Sal-
       mon River, New Brunswick. *J Fish Res Board Can.* 33: 829–833.

KANIS, E, REFSTIE, T & GJEDREM, T. A genetic analysis of egg, alevin and
1976   fry mortality in salmon *(Salmo salar)*, sea trout *(Salmo trutta)*,
       and rainbow trout *(Salmo gairdneri)*. *Aquaculture* 8: 259–68.

KOMOURDJIAN, M P, SAUNDERS, R L & FENWICK, J C. Evidence for the
1976   role of growth hormone as a part of a 'light-pituitary axis' in
       growth and smoltification of Atlantic salmon *(Salmo salar)*. *Can J
       Zool.* 54: 544–51.

LINDROTH, A. Heritability estimates of growth in fish. *Aquilo Ser* Zool 13:
1972   77–80.

McASKILL, J.Personal communication.

MEISTER, A L. Personal communication.

MØLLER, D. Transferring polymorphism in Atlantic salmon *(Salmo
1970   salar)*. *J Fish Res Board Can.* 27: 1617–25.

MØLLER, D, BJERK, O & HOLM, M. Comparative growth studies, II.
1976   *Internat. Counc. Explor. Sea C.M.* 1976/E:36.

NAEVDAL, G, HOLM, M, MØLLER, D & OSTHUS, O D. Experiments with
1975   selective breeding of salmon. *Internat Counc Explor Sea CM.*
       1975/M: 22.

NAEVDAL, G, HOLM, M, MØLLER, D & OSTHUS, O D. Variation in growth
1976   rate and age at sexual maturity in Atlantic salmon. *Internat Counc
       Explor Sea CM.* 1976/E: 40.

NAEVDAL, G, HOLM, M, LEROY, R & MØLLER, D. Individual growth rate
1977   and age at first sexual maturity in Atlantic salmon. *Internat Counc
       Explor Sea CM.* 1977/E: 60.

NAEVDAL, G, BJERK, O, HOLM, M, LEROY R, & MØLLER, D. Growth rate
1978   and age at sexual maturity of Atlantic salmon smoltifying at one
       and two years of age. *Internat Counc Explor Sea CM.* 1978/F: 23.

NYMAN, L. Protein variations in Salmonidae. *Rep Inst Freshwater Res.*
1967   Drottningholm 47: 5–38.

NYMAN, O L & PIPPY, J H C. Differences in Atlantic salmon *Salmo salar,*
1972   from North America and Europe. *J Fish Res Board Can.* 29:
       179–85.

PAYNE, R H, CHILD, A R & FORREST, A. Geographical variation in the
1971   Atlantic salmon. *Nature* (London) 231: 250–52.

PIGGINS, D J. The results of selective breeding from known grilse and
1973   salmon parents. *Ann Rep Salmon Res Trust of Ireland.* No 18,
       Appendix 1, 35–39.

POPE, J A, MILLS, D H & SHEARER, W M. The fecundity of Atlantic salmon
1961   *(Salmo salar* Linn*).* *Freshwater and Salmon Fish Res.* 26: 1–12.

PORTER, T R & MEERBURG, D J. Upwelling incubation boxes for Atlantic
1977   salmon, *Salmo salar. Internat Counc Explor Sea CM.* 1977/M: 22.

RALEIGH, R F. Genetic control in the lakeward migrations of sockeye
1967   salmon *(Oncorhynchus nerka)* fry. *J Fish Res Board Can.* 24:
2613–22.

REFSTIE, T, STEINE, T A & GJEDREM, T. Selection experiments with
1977   salmon. II. Proportion of Atlantic salmon smoltifying at 1 year of
age. *Aquaculture* 10: 231–42.

RICKER, W E. Hereditary and environmental factors affecting certain
1972   salmonid populations. In *H R MacMillan Lectures in Fisheries.* The
stock concept in Pacific salmon. (Eds R C Simon and P A Larkin)
University of British Columbia, Vancouver, BC 19–160.

RITTER, J A. Preliminary observation on the influence of smolt size on tag
1972   return rate and age at first maturity of Atlantic salmon *(Salmo
salar). Internat Counc Explor Sea CM.* 1972/M: 14.

RITTER, J A. Lower ocean survival rates for hatchery-reared Atlantic
1975   salmon *(Salmo salar)* stocks released in rivers other than their
native streams. *Internat Counc Explor Sea CM.* 1975/M: 26.

RITTER, J A. Relationships of smolt size and age with age at first maturity
1975   in Atlantic salmon. *Tech Rep Ser No Mar/F* 175.5. Res Dev Branch,
Maritimes Reg, Environment Can, 7 p.

RITTER, J A & NEWBOLD, K. Relationships of parentage and smolt age to
1977   age at first maturity of Atlantic salmon *(Salmo salar) Internat
Counc Explor Sea CM.* 1977/M: 32.

RYMAN, N. A genetic analysis of recapture frequencies of released young
1970   of salmon. *Hereditas* 65: 159–60.

SAUNDERS, R L. Unpublished data.

SAUNDERS, R L. Seasonal pattern of return of Atlantic salmon in the
1967   northwest Miramichi River, New Brunswick. *J Fish Res Board Can.*
24: 21–32.

SAUNDERS, R L. Contributions of salmon from the northwest Miramichi
1969   River, New Brunswick, to various fisheries. *J Fish Res Board Can.*
26: 269–78.

SAUNDERS, R L. Sea ranching – a promising way to enhance populations
1977   of Atlantic salmon for angling and commercial fisheries. IASF.
Special Publ Ser No 7. pp 17–24.

SAUNDERS, R L, KERSWILL, C J & ELSON, P F. Canadian Atlantic salmon
1965   recaptured near Greenland. *J Fish Res Board Can.* 22: 625–29.

SAUNDERS, R L & HENDERSON, E B. Influence of photo-period smolt
1970   development and growth of Atlantic salmon *(Salmo salar). J Fish
Res Board Can.* 27: 1295–1311.

SAUNDERS, R L & SREEDHARAN, A. The incidence and genetic implica-
1977   tions of sexual maturity in male Atlantic salmon parr. *Internat
Counc Explor Sea CM.* 1977/M: 21.

SCHAFFER, W M & ELSON, P F. The adaptive significance of variations in
1975   life history among local populations of Atlantic salmon in North
America. *Ecol* 56: 577–590.

SCHIEFER, K. Ecology of Atlantic salmon, with special reference to
1971   occurence and abundance of grilse in north shore Gulf of St
Lawrence Rivers. PhD Thesis. Univ of Waterloo, Ont. 129 p.

SIMON, R C. Genetics and marine aquaculture. *In* W J McNeil ed. *Marine*
1970   *Aquaculture,* pp 53–63. Oregon State Univ Press, Corvallis, OR.
        172 p.

SOLOMON, D J. Some observations on salmon smolt migration in a chalk
1978   stream. *J Fish Biol.* 12: 571–74.

THORPE, J E. Early maturity in male Atlantic salmon. *Scott. Fisheries Bull.*
1975   42: 15–17.

THORPE, J E. Bimodal distribution of length of juvenile Atlantic salmon
1977   *(Salmo salar* L) under artificial rearing conditions. *J. Fish Biol* 11:
        175–84.

WENT, A E J & PIGGINS, D J. The absence habits of some grilse kelts – II.
1968   *Ann Rep Salmon Res Trust of Ireland.* No 13, Appendix II, 25–32.

WILKINS, N P. Biochemical genetics of the Atlantic salmon, *Salmo salar.*

ZARNECKI, S. Differentiation of Atlantic salmon *(Salmo salar* L) and of
1963   sea trout *(Salmo trutta* L) from the Wisla (Vistula) river into
        seasonal populations. *Acta Hydrobiol.* 5: 255–94.

5 Discussion

L Stewart, (Salmon and Trout Association) opened the discussion as follows

Mr Stewart claimed that ocean ranching could have little or no influence in the matter of increasing natural stocks of salmon in rivers. Ranching, as at present practised, is a developing industry for the production of salmon for human consumption and, as such, is carried out solely as an economic venture based on sound commercial principles. It seemed to him that no company or other interested party would, at the present time, artificially rear salmon to the adult stage and liberate them in rivers where stocks were depleted; further, it seemed unlikely that such a practice would develop in the future.

According to European figures, it took at least 6-7 tonnes of fish and fish offal to produce one tonne of salmon flesh. If pellets were fed, then production costs were higher. In coastal units, where pumping was necessary, fuel charges (petrol/oil) amounted to half a tonne of fuel per one tonne of fish produced and inshore freezing units used two tonnes for each tonne of fish produced. On these figures, Mr Stewart asked, how could any commercial enterprise develop adult salmon for liberation into rivers? Instead, might not the production of extremely large tonnages of salmon for human consumption take much, if not all, of the netting and angling pressure from salmon rivers throughout the Northern Hemisphere?

On the subject of sea-rearing of coho salmon *Oncorhynchus kisutch* instead of Atlantic salmon, about which there had been a great deal of discussion recently in this country, he was of the opinion that economic considerations must play a part here because any commercial enterprise had to quantify production costs per unit. According to Norwegian figures, the price of a reared coho salmon smolt was apparently 5.8 pence as against 35 pence for an Atlantic salmon smolt. On this basis, the costs of rearing 500,000 smolts of each of the two species would be in the region of £29,000 and £175,000 respectively. These figures gave some indication as to why the ranching of coho salmon could seem an attractive proposition for development in this country, though a difficulty here would be the prevention of escapement of coho salmon into rivers holding Atlantic salmon.

D H Mills (University of Edinburgh) said that with the increase in the numbers of cage-reared salmon coming on to the commercial market is it possible that the cost of them could influence the price of wild salmon. This could be an advantage at least if, by reducing the price of the Atlantic salmon, the incentive to poach was reduced. On the other hand, if the price was reduced it would affect anglers who fish either for profit or to sell their fish to meet the cost of high rod rents.

J R W Stansfeld asked Mr Thorpe whether, in view of the theoretical genetical factor in grilse maturation postulated by Drs Gunnes and Saunders, he had achieved any reduction in the percentage of grilse maturation on his fish farms.

Mr Thorpe replied that it was too early to express an opinion on this matter.

A S Gee (University of Wales Institute of Science and Technology) asked whether there were genetical consequences of differential exploitation of different runs of salmon within one major system. On the River Wye, for example, exploitation by rods on the three sea-winter salmon, which enter the river in the early spring, is much higher than on grilse, which are late summer fish.

Dr Saunders replied that different runs of salmon can be at least partly racially segregated. Over-exploitation of spring run salmon in part of the Miramichi system has resulted in the loss of the early run so that only the fall run now remains.

W T W Potts (University of Lancaster) said that intensive animal rearing on land usually leads to serious problems of waste disposal. It would be interesting, therefore, to know what is the state of the sea bed under the salmon-rearing cages and whether there is any danger that the oxidative capacity of Scottish sea lochs might limit the expansion of sea fish farming.

Dr Young replied that problems had not arisen in this regard.

G S Scott (Clyde River Purification Board) suggested that examination of the ocean resources of fish food might be worthwhile studying. There seemed no lack of ocean plankton which had been extensively studied by plankton recorders but the size of the stocks of fishes such as cod and herring might have some influence on the abundance of salmon.

Y Harache (CNEXO, France) said that Pacific salmon held in captivity for several weeks after the normal smoltification period when transferred to sea cages tended to lose their migratory habit and remain in the vicinity of the cages for some time. This technique has enabled a marine sport fishery to develop based on semi-sedentary populations of Pacific salmon. If such a habit occurs in the Atlantic salmon there are possibilities for developing further sports fisheries.

Dr L Stewart (Salmon and Trout Association) said that he had been actively involved in attempts to establish migratory runs of Atlantic salmon and sea trout in the Falkland Islands, and his subsequent investigation into the Islands' fisheries revealed that, though salmon had not been established, sea trout of up to 20 lbs in weight were caught in some of the Falkland rivers.

In addition to the investigation into the Falkland fisheries, he had carried out a survey of rivers in Tasmania and New Zealand where salmon acclimatization experiments had taken place from the nineteenth century onwards. None of the attempts to introduce migratory runs of either Atlantic or Pacific salmon species in Southern Hemisphere rivers appeared to have met with success, except one instance – sea going runs of quinnat salmon

Oncorhynchus tschawytscha had eventually been established in certain east coast rivers of New Zealand's South Island early this century. From his investigations in Tasmania, New Zealand and the Falkland Islands, he had reached the opinion that the theory of a salmon's so-called 'homing instinct' capable of operating over long distances could largely be discounted and that the real explanation for the return of adult salmon from the sea was likely to be of a simple physical nature. Briefly, it was possible, in his opinion, that when a salmon smolt left the offshore waters it would meet up in the ocean with a rotating current (gyre) in which it would drift along with other species of fish fauna. During this time, the smolt would be predating upon marine aquatic organisms, the degree of feeding increasing or decreasing according to the physiological condition of the fish; its life cycle would thus be controlled by the rotation of the gyre and be related to ovary or gonad development, the fish could leave or rejoin or even transfer to other associated gyres. The ultimate result, if it kept within its originating gyre, would be its return to the point at which it embarked as a smolt. It was possible that, at the adult stage of its life, a smell imprint took over and acted as a signal for the salmon to change its offshore habitat for that of freshwater and that, as it closed in to the river of its birth, the flows therefrom were detected. It then followed the coast until it recognized the familiar pheromone which impelled it to enter its natal stream. If this passive drift theory was valid, then the explanation of the failure to establish the sea going runs of salmon might be related to the absence of integral land masses in the Southern Hemisphere and the lack of suitable oceanic gyres developing as a result. It was thought that the localized success of the quinnat salmon runs in New Zealand might be dependent upon two small gyres producing circular flows which had been found in the area of the Canterbury Bight.

He agreed with Dr Thorpe that there were two factors influencing salmon migration, *ie* the environmental factor and the imprinting factor. One without the other would preclude success in attempting naturally to increase our salmon stocks.

I F West (Fisheries Research Division, Ministry of Agriculture and Fisheries, New Zealand) directed a question to Mr Thorpe regarding what is known of the limits of the marine feeding resource used by the Atlantic salmon. He asked if it is not possible that the ecological niche vacated by the declining salmon may have been filled by another species? Consequently with a finite resource ranched salmon could eventually compete for marine resources with wild fish.

Mr Thorpe replied that no clear answer could be given to this question although it was thought unlikely that ranched fish would compete unduly with wild fish.

Mr West then went on to discuss quinnat salmon in New Zealand.

1 Salmon research – the treasure chest

P F Elson, Fisheries Research Board of Canada

Introduction

During the last half century there has been an impressive accumulation of knowledge pertinent to better management of Atlantic salmon resources.

Up to the end of the first quarter of the 20th century, most management was based largely on intuitive reasoning. Research concentrated mostly on basic life history of the species. Catch records were maintained for many commercial and some sport fisheries. But these records received only limited use in terms of their potential contribution to improved management.

Beginning in the late '30's more intensive studies of the ecology of salmon were begun. Some, utilizing tagging techniques, involved movement of adults from the sea to and up rivers. Others focused on the ecological requirements, behaviour and survival of the young in rivers.

The quantitative aspects of salmon production thus begun opened the door for management based on science, as opposed to the empirical and intuitive approaches of bygone years.

This is not to belittle the contributions arising from long experience and keen observation by earlier managers. Enlightened management will always need the wedding of experience and science. Essential contributions from science must include not only broadly based biology, but also inputs from the economic and social fields, all welded together through appropriate legal procedures.

There is at this time distressing, indeed almost tragic,

failure to fully utilize the vast amount of knowledge that could lead to far more effective management of our Atlantic salmon resources. Why? Poor communication!

Unless new knowledge is transmitted from the gatherer to the potential user it has no current value. The researcher, in whatever field, may write the most concise and clear report of his work, but unless the manager and administrator read and digest what he writes, it can contribute little to progress.

Scientific reports are usually couched in the esoteric jargon characteristic of a particular field of research. This leads to ready and clear communication between scientists in the same or similar fields. Unfortunately, those involved in management are often too busy with administrative concerns to spend the time and effort needed to convert the specialists' report into manageable ideas which can be used. In addition, the scientist may not even be interested in whether the administrator can use his findings. He might only be concerned with organizing a scientific presentation that meets the approval of his scientific peers, his bosses, and the specialist journal which he hopes will publish his report and he may think his success depends on acceptable scientific publications. Here are two examples of failure to achieve effective communication:

1. Some years ago I was asked to divert a substantial portion of my time from active research to assemble a review of research literature on Atlantic salmon. In the review I referred to two similar reviews, one by Pyefinch (1955) less than ten years old at the time and the other by Dymond (1963), less than five years old. Some months later, when a preliminary draft had been examined by one of the instigators (a biologist and administrator) of the request, it drew the comment, 'Gee, if I'd known those were available I'd not have asked for another review!'

2. Between 1973 and 1975 I had occasion to analyze and report in some detail on the salmon fisheries of the River Foyle in Northern Ireland (Elson and Tuomi, 1975). One of the analyses involved examination of available data using Ricker's stock-and-recruitment method, (1958). A by-product of such analysis is an estimate of possible maximum

exploitation rates. But my text emphasized that the Foyle (or any salmon river for that matter) could not be effectively managed through using exploitation rates as a focus. Rather, the fishery must be managed to assure, as nearly as possible, an appropriate spawning escapement, which was defined. A reviewer (Ruggles, 1977) of this long and complex report, who was an administrator first trained as a biologist, completely missed this key point and focused on possible damage from using the high exploitation rate against which the text had clearly warned! I submit that in these two cases the readers should have been professionally competent to locate the literature and digest it, but failed to bring enough attention to bear.

An important body of scientific literature has accumulated in the last few years concerning the importance of fishing strategies and how they can and should be manipulated in order to discover more effective management for many of our fisheries. Those I have read are compiled in the jargon of the statistician, usually involving complicated equations of differential and integral calculus. But they do offer approaches which are extremely important in maintaining Atlantic salmon fisheries in years ahead (eg Silvert, 1977 and 1978; Walters and Hilborn, 1976). Biologists and administrators who expect to be concerned with Atlantic salmon resources five or ten years hence can ignore such papers only at the peril of future resources. In some cases it will doubtless be necessary, but eminently worthwhile, to seek the assistance of a competent interpreter.

Parochial attitudes
Administrators responsible for decisions about Atlantic salmon fisheries have frequently taken extremely parochial, even chauvinistic, approaches to their problems. This leads to little thought being given to sharing mixed stocks with fisheries more advanced in migration. It has also meant that insufficient thought was given to perpetuating the resource by assuring appropriate spawning escapement in rivers. There is evidence in some areas that this situation was worse in publicly owned 'open-entry' fisheries than in some privately owned fisheries, as in parts of Europe. Pub-

licly owned fisheries are not necessarily improvident, but decision-makers for these fisheries too seldom think beyond the immediate short-term value of their own fishery. This can be particularly damaging in a mixed-stock fishery (Elson and Tuomi, 1975). Unhappily, examples of such parochial attitudes are common.

Early this year I contributed to an analysis of the potential and time frame of the drastically reduced salmon stocks of New Brunswick's Saint John River to support a renewed commercial fishery for Atlantic salmon (Underwood McLellan (1977) Limited, 1978). The fishery has been banned since 1972. The stocks, which had suffered drastic reduction from a combination of man-induced environmental changes, are recovering. The study was commissioned by the provincial department which administers commercial fisheries. Another department which administers recreational fisheries and watches salmon recruitment was not consulted at all, nor was there any suggestion from the commissioning department that any consideration be given to upriver stocks. Needless to say, any such study had to, and did, include all segments of the Saint John River population.

The effects of the recently developed Greenland fishery for Atlantic salmon have been well studied and documented on both sides of the north Atlantic. This indicated that the salmon was indeed being placed in biological jeopardy, and that home fisheries were noticeably reduced, before international agreement succeeded in bringing about a reduction of the catch. In one Quebec experiment (Tétreault and Carter, 1972), 42 percent of tagged smolts were taken in Greenland, 42 percent in Newfoundland, presumably on the way home, and only 16 percent in home waters. A detailed statistical study of tag returns from New Brunswick and Nova Scotia fish (Paloheimo and Elson, 1974) indicated that the Greenland fishery may have taken as much as 27-38 percent of New Brunswick large salmon and 32-68 percent of Nova Scotia large salmon. Of even more concern is that spawning stocks were reduced to hazardously low levels by the combined distant and residual home fisheries (Paloheimo and Elson, 1974; Elson, 1974).

Even though the catch by the Greenland fishery has dropped to about half its peak period, the Newfoundland fishery has continued to take almost as many mainland salmon as in the late '60's and early '70's. This continues in the face of still demonstrably deficient mainland spawning stocks. The Newfoundland catch of northwest Miramichi large salmon, tagged as smolts in 1973, was 37 percent of all such returns, nearly three times the average for the preceding 11 years, while the Greenland fishery took 53 percent of the same group (Elson and Williamson, 1975). With the post-1976 reduced Greenland fishery, there is every reason to believe that the Newfoundland catch is now proportionately higher and contributes to delaying the recovery of mainland stocks. This situation seems even more absurdly chauvinistic because the Newfoundland fishery and mainland stocks are both under charge of the federal government. Recently a senior fisheries officer of the federal government, stationed in Newfoundland, said in an open meeting that there was no reason to reduce the Newfoundland fishery, 'it was purely a matter of allocation rather than conservation'. No plans to reduce Newfoundland seasons so as to permit more mainland spawning to escape homeward are envisioned for the foreseeable future (Chadwick et al 1978). The Newfoundland salmon fishery is, for many outport fishermen living at subsistence levels, a type of welfare programme. Such programmes are seldom managed in the best interests of the resource. (Sinclair, 1978). Federal officials in both Ottawa and Newfoundland would show a much greater degree of responsibility to the resource owners, the nation's taxpayers, by devising plans to better perpetuate and use this common resource.

Greenland and North America are not the only areas where salmon of mixed stocks are fished far distant from their natal rivers. The early '60's saw the burgeoning development of an offshore drift net fishery on the west coast of Eire. Results of earlier tagging studies showed that some of the fish in this area, even some taken near shore, were subsequently caught far to the north and east. Many appear to have originated in the extremely productive River Foyle, others were apparently bound towards more distant rivers in Northern Ireland, England, Wales and Scotland. The pattern of expansion in this fishery and concomitant decrease in the distant homewater fisheries somewhat resembles the comparison between the Greenland and the Canadian mainland fishery. Inter-relations are examined in some detail by Elson and Tuomi, 1975. As far as I have learned, the attitude of Eire authorities to possible damage of distant resources is quite as chauvinistic as that of Canadian authorities regarding interaction between Newfoundland and mainland fisheries. An unhappy facet of these heavy, distant mixed-stock fisheries is that by reducing recruitment distantly they may well be doing long-term damage to a more reasonable home fishery of their own. Much valuable research is essentially buried because of these parochial attitudes.

Biology and environmental change

There is a mass of scientific literature on many aspects of salmon biology. The two reviews mentioned earlier (Pyefinch, 1955; Dymond, 1963) are still very useful. Much useful information and comprehensive lists of references are to be found in Banks' review of literature on upstream movement (1969) and Gardner's review of literature on sea-age and maturation (1976). Many publications, particularly those that tend to cover broader aspects and hence be somewhat long, contain much more information than their titles imply and fail to get sufficient attention. Jones' excellent, if somewhat dated, book 'The Salmon (1959) may be an example. Several other examples occur in my own writings. Publications on predator-prey relationships and on effects of forest spray on wild populations of young (Elson, 1962 and 1967) contain much basic information on natural salmon production in rivers, required as background for title focuses. Another on salmon of the River Foyle (Elson and Tuomi, 1975) brings together a substantial mass of literature on various aspects of biology and environment pertinent to productivity of salmon rivers. A third, more general paper on smolt production and optimal spawning (Elson, 1975) summarizes much information on these aspects and suggests a method for transferring some of the recruitment lessons learned from the mostly single year-class life history of Foyle salmon to the more complicated life history of some Canadian salmon. Such papers and many others of like ilk deserve far more study than they appear to get. Moreover, not just the texts, but the substantiating list of references, warrant careful examination by those who must decide in areas of research and those who make administrative decisions about managing fisheries.

In terms of natural production from rivers I wish to emphasize two specific points:

The first is the importance of sufficient spawning. Often managers fail or are unable to assure this essential. Up to the present, the best general guideline is that eggs should be deposited at a general rate of about 140/100 yd of the river bottom. Because all areas of many streams, *eg* deep pools, lakes or long deep still waters, are not good spawning or rearing areas, actual rates of deposition on the latter will be somewhat heavier (Elson and Tuomi, 1975; Elson, 1974 and 1975).

The second is that such spawning must be well spread over all rearing areas of a system. Evidence is now accumulating that this may be best accomplished by assuring that the various genetic strains of a river system's salmon population be encouraged to reach their historic spawning grounds. Introductions of foreign strains may help when original populations are nearly or actually extinct. But such introductions are a second choice to revitalizing the original strain (Elson, 1973; Saunders, 1967).

Man-induced environmental change on a scale large enough to affect the ecology of many animals must now be accepted as a fact of life. Salmon, even in remote rivers, have not escaped the ravages of such environmental degradation. Sometimes these changes can be at least partially remedied, sometimes not. Such changes can be classified in two categories – water borne pollution and physical alteration of rivers. The former includes discharge of harmful chemicals and other industrial, agricultural and urban pollutants, the latter includes drainage operations or channelization, hydro-electric development, siltation from road building and many other abuses of a natural river. Two references (Elson and Tuomi, 1975; Elson, 1974) discuss both types of degradation for an Irish and a Canadian river. Elson *et al* (1973) elaborate on a variety of chemical pollutants in North America and another report discusses both physical and chemical degradation resulting from forest industry practices (Elson, Saunders and Zitko, 1972). Not all harmful pollution is lethal as shown by aberrant behaviour of returning salmon in a polluted estuary (Elson, Lauzier and Zitko, 1970).

Degradation in rivers occurs throughout the range of Atlantic salmon. An interesting case is that of the Richlea River in northern Sweden where heavy metal discharge from industrial operations caused a great decrease in invertebrate fauna. A severe drop in the population of young salmon was attributed largely to a dearth of food for the young (Södergren, 1976). Pollution-induced stress can directly affect the physiology of fish, hence their reaction to succeeding stresses: even short-term stress may produce a long-term response, (Mazeaud, Mazeaud and Donaldson, 1977).

In the last few years, with growing consciousness of man's ability to damage environments, environmental impact statements are sometimes demanded before beginning engineering or other changes to environments. One problem is to assure that input into the impact study covers the required needs. Walters (1975) describes instances where a series of workshops of multi-disciplinary nature, assisted by ready access to computers, greatly enhanced the value of what could have been rather unproductive advance impact statements.

Lists of references at the ends of scientific papers can be very helpful, but each is limited by the author's concept of his subject matter at the time of writing. A Canadian Fisheries Library provides a useful Atlantic salmon bibliography (Anon, 1974), updating it from time to time. It should not, of course, be expected to contain references not directly mentioning Atlantic salmon.

New fishing strategy essential

There are many areas where new salmon research is needed. A better understanding of the productivity levels of specific rivers is desirable. Responses to and long-term effects of many sub-lethal pollutants, *eg* chlorinated hydro-carbons, need attention. Development of aquaculture for salmon, with associated studies in physiology, pathology and genetics, can help to fill the void that will inevitably be left by decreasing natural production.

But the one essential need is for a change to a more realistic philosophy for salmon fisheries and development of new fishing strategies for individual systems. Many of the needed tools are available. But the current state of most fisheries indicates that the necessary political and administrative will and courage are lacking.

To begin, there needs to be a re-alignment of focus. Making a good catch next year, or even five years from now will no longer assure a continuing renewable resource. The concept of optimum sustainable yield has gained increasing support from enlightened fisheries scientists and economists (Roedel, 1975). The older concept of maximum sustainable yield served a useful purpose in preserving many fisheries, though I am not aware that it was ever applied to salmon. But its deficiencies begin to emerge as socio-economic problems take on more importance (Larkin, 1977). It is these social and economic problems, especially, that frustrate the biologist in his attempt to provide bases for conservation of the salmon resource. No matter what information he reveals, environmental degradation becomes worse and commercial fisheries take more and more of the stocks. New fishing strategies *must be* developed.

My list of references includes five specific to the development of new and better fishing strategies (Silvert, 1977 and 1978; Walters and Hilborn, 1976; Sinclair, 1978; Gulland, 1978). Space prevents summarizing them here and in any case they should all be thoroughly read and digested by those making new decisions on fishing strategy. A paper on the economics of overfishing points out the danger of extinction if present values are maximized (Silvert, 1977). This sounds perilously close to what happened in New Brunswick and seems to be happening in some Irish fisheries. Suggestions for avoiding disaster are put forward. Gulland (1978) emphasizes that the age of simplicity is over and that scientists and managers will have to co-operate more closely. Salmon fisheries, where the scientist can have his finger on the pulse of the resource, especially in rivers, probably offer more opportunity in this regard than most marine fisheries. Even useful midseason changes in strategy can be developed (Elson and Tuomi, 1975, section 1). Silvert (1978) offers a stimulating discussion on fisheries management as a research tool. He discusses the value of harvesting at different levels in order to develop improved knowledge about recruitment needs and better long-term management. His mathematical diversions need not deter the reader from grasping the pith. The paper by Walters and Hilborn (1976) on adaptive control of fishing systems involves some complex mathematical treatment. But most managers doubtless have access to professional interpreters to assist them to grasp the essential guidelines for periodic manipulation of fishery effort to gain long-term advantage. The paper by Sinclair (1978) is straightforward reading. It too emphasizes the need for change in current fishing practice.

I hope this paper will bring some readers to the realization that there is a vast hoard of useful but *unused* research. I have not tried to provide a bin full of facts, but merely to indicate something of what is available, how to uncover it, and a few reasons why much has been ignored. If I were to suggest three reasons why so much of value lies buried, they would have to be mental laziness of readers, parochial, even chauvinistic attitudes and lack of administrative and political courage, perhaps in that order.

References

ANONYMOUS. *Atlantic salmon references, Vol 2, 1974.* (Supplants Vol 1.)
1974 Environment Canada – Fisheries, Maritimes Regional Library, P O Box 550, Halifax, Nova Scotia.

BANKS, J W. A review of the literature of the upstream migration of adult
1969   salmonids. *J Fish Biol* 1: 85–136.
CHADWICK, M, PORTER, R & REDDIN, D. Newfoundland and Labrador
1978   Atlantic salmon management programme, 1978. *Atl Salmon J*
        1978 No 1: 9–15.
DYMOND, J R. *Family Salmonidae.* Memoir Sears Fund For Marine
1963   Research, New Haven. No 1 Part 3: 457–502.
ELSON, P F. Predator-prey relationships between fish-eating birds and
1962   Atlantic salmon. *Bull Fish Res Board Can.* 133: 87 p.
ELSON, P F. Effects on wild young salmon of spraying DDT over New
1967   Brunswick forests. *J Fish Board Can.* 24: 731–67.
ELSON, P F. Genetic polymorphism in northwest Miramichi Atlantic
1973   salmon, in relation to season of river ascent and age at maturation
        and its implication for management of stocks. *ICNAF Res Doc*
        73-76: 6 p.
ELSON, P F. Impact of recent economic growth and industrial develop-
1974   ment of the ecology of northwest Miramichi Atlantic salmon
        (Salmo salar). J Fish Res Board Can. 31: 521–44.
ELSON, P F. Atlantic salmon rivers, smolt production and optimal spawn-
1975   ing: an overview of natural production. *IASF Spec Pub* No 6:
        96–119.
ELSON, P F, LAUZIER, L M & ZITKO, V. A preliminary study of salmon
1970   movements in a polluted estuary. FAO Technical Conference on
        marine pollution and its effects on living resources and fishing,
        Rome, Italy. Fishing News (Books) Limited, London. p. 325–30.
ELSON, P F, MEISTER, A L, SAUNDERS, J W, SAUNDERS, R L, SPRAGUE, J B
1973   & ZITKO, V. Impact of chemical pollution on Atlantic salmon in
        North America. Int At Salmon Symp 1972. *IASF Spec Pub* No 4:
        83–110.
ELSON, P F, SAUNDERS, J W & ZITKO, V. Impact of forest-based indus-
1972   tries on freshwater-dependent fish resources in New Brunswick.
        Fish Res Board Can Tech Rept. 325: 26 p.
ELSON, P F & TUOMI, A L W. The Foyle Fisheries: new bases for rational
1975   management. Section 1 – The impact of fisheries and environ-
        mental changes on the management of Atlantic salmon of the
        Foyle River system, Ireland by Paul F Elson: 1–194. Section 2 –
        Institutional and economic aspects of Foyle fisheries manage-
        ment by A W L Tuomi: 195–210. *Special Report to the Foyle Fisheries
        Commission,* Londonderry, Northern Ireland. 224 p.
ELSON, P F & WILLIAMSON, A (unpub). Exploitation of northwest
1975   Miramichi salmon by Newfoundland commercial fisheries. 19 p
        plus tables.
GARDNER, L G. A review of factors which may influence the sea-age and
1976   maturation of Atlantic salmon *(Salmo salar L). J Fish Biol.* 9:
        289–327.
GULLAND, A. Fishery management: new strategies for new conditions.
1978   *Trans Am Fish Soc* 107 (1): 1–11.
JONES, J W. *The salmon.* Collins, St James Place, London. 191 p.
1959

LARKIN, P A. An epitaph for the concept of maximum sustainable yield.
1977 *Trans Am Fish Soc.* 106 (1): 1–11.

MAZEAUD, M, MAZEAUD, F & DONALDSON, E. Primary and secondary
1977 effect of stress in fish: some new data with a general review. *Trans
Am Fish Soc.* 106 (3) 201–11.

PALOHEIMO, J E & ELSON, P F. Effects of the Greenland fishery for
1974 Atlantic salmon on Canadian stocks. *IASF Spec Pub Ser.* 5(1): 34 p

PYEFINCH, K A. A review of the literature on the biology of Atlantic
1955 salmon *(Salmo salar* L) *Sci Invest Freshwater Fish Scotland.* 9: 24 p.

RICKER, W E. Handbook of computations for biological statistics of fish
1958 populations. *Bull Fish Res Board Can.* 119: 300 p.

ROEDEL, P M (Ed). The optimum sustainable yield as a concept in
1975 fisheries management. Proceedings of a Symposium of Am Fish
Soc, Honolulu, Hawaii, 9 September 1974. *Am Fish Soc Spec Pub
No 9:* 89 p.

RUGGLES, C P. Foyle Fisheries: new basis for national management,
1977 reviewed in *Trans Am Fish Soc* 106 (5): 502–3.

SAUNDERS, R L. Seasonal pattern of return of Atlantic salmon in the
1967 northwest Miramichi River, New Brunswick. *J Fish Res Board Can.*
24: 21–32;

SILVERT, W. The economics of overfishing. *Trans Am Fish Soc.* 106 (2)
1978 121–30.

SILVERT, W. The price of knowledge: fisheries management as a
1978 research tool. *J Fish Res. Board Can.* 35: 208–12.

SINCLAIR, W F. Management alternatives and strategic planning for
1978 Canada's fisheries. *J Fish Res Board Can.* 35: 1017–30.

SODERGREN, S. *Ecological effects of heavy metal discharge in a salmon river.*
1976 Inst Freshwater Res, Drottningholm. 55: 91–131.

TETREAULT, B & CARTER, W M. Adult salmon recaptures from a 1968
1972 smolt stocking programme. *ICNAF Res Doc.* 72/49, *Ser No* 2786,
Ann Meet 1972.

UNDERWOOD McLELLAN (1977) Ltd. *An economic evaluation of the Saint John
1978 River fisheries.* 279 p.

WALTERS, C. An interdisciplinary approach to development of
1975 watershed simulation models. *J Fish Res Board Can.* 32: 177–95.

WALTERS, C J & HILBORN, R. Adaptive control of fishing systems. *J. Fish
1976 Res Board Can.* 33: 145–59.

2 Ensuring the Atlantic salmon's future

W M Carter, The International Atlantic Salmon Foundation (IASF), Canada

Misconceptions about salmon
There are misconceptions about salmon and salmon fishermen. I am going to try and strip some of these away to see if I can state, in simple terms, some of the obvious problems and their apparent solutions.

One of the common misconceptions about Atlantic salmon is that the fish is a snob and that one needs to be wealthy and priviliged to fish for it. Monty Montgomery dispelled this fallacy in these simple, eloquent words, published in the Boston Globe on June 9, 1978:

'If the Atlantic salmon wore hats they would be tweed hats . . . If they wore shoes they'd wear cordovan loafers . . . The Atlantic salmon isn't a snob fish; it's just a perfectly secure fish with no need to be trendy . . . The Atlantic salmon is simply the greatest game fish in the world. Surely God could have made a better fish, and surely he chose not to. The Atlantic salmon is what a trout meant to be but failed to be.'

Value of the recreational fishery
If fishing for recreation and pleasure labels the participants 'elitists' then the world must be filled with them. No doubt it's good that anglers are so abundant, because collectively they create a huge and lucrative industry that helps put bread and butter on the table for thousands.

Angling is big business in many countries. In a recent address to the Canadian Wildlife Federation, Fisheries Minister LeBlanc left no doubt that sport fishing is a big industry in Canada. He revealed that 25 percent of all Canadians went sport fishing during 1975, fished 75 million days and caught 250 million fish (including 82,585 Atlantic salmon). In the process they spent an estimated $1 billion in pursuit of their quarry, $150 million of it in the Province of Quebec where some of Canada's finest Atlantic salmon rivers are located. Anglers invested another $1 billion that year alone in major durable items, such as boats, motors, camping gear, land, buildings, vehicles, *etc.* (LeBlanc, 1978.)

The approximate annual world catch of Atlantic salmon is 25 million pounds. Anglers take less than 10 percent of this total. They contribute, in the process, as much as 90 percent of the total value of the entire Atlantic salmon fishery in some countries including both Canada and the United Kingdom. Anglers often work like beavers perfecting their skills. They view fishing as a challenge, not a meat market. All over the world anglers lend leadership to conservation. In their tireless pursuit of an often elusive, sometimes illusionary, quarry they create untold man-years of employment for others, many of whom don't care if their only real contact with fish is in a can.

I have respect for the professional commercial fisherman. My boyhood summers were spent apprenticing the trade. But it is high time we put an end to the invidious comparison between the motives and relative needs of the commercial fisherman and the angler. They can share salmon. Fisheries managers have a responsibility to ensure, by good management policies, that they do.

The many thousands of people who have jobs today because there are so many die-hard anglers around don't appreciate attempts, by government or anyone else, to remove their principal means of putting bread and butter on the table.

The myth that anglers are snobs and their sport a frivolous luxury is exactly that – a myth, and it discredits those who continue to exploit the fallacy.

The commercial fishery

Another common misconception is that the Atlantic salmon

is so valuable to the angler that it should be declared a game fish, and all commercial fishing prohibited, permanently.

Nothing could be more wasteful, or more irresponsible. Where salmon fisheries are properly managed and the breeding stock protected, a healthy salmon river can produce sufficient numbers of fish to supply both the commercial and angler demand. Indeed, there are some areas, both here and in Canada, where anglers could not crop 20 percent of the annual run if they were allowed to fish without restriction. And there are fishermen in remote areas of Canada who, if deprived of the opportunity to fish for salmon commercially, would literally go hungry.

It would be absolutely unacceptable, politically, to advance such a proposal anywhere today, except perhaps in the New England States. There, slow but encouraging progress to restore destroyed runs precludes any commercial fishing pressure. But the salmon was extinguished before any real effort to restore it was undertaken.

Iceland, where commercial salmon fishing has been banned since 1922, is a special situation. All the rivers are owned by farmers and they, supported by their government, have decided that angling is their most profitable method of harvesting.

Native peoples' food fishery
There is a misconception in Canada that all native people are conservationists and are entitled, by treaty, to an unlimited harvest of fish and wildlife.

Native people still living off the land in their traditional manner may indeed have a legitimate claim. It is questionable if the rest, supported on reservations by a generous welfare state, can in fact claim any special preference whatsoever to a salmon food fishery.

What is now being perpetuated in some areas of Canada, under the guise of historic native people's rights, is instead an illegal and uncontrolled commercial salmon fishery and a black market, supported by every person who purchases from this illicit trade.

If, in its generosity toward the original peoples of Canada, the government wants to provide a *per capita* allotment of salmon for food, it could do so by purchasing the required quantity from the licensed commercial fishery and distributing it among the tribes. This method would quickly resolve the acrimonious debate and end the wholesale slaughter now being carried on under the cloak of a food fishery, as well as provide an additional outlet for salmon caught by legitimate commercial fishermen.

Observe what animals do
Some of the best advice I ever received came from the late A G Huntsman in a letter he wrote to me soon after I had graduated as a young biologist, laden with more hope and textbook theory than common sense or experience. 'Observe what animals do, where and when', wrote A G, 'and you will soon know more about biology than has ever been written yet'.

'Observe what animals do', said A G. But we look and don't see.

Watch a flight of geese and see a study in aerodynamics. Watch all animals in the forest flee at the sight of a porcupine – but one, the fisher, and ponder why one animal alone has developed the fearless knack of flipping the walking pin cushion over on its back to reach its vulnerable, unprotected belly. Observe the beautiful Monarch butterfly with its potent poison which can paralyze birds, frogs and bats. If you look again you may find that it is not a Monarch at all, but another harmless species which has adapted the Monarch's copper-coloured appearance to deceive its predators.

Sit and watch salmon attempting to leap a waterfall, and note carefully their route as they jump. Then you can prevent an engineer, who may think he knows more than a fish, from building a costly fishladder at the wrong location.

Watch salmon abandon a long-travelled channel to continue their upstream migration against the opposite bank. They may be telling you that their sensitive noses have detected a pollution source, one that you know exists, but haven't seen.

My grandfather, who knew nothing about biology, but who was a fine sailor and very wise in the ways of salmon, told me, long before we suspected how salmon navigated, that they were guided by the stars. 'Each year that the ice cover off Newfoundland is late breaking up', he said, 'I have noted that the salmon coming to my nets are delayed. It can only be that they could not observe the stars'.

Genetic and environmental influences

Some Atlantic salmon look different. Some are short and squat, others long and streamlined. Some run early, others late. Some stay at sea one year to return as grilse, others two, three or even four years before returning. In some rivers almost all Atlantic salmon spawn once and never return. Yet some will successfully return two, three, four, five – even six or more times.

In some rivers all grilse are male. Others will produce as many females as male. Some produce no grilse at all. What does it all mean?

Essentially it means that salmon stocks are not homogeneous, as we once thought them to be. No, a salmon is not a salmon is not a salmon. This may be the single most important thing we have learned about the salmon.

North American Salmon Research Center

With very generous support from the Canadian Government and some farsighted citizens in Canada and the United States, we now have, at St Andrews, a co-operative programme between The International Atlantic Salmon Foundation and the Department of Fisheries which seeks to answer those questions and tell us if the special characteristics we want in future salmon stocks are inherited, and can be transmitted from one generation to the next by selective breeding, or if those qualities are environmentally controlled.

Can growth rate, migratory routes, time at sea, disease resistance, spawning frequency and other attributes be transmitted from one generation of salmon to the next, or to hybrid races, by controlled selective breeding? If we can do this, think of the immense importance it would have for commercial fishing, angling, sea ranching and salmon farming. Think of the benefit to our hatcheries if we knew the heritable characteristics of stocks, so we could choose to raise only those with known traits instead of continuing into another 100 years of a hit and miss rearing programme.

If we are successful we believe we can substantially influence future salmon management but we need to know the answers to these questions. Then we can use that knowledge to increase and enhance salmon stocks, knowing, instead of guessing, at what we are doing.

A changed harvesting policy

Knowing now that salmon stocks are discrete groupings of identical individuals (there may be a dozen or more different gene groups in a single river system), why haven't we made a fundamental change in management to recognize this? Lord Hunter, in his report on the Scottish Salmon and Trout Fisheries in 1965, first suggested the importance of harvesting salmon stocks of known origin. There is only one way to do this, but we have made no real attempt to do so, even as an experiment in management.

Agriculture, instead of the imaginative success it has become, would be a bankrupt science now if land resources were managed with the same blindness.

Use, as an analogy, two farmers who sow identical crops in adjacent fields. One prepares the soil carefully, plants selected seed and nurtures the young growing stock with knowledgeable attention. The other, indifferent and perhaps lazy, plants his barren soil too early (or too late) and then abandons it to nature's care.

In the agricultural world, the prudent farmer will usually harvest a bumper crop, market a surplus, store away sufficient for his own use and set aside seed for next year's planting.

The other, if he has any harvest at all, will produce a small crop of low quality. There will be no surplus. If there is any left for seed it will be small, stunted and probably diseased.

If we apply our present salmon management practices to the harvesting of those adjacent fields, the fences would be taken down, both would be harvested together, the crop would be mixed and each farmer would share equally. The seed reserved for next year would be a mixture of good and

bad, diseased and healthy, big and small. After several years
of this management approach both fields would be producing a stunted and diseased crop. Eventually there would be
no crop at all.

Political and economic reality
There is a political and an economic reality to be faced if we
want to change our approach to salmon harvesting. We
cannot do it overnight. Between agreement in principle
and implementation in practice there can be hesitation and
even procrastination. There will be regions where one
method will work well while another will not succeed at all.
But our present course does not do justice to our knowledge of salmon. Until we begin to make fundamental
changes in harvesting policy we will, without doubt, see
salmon stocks continue to decline and then disappear.

What then are these change?

New management policies
(a) Governments of salmon producing countries must
use their united bargaining power to entrench the prohibition of Atlantic salmon fishing in the sea in international
waters.

(b) Individual salmon producing countries should
gradually withdraw their own Atlantic salmon fisheries to
coastal regions near, or preferably to areas within, river
estuaries.

(c) Wherever practicable, national salmon policies
should incorporate flexibility to manage stocks on a watershed basis. In this way abundant runs can be cropped more
generously and those in jeopardy can be protected and
restored.

Sea ranching
There is a simple technique to increase Atlantic salmon
stocks that should now be used more widely.

We have known for a long time that the salmon has a
superbly well developed navigational system, though all of
the components are still not well understood. But the salmon does return home from the sea to the last freshwater

river it left as a smolt, and there is the trump card we have not yet played. When we do, we can increase salmon stocks in the sea, at moderate cost.

Research conducted in Iceland, supported by grants from IASF, first demonstrated that the technique of sea ranching could be economically attractive and at the same time increase salmon stocks for other fisheries.

Adult salmon returns as high as 10.5 percent from some groups of planted smolts, were reported by Gudjonsson at the First International Atlantic Salmon Symposium in 1972. In Ireland, Piggins has reported that the best achieved rate was 4.2 percent. It is believed that sea ranching survival rates can be substantially improved by applying new genetic knowledge in stock selection.

The same technique, with Pacific salmon, is widely used in Japan. Major new sea ranching programmes are planned on the west coast of North America.

It has been demonstrated at the North American Salmon Research Center in St Andrews that sea ranching will work on the east coast of Canada as well. Close to three hundred salmon and grilse have returned to the Research Center this year. Products of the genetics crossing programme there, some of the returning fish exhibit exceptional growth. One grilse measured 69 cm. When weighed it would be close to 10 lbs.

Using selected salmon of known genetic traits, a number of small rearing stations could produce large numbers of smolts for planting in the numerous tiny barren rivers emptying into the sea. After growing to maturity on free energy gathered in the ocean, the returning adults could be harvested in commercial traps as they seek to re-enter the small rivers that had sent them on their way to sea as smolts.

The attraction outflow does not need to be high – at St Andrews it falls as low as 1,500 IGM.

Supplementing natural river production with sea ranched salmon now appears to be one of the most promising methods of increasing salmon stocks for the commercial and the recreational fisheries.

226 THE FUTURE

Regulation
There are too many people chasing too few fish. Both commercial fishermen and anglers must accept the necessity of even stricter regulation. People simply will not police themselves.

One area of increased regulation we want is some functional control on the purchase and sale of salmon. It is an urgent need.

Poaching, which has now become a very real threat to Atlantic salmon, must be contained, and quickly. We don't need new laws to do that, the ones we now have are adequate when they are applied.

Break the market for illicit salmon by vigorously prosecuting *both* the seller and the purchaser, and this will be far more effective than an army of new wardens.

Convince the prosecutors and the judiciary that the future of this valuable resource rests with them more than any other sector of society, and we will achieve a major breakthrough.

That is the challenge for conservation organizations and for anglers and commercial fishermen alike.

Organize and pressure
I have followed Dr Huntsman's dictum during my professional career as a salmon biologist. I have observed what salmon do, where and when, and I believe I understand the messages that the salmon have been sending.

But it is not the biologist or the fishery manager who has the last word. It is the administrator and our elected representatives. We must convince them to do what should be done. If we cannot first do that, then there is not much hope of preserving or increasing salmon stocks.

How can we do this? Let me quote from a speech given by Canada's Minister of Fisheries on 2 March, 1978, to a herring fisherman's co-operative (LeBlanc, 1978).

'Your main power lies in one simple, overriding fact: you have organized, you can regulate yourselves, and you can pressure others. You can bargain and you can influence . . . government.

'Being organized is no guarantee that you will get

everything. But being unorganized is almost a guarantee you will get next to nothing . . .

At the signing of the American Declaration of Independence, Benjamin Franklin said, ". . .we must indeed all hang together or most assuredly we shall all hang separately".'

And finally, M LeBlanc said,

'If I had to write the manual for dealing with Government, I would put two main rules of the road: carry a big flag – that is, have an organization – and sound your horn. Let people know you are there. Push the officials; I will tell you a secret: they like it. Anyone in an office all day long needs action. The more you make known your views the less likely will an official make some horrible mistake out of ignorance and end up transferred to a broom closet.'

Amen. The message could not be clearer.

Earlier this year when IASF decided to sponsor an information workshop involving voluntary salmon organizations in New Brunswick, we discovered, to our amazement, that there were 17 different groups in that tiny Canadian Province, claiming the Atlantic salmon as their 'raison d'être', and some had never heard of any of the others!

Conclusion

Find a basis of common ground and agreement among all the legitimate users of the Atlantic salmon resource. Then find a bridge to connect those many small, independent voices in each salmon producing country into one loud, united voice and you will be much more successful in convincing government to do what you know needs to be done.

First organize to become one effective voice. Then the other salmon management needs I have suggested will come more easily. A conservation miracle is within reach, but it must be grasped. Governments can be made to do many of the things you want. M LeBlanc has told you how.

Long ago, when there were far fewer people, and man had not yet begun his greedy thrust, possessed with his own perceived welfare, salmon swam freely in the Seine, the

Rhine, the Thames and the Hudson. And all creatures did a pretty good job of living together and sharing – a word we don't understand. Now having messed it all up it's ironic that man, the perpetrator, is the salmon's only hope.

References

GUDJONSSON, T. Smolt Rearing Techniques, Stocking and Tagged Adult
1972   Salmon Recaptures in Iceland. *Proceedings of International Atlantic Salmon Symposium, 1972.*

HUNTER. *Hunter Committee Report on Scottish Salmon and Trout*
1965   *Fisheries.*

HUNTSMAN, A G. Personal Communication.

LEBLANC, R. *Address to Canadian Wildlife Federation, 20 May, 1978.*
1978

LEBLANC, R. *Address to the Atlantic Herring Fisherman's Marketing*
1978   *Co-operative, March 1978.*

MONTGOMERY, M. Boston Globe, 9 June, 1978.
1978

PIGGINS, D J. Atlantic Salmon Aquaculture: Costs, Comparisons and
1977   Future Trends. *IASF Spec Pub No 7,* Nov 1977.

SCOTT, SIR PETER. Origin and date unknown.

3 The implementation of policy

Sir Hugh Mackenzie, The Atlantic Salmon Research Trust

Introduction

For many weeks I have been looking at these four words *The implementation of policy* and wondering (a) what interpretation you would put on them and (b) what construction I should give them. The Advisory Committee planning the Symposium agreed on such a title, persuading me to give a paper by arguing that its title would give me freedom to say anything I liked! I will stick to the theme of the Symposium and I will give some thoughts, comments and suggestions on the theme and what we should aspire to get out of the wealth of facts, information and opinions which have been presented to us over the last two and a half days.

This tremendous wealth of knowledge made available to us, and which will reach a much wider circle when the Report of the Proceedings is published, cannot fail to benefit salmon and salmon fisheries if given the proper attention by our legislators and administrators. Ultimately governments must be brought in if some of the measures which the Symposium has clearly demonstrated as needed are to be translated into effective action.

But just saying and expressing this is not enough. Of course we have all gained individually from what we have heard and discussed and I venture to think that as a means of exchanging and gaining knowledge the Symposium has been a success. But do not let us all depart in a spirit of euphoria and allow the Symposium to descend to having been just a 'talking shop'. We must do better; we must ensure that it has some lasting benefit for salmon, not just for ourselves.

I confess to some disappointment that all the talent displayed at the First International Symposium in 1972 failed to initiate any positive action. The conclusions seemed very obviously of potential benefit to salmon. It was a pious hope, seemingly, that this might happen through the agencies, bodies and organizations represented there.

What to do now to avoid a lamentable repetition? How do we induce Governments to move, or set other wheels in motion to take advantage of what has come out of the Symposium? I will return to this later.

The first step

Following what I was taught some 40 years ago, we must first *define the aim*. Surely, after these two and a half days, there can be no argument that to satisfy all interests our aim should be: that in the world of tomorrow there are salmon for our children and grandchildren, and their children, to enjoy in all the various ways possible – I should add 'legally' possible – and that salmon will at least be as numerous for them as they are now, and preferably far more numerous. This may be a blinding glimpse of the obvious, but let's not lose sight of it. The way ahead is confused and strewn with obstacles and we must keep it in the forefront of our minds.

Salmon are being heavily exploited – in certain areas more than their present spawning escapement can sustain. If we are to learn from this and prevent disaster from becoming more widespread, then we must not be foolish enough to ignore the clear evidence before our eyes: that positive, remedial action is vital. The case for new measures to control or ban fishing in international waters and to ban all drift netting has been amply substantiated throughout the Symposium.

How best to put policy into practice? Internationally the scene is very diffuse and confused. With the demise of International Commission for the Northwest Atlantic Fisheries (ICNAF) and Northeast Atlantic Fisheries Commission (NEAFC) we have a vacuum, not likely to be filled in the immediate future by the EEC Common Fisheries Policy – which in any event will not apply across the Atlantic – or by the United Nations Law of the Sea Conference. Nationally, and here I can speak only for the United Kingdom, a revision and bringing up to date of salmon legislation, to match the current state of affairs so amply demonstrated during the Symposium, seems very necessary.

Unilateral action in international affairs contributes nothing – it only adds to national rivalries. Fully co-ordinated action from the salmon producing countries is essential, but governments on their own will never start to achieve this. They must be primed by some means. And if the salmon hasn't a vote we must supply it.

There is an urgent role for voluntary bodies such as the Salmon and Trout Association, the Atlantic Salmon Association, and kindred organizations. I suggest they should immediately consult together so as to produce an agreed and fully co-ordinated doctrine for the optimum management of salmon fisheries, following up the proposals made by Dr Carter in his address to the Salmon and Trout Association at their annual conference in November/December 1977. Their arm will be infinitely strengthened if they can evolve such an agreed policy.

Proposal

I suggest the setting up of a North Atlantic Salmon Convention somewhat on the lines of the now virtually defunct ICNAF and NEAFC, but confined to salmon only. I do not know whether it would be practicable to extend membership to include representatives of voluntary bodies in addition to the Government representatives one would expect, but I should like to see it. I believe there is everything to be gained from the Symposium proposing and approving a resolution to set up such a Convention. Should this be done, I undertake – and am authorized to say this – that the resolution would be transmitted in the most resolute terms possible by Atlantic Salmon Research Trust (ASRT) and International Atlantic Salmon Foundation (IASF) to all governments concerned. In this way I believe we might start the ball rolling in the right direction.

To go further, before it can achieve anything useful, such a Convention must be prepared to follow a certain doctrine or set of principles, which, I suggest, should include the following:

   (a) The management of *all* salmon fisheries should be based on the now accepted fact that each and every river has its own particular strain of salmon. This is absolutely fundamental, and although it may have seemed common sense before, scientific proof of it is probably the most important advance in knowledge that there has been in the past 10 years.

   (b) Following on from (a), fishing for salmon at sea should be phased out over a period of years so that in due course each river system has complete control of its own crop of salmon, within its own waters.

Enforcement

There is also a very urgent need to press for greatly improved enforcement of existing national laws for the protection of salmon, and amendment of these laws where necessary. It was tragic that the 'Sale of Salmon' Bill proposed by the Salmon and Trout Association was 'talked out' in Parliament – and by the Minister of all people – when introduced in the early months of 1978. But for this utterly deplorable action, we could now in this country have in full swing an advertising campaign showing the full penalties for the disposal of illegally caught fish, as now obtains in Canada.

Effective enforcement will be costly in money and resources, but the provision of adequate means to enforce legislation, in both the national and international fields, is absolutely essential. Any Convention which may be established must urgently tackle this, and Governments must be hounded relentlessly until they produce what is needed in both fields.

Research

To all this should be added the important point that any such Convention must strongly support in every way open to it all research leading to more knowledge, and give full encouragement to new enterprises and developments such as salmon farming, which itself is of particular importance through its potential for relieving the pressures on 'wild' salmon.

Conclusion

Of course there will be objections and arguments, and there are many details which must be resolved. Time does not permit me to develop the arguments further, but in my view the proposals now put forward are fully in accord with the majority of really significant points raised during the Symposium and represent a consensus of opinion as revealed in the discussions of the past two days.

4 Closing address

Hon Romeo LeBlanc, Minister of Fisheries and Environment, Canada

Early history
This conference on Atlantic salmon maintains a long tradition. Take for example, the subject of fishing bans. In 1030 AD, King Malcolm the Second of Scotland instituted just such a ban. King Malcolm's closure began on the Feast of Assumption and it ran through to Martinmas. History does not record whether or not it was effective.

Later, we find that Richard Coeur de Lion was also concerned with this problem, despite his Crusading concerns. Regulations issued in his time required that midstream channels of streams in which the salmon spawned be kept free of obstruction. And one cannot help envying the clarity of the guidelines: a well-fed three-year-old pig had to be able to stand sideways in the water without touching the sides of the stream.

Another thing we learn from history is the extent of man's fascination with the salmon. People have been aware for a very long time that, in the salmon, they had something quite extraordinary in the way of natural assets. They were prepared to go to great lengths to protect him.

The Atlantic salmon cult
Indeed here today in Edinburgh I have the distinct feeling that I am attending less of a symposium or conference than taking part in some sort of liturgical ceremony. I get the impression that the Atlantic salmon preoccupation has taken on somewhat the form of a cult, with its ordained priests and with its faithful.

I am not an ordained priest myself and in fact I will insist on dragging into this hall of worship many of the great unwashed in the form of commercial fishermen. You must understand this bias in the very beginning. Although I am by nature in favour of religious pluralism I am, by the laws of the country, charged with the responsibility for many rather than just one congregation.

Progress in Canada
In Canada we are at a time of change in fisheries management – not just where salmon is concerned, but across the board. In the case of Atlantic groundfish we are rebuilding stocks behind the wall of our 200-mile zone. Out on our Pacific coast, we are in the first phase of one of the most ambitious fish stock rebuilding programmes in the world – an enhancement programme which we hope will double salmon production from 25 million to 50 million fish in the next 20 years. We are learning much about the effectiveness of various techniques and we are developing some new ones besides. However, I would prefer to spend my time with you discussing our general approaches to salmon management rather than specific techniques.

Our approach to fisheries management is simple: we think about fish first and foremost in terms of what they mean to people. The fact is that our approach is based on a recognition that the fate of people and the fate of natural renewable resources are intertwined. We also base everything we do on the premise that fish are a common property resource – they belong to the people in general. The yardstick we use to measure our success – whether in the setting of catch levels, or in judging how large a fishing fleet we need – is in the contribution made to society in general.

The salmon's indifference to international boundaries pushes us one step further. It forces us to recognize that the species must be managed in co-operation with the people of other nations, some close, some very far away.

In Canada we have learned our lessons painfully and slowly. From 1920 until roughly 1952 the total Canadian catch of Atlantic salmon was over five million pounds per year.

During the 1930's this figure often went up over thirteen million pounds. After this the situation got worse, not better, and there isn't much mystery about why. Two human impacts were responsible. One was environmental abuse – the wrecking of habitats, the damming of rivers, the insidious inroads of silent, undetected chemical pollution over the years. It came in the form of polluted waterways, and in the form of river bottoms cluttered with bark, woodchips and other sedimentation we supplied through our excesses. To some extent, the problem of Atlantic salmon was not so much the rustling of the livestock but the death of the pastures.

The other problem was, of course, over fishing – some of it Canadian, much of it foreign. The same sort of problems were being faced on our Pacific coast as well as across the Atlantic.

We have now begun to turn this general situation around. We are replenishing the species. We are restoring the waterways. On the Pacific, for example, our salmon enhancement programme is off to a good start. We see this, in one sense, as a stepping stone to the Atlantic. We have learned much in the west, not only about multiplying salmon, but about the socio-economic 'spinoffs' and therefore the social justification for programmes of salmon enhancement. And these are all lessons that can be transferred to our eastern shore.

In the first seven years we are committed to spending $150 million for salmonid enhancement on the Pacific coast. In the succeeding years of the second phase we will probably invest up to $60 million each year – assuming of course, that we are getting results.

This is a huge investment. The fact that we are making it – plus an investment of about $17 million on Atlantic salmon during the past two years on research, development and enforcement – says more than mere words can about the importance Canada attaches to salmon.

It also reflects our ability to see, and more than that to sell, the truth that salmon goals and social goals must be in harmony.

At one point in the early planning of the Pacific programme some of our people took an imaginary one million pounds of enhanced salmon and asked themselves, in effect 'What have we got here' – 'What' meaning benefits to society. 'We' meaning Canadians as a people. We discovered some interesting facts. We found, for instance, that a million extra pounds of salmon meant ten weeks of steady work for 100 people. By the year 2007, the salmon enhancement programme could yield four million man days of work for Canadians.

And that was only the economic side of it. We were able to make comparisons of the choice itself, the value of the salmon option. Salmon versus heavy industry, salmon versus factories by the water, salmon versus energy uses. These comparisons were very favourable to salmon.

Obviously this was no either/or proposition. In the real world hard choices must be made. The world still runs on oil and hydro-electric power. An industrialized society needs factories. But we could make a very strong case for the advantages of salmon development. Because we could make this case, we have been better able to avoid excesses and irreversible acts. We could say accurately and simply that by making waters right for salmon, we are making our own life support systems more secure – we're improving the quality of our lives, and we're keeping our options open.

Perhaps our most important success of all has been in getting, and so far keeping, popular support for salmon enhancement. Without this backing, the programme would be another of those fleeting phenomena that dot the history of the species. With popular support, salmon keeps its high priority among public concerns – enhancement and conservation become a way of life. So before we began the programme we went to the people in a series of town-hall type meetings in the heart of the salmon country, which means most of British Columbia.

Since then we have worked to keep the public involved. Individual schools have adopted salmon streams for clearance. Indian bands have worked in concert on stream clearance. We work through the schools and through service groups on public education projects.

But let us not forget this: enthusiasm for salmon

enhancement grows out of a reasonable degree of self-
interest – a conviction on the part of the enthusiast that
there is something in it for him. We cannot expect people to
participate in rebuilding salmon unless they can participate
in the rewards. And this is as true in eastern Canada as in
western Canada.

We are also working to repair those impoverished pastures I mentioned earlier. Industrialization and population
growth have had an impact on the habitats, particularly on
the delicate estuary and foreshore areas. It has been said
that changes in law necessarily lag behind changes in technology. This may be so, but surely the lag need not be as
great as it has been. In any case, Parliament has recently
rewritten the law to match the current realities. The
Fisheries Act of Canada has been amended to build in new
habitat protection. In general what the law now tells
developers is that if they want to build, dredge, pave-over
or otherwise make major changes in these critical zones,
they must first get a green light from fisheries experts. The
penalties are very tough indeed; they include not only fines
for violators but, in some cases prison sentences.

Here in Edinburgh over the past few days you have heard
about concern in many countries over illegal fishing. You
have heard about our own problems in Canada with poaching. We certainly have made it a much more expensive
pastime than it used to be. The law is tougher now. It says
that the convicted poacher will lose not just dollars but all
his poaching equipment including boats and vehicles.
These are measures of unprecedented toughness. They
signal our determination to deal effectively with the problems.

Tough decisions
Now I come to the most serious problem of all, the end
result of all the abuses – the depletion of Atlantic salmon
stocks.

Since 1972 all commercial salmon fishing has been at a
halt in three key areas of our Atlantic coast. Taking this
action was not an easy thing for my predecessor to do. It
involved suspension of commercial fishing in and near the

Restigouche, Miramichi and Saint John Rivers of New Brunswick and the rivers of Quebec. In southwest Newfoundland we had to close down the drift net fishery permanently.

It has been bitter, costly medicine. In the riding which I represent in New Brunswick there are fishermen who have hung up their nets, nets which are rotting from disuse. To them, the ban was and is an interruption of what they consider to be not a privilege but an ancestral right. This is understandable because very early in the 17th century my Acadian ancestors fished salmon with the Micmac Indians at the entrance to Richibucto River in New Brunswick. The ban has been costly for the people of Canada in general who have paid the bill for compensation of some 700 commercial fishermen since 1972. In some cases this compensation has taken the form of regular cheques to reimburse fishermen for the temporary loss of their right to fish. In other cases, money has gone to purchase the gear of some fishermen, – to buy them out of their calling permanently. The total bill for all these measures in the seven years of the ban has been $12 million. And of course that total does not count lost fishing earnings – seven years of revenues lost.

These are Draconian measures. Canadian fishermen accept them as a need of the hour. But no fisherman, no official, no Minister of the Government of Canada, is disposed to making them a permanent insitution. As fast as possible we want to return to normalcy.

International agreement
We know however that it isn't all up to us. Some of these problems cannot be solved within Canada or even within the 200-mile zone.

For instance we could not, by ourselves, solve the problem of Canadian salmon taken off west Greenland. Here what successes we have achieved have been successes of accommodation and understanding. I am talking of course about the agreement reached by the International Commission for the Northwest Atlantic Fisheries (ICNAF) in 1971 to phase out non-Greenlandic fishing for salmon. The current catch restriction at west Greenland of 1,190 tons represents progress. But it is still a heavy burden on Canadian stocks and on Canadian fishermen. Our experts estimate that at least 40 out of every 100 tons of salmon caught off west Greenland are North American in origin. Virtually all of these fish are Canadian – most of them are fish spawned in rivers that flow into the Gulf of St Lawrence. We contribute, in fact, about 500 tons of salmon to the Greenland fishery each year. To understand what this means to us, you need to remember that, before the ban, the annual commercial catch for the Maritime provinces and Quebec was around 150 to 200 tons.

For some time we have been negotiating a bilateral fisheries agreement with the European Economic Community. In the texts we have worked out, we have reached an accord on principles regarding salmon. The Community and Canada agree that salmon producing nations have the first interest, and the prime responsibility, for the resource. We agree that salmon should not be pursued on the high seas. In the negotiations, we have focused particularly on the salmon fishery off west Greenland, with a view to establishing controls which will protect the interests of all states, including EEC member states.

And these principles are clearly visible in the new international regime that is taking shape with agonizing slowness at the Law of the Sea Conference. From the start of this historic meeting, I think it is accurate to say that Canada has been perhaps the most activist salmon nation. The Salmon Article which has now been worked out at the Conference comes very close to matching what we see as the ideal solution. It provides a virtual ban on fishing for salmon on the high seas beyond 200 mile fishing limits. And the primary interest and responsibility of the state of origin is recognized in cases where these species are fished by other countries, and in the economic zones of other countries.

I want to make it clear that we do not see this promising trend as a victory for Canada, or even as a victory for salmon producing nations. It's a victory for common sense. It is obvious that, unless salmon producing nations make the commitment to keep the stocks alive, salmon will continue to slide into decline. The decision to invest in keeping

salmon alive is a matter of national priorities – a matter,
bluntly, of what's in it for us. The cost of an enhancement
programme cannot be justified without a strong assurance
that the fish we produce and fatten will not wind up in
someone else's nets.

It looks as if these facts of life have finally been accepted.
If this is so, if our own salmon fishing ban continues to pay
dividends in restoring the stocks, we are ready to consider a
more complete rebuilding job.

The future
Late last year I set in motion a process which could lead to a
salmon enhancement programme on the Atlantic coast.
Our first step has been to make a systematic review of the
Atlantic salmon situation – the biology; the sociology; the
economics; that is the whole picture. The task force
assembling this data is working in close co-operation with
the governments of the provinces concerned, and with the
users of the resource. Fishermen, commercial and recreational, are involved in this study, as are citizens at large in
communities most concerned with salmon. I should point
out that in Canada this kind of consultation isn't a matter of
good manners – it is simply what is needed in order to get
things done.

This task force is looking at the present state of the stocks.
They will make forecasts for the future. We are examining
questions of how the fish should be shared – who gets what,
and how much. We are including in these calculations the
additional fish that could be produced in a successful
enhancement programme. We are also examining harvesting – how to get, area by area, the best possible mix of
catches.

That is the first step, and two months from now we move
to the second. I am convening an Atlantic salmon seminar.
This national salmon forum will bring together both government and private citizens to examine the insights and
data developed in our review. We will relate all this to the
logistics of a long-range enhancement programme for the
Atlantic salmon.

Out of this may come a programme shaped by hard facts

and data, and shaped also by the principle I mentioned earlier – of managing the fisheries for the greatest public good.

It goes without saying that in such a programme, the public has a right to expect not only to participate in the cost of enhancement but in the subsequent rewards.

This seems to be an appropriate point at which to comment on the interesting and imaginative concept of confining salmon fishing to the waters off the mouths of rivers.

To the extent that we could adjust our fishing effort in this way without making life harder for our already heavily-laden Atlantic fishermen, we're in favour. There is no question about the immediate operational logic of the concept. I have not forgotten that this was the way the original North American Indians fished – the resource lasted and it certainly sustained their way of life.

But we have a way of life to sustain too. What about those fishermen, thousands of Newfoundland and Labrador alone, who do not live near salmon rivers. Fishermen who toil to bring back a mixed catch, adequate but not much more than adequate. Tell these people they have to stop catching salmon and their catch isn't adequate any more – their margin is wiped out. The headland idea would be for these people a salmon prohibition, but an unacceptable prohibition at this point. They pay taxes too!

There are biological questions about the headland concept that also need to be answered. Mistakes made at the mouths of rivers could be even more disastrous than those committed further out. Let us not close our minds to any idea at this point, but let us remember that there is more to this problem than fish and let us look at all angles. We have to look at this idea more closely before we can make decisions about whether, when and how we can implement it. I am certainly not ready now to demand any more sacrifice of our fishermen in the name of a quick solution to one aspect of a complex problem.

I made it clear at the beginning of this talk that Parliament charges me with the responsibility for the commercial fisheries. As Minister of Fisheries, the interests of those who depend on fish for their livelihood must receive a major share of my attention. But I am also very much aware that we have in the salmon one of the most sought after sport fish in the world. We have many examples in Canada to show that, with careful management, sport fishing and commercial fishing can not only co-exist, they can thrive on each other's success. And from what I've been told, Scotland's District Salmon Fishery Boards support such a premise. In British Columbia, the vast support that I have received for salmon enhancement comes from the fact that all users, present and potential, recognize that if they join together to get more fish, they all benefit. It will be easier to share more fish than to fight over less. With this in mind, whenever I meet with fisheries groups of conflicting interests I refuse to choose between them. What I say is 'let's get together and produce more fish.'

In short, the case of the salmon is one of those situations where the principles of fair play and great reward coincide happily.

The basic philosophy of any minister of the crown is that he or she cannot give in to any one pressure group. A fisheries minister cannot favour angler over fisherman, or inshore fisherman versus offshore. The message to all contenders must be clear: There can be no winners in a game of power plays.

Likewise, all the ills of the species cannot be blamed on one group or one cause. To those who like to assign all blame to the Indian food fishery I must say that I am left without an answer when Indians remind me that before we came on the scene, the salmon was plentiful. Yet while I recognize the need of native people to participate in the fisheries, this does not mean that we can accept the misuse of the special fishing privilege or the operation of disguised commercial fishery, nor can we accept the actions of those who trade in illicit fish.

As I have said earlier, Parliament has shown its readiness to legislate by giving the Minister of Fisheries extraordinary powers to protect the resource. But a policy based simply on response to acts of wrong-doing is negative at its core, and ruinously inefficient. Short of military personnel standing shoulder-to-shoulder along our rivers and streams there is no way that the state can police this problem out of existence. We do not want to get into the situation of a community which has spent so much on its police force that it cannot afford any of the other amenities. We must search instead for a co-operative way.

If we begin by building, within Canada, and in a transatlantic context, an alliance rather than a tug-of-war between salmon users, we can start thinking in terms of benefits more than of costs. And I am profoundly convinced that the cement for such an alliance is public participation – public discovery of the public interest in salmon. And this means, among other things, giving as many people as possible the chance to experience the thrill of catching a salmon. If we expect collective attitudes to change without this sharing of the wealth and the joy, we are spitting against the wind.

I know there are those who believe sincerely that privately held salmon pools are a positive force for conservation. This may be so, but it is not universally accepted. Although most streams in Canada are available to the general public, a small number of privately controlled streams do exist. I know from personal experience that the most enthusiastic sermon on conservation is stopped short by the kind of question posed to me by a schoolboy in Kedgwick, New Brunswick. He said, 'If the salmon are so beautiful why don't we have a chance to catch one?'. Why indeed, since the river flows right through their village.

Having said all this, let me assure you that we in the Federal Government understand that sports fishing even though it is a pastime, plays an important part in the lives and the earnings of Canadians. Recently we organized a national survey of sport fishing – 50,000 questionnaires were sent to anglers across Canada. We found out how much money these people spent in Canada, where they came from, where they went, and why they came. We counted not only dollars spent on hooks and lines and fishing flies. We looked at money spent indirectly on angling. For instance, the cost of getting to and from the fishing grounds, motel and hotel accommodation, food bills and other items. The estimate at this point was about $900 million a year. We found out too from one end of Canada to the other that over six million people indulged in sport fishing in all seasons. Close to one quarter of our total population fished in 1975.

Sport fishing in short is not an industry we take lightly, nor one we can afford to lose. It plays an important part in the fortunes and lifestyle of a large base of the population. And, of course, it is inextricably tied to the availability of the greatest angling prize of them all – the salmon.

Before I close, let me leave this thought with you. Earlier I said that the interests of the salmon were best served when competing interests did not tear the species apart in their own tugs of war. Surely what is valid within national frontiers is valid beyond them.

Salmon problems cannot be solved on one side of the ocean alone. Those who prevent the salmon from returning to spawn exercise a veto on the resource. Those who do not protect the spawning rivers exercise a veto at the other end. We should not be hypnotized by lines on maps – these are concepts understood only by creatures living above the water – they do not influence the fish and they do not by themselves help us to manage them. The ocean offers us no fences.

We have an ICNAF agreement on limiting catches off Greenland that may expire this year. We hope to have an agreement with the European Economic Community that will ensure that adequate control is maintained in 1979. After that, the picture becomes a little foggy.

There has been the suggestion of a multilateral fisheries treaty on Atlantic salmon – an international effort aimed at management, at development, at exchange of technical information. In my view this idea is worth pursuing.

It seems to me that the time may be ripe to pick up the principles emerging from the Law of the Sea Conference and give them effect within the North Atlantic. This wouldn't necessarily mean the creation of another organization to add to the many which are now concerned with salmon, but might at least define the rules by which the international game is played. If the salmon can so easily transcend the fences of jurisdiction we should be able to do as well when it comes to its protection. I have a feeling that nothing less than a transatlantic approach will ever bring effective resolution to these problems. This is the lesson that the long history of salmon management seems to be trying to tell us.

5   Discussion and resolution

Lord Hunter opened the discussions by giving an outline of the report of the Departmental Committee over which he presided.

D Lank (Atlantic Salmon Association) said that we must be practical in our outlook to persuade people who have responsibility for salmon affairs to take an enlightened view of the problems. Some people in Canada wanted to use sanctions against those countries which offended against the best interests of the Atlantic salmon. The USA did actually exert pressure on Denmark. Canada has been prepared to make sacrifices. All of us must be realistic and we must break the myth that salmon fishing is a wealthy man's sport. He expressed the hope that the Greenland catch could be determined for more than one year.

Sir Richard Levinge (Salmon and Trout Association) said that Canada has unique advantages as regards the salmon because it has shown interest in the species. An international salmon convention must have a depository government and Canada seems to be eminently suited as such.

D L McKernan (Institute of Marine Studies, University of Washington, Seattle) felt that what is necessary is an international convention which would apply to the whole of the north Atlantic and *inter alia* ban all salmon fishing beyond 12 miles from base lines. There would be difficulties in getting agreement but nevertheless those interested should persevere.

L Stewart (Salmon and Trout Association) said that everyone believes there should be an international convention and that it was necessary to do something now.

G D F Hadoke (Foyle Fisheries Commission) said that the two bodies sponsoring this symposium should sponsor a resolution calling for an international convention. (This view was endorsed by the Directors of both the International Atlantic Salmon Foundation and the Atlantic Salmon Research Trust).

Resolution adopted by the Assembly

D L McKernan then read out a draft resolution as follows: The symposium resolves that for effective protection of north Atlantic salmon and in order to encourage the rehabilitation and enhancement of Atlantic salmon wherever they are found or once occurred, and for the national management of salmon fisheries, an International Convention for Atlantic Salmon be established by those countries bordering the North Atlantic and its connected seas that produce and/or fish for Atlantic salmon.

The Symposium further resolves that such convention should include *inter alia*, provisions to:

(1) Ban fishing for Atlantic salmon beyond 12 miles;
(2) Provide for co-operation among all countries in conservation, regulation and enforcement measures and
(3) Provide a forum for international co-operation in research and the exchange of data on Atlantic salmon.

Discussion on the resolution was then invited.

A J Aglen asked to what extent the research aim might be left to the International Council for the Exploration of the Sea, and a number of persons felt that in due time that course would be adopted. One participant in supporting the resolutions asked whether more details should be given as to the terms of the Convention.

W M Carter expressed the view that no attempt should be made to draft a convention at this stage, a view generally accepted by the Symposium.

After further discussions, the resolutions as proposed by Mr McKernan were put to the Symposium and passed unanimously.

The proceedings concluded with a vote of thanks to all those who had taken part in the work of the Symposium.

Index

**Other books published by Fishing News Books Limited
Farnham, Surrey, England**

Free catalogue available on request

Advances in aquaculture
Aquaculture practices in Taiwan
Better angling with simple science
• British freshwater fishes
Commercial fishing methods
Control of fish quality
Culture of bivalve molluscs
The edible crab and its fishery in British waters
Eel capture, culture, processing and marketing
Eel culture
European inland water fish: a multilingual catalogue
FAO catalogue of fishing gear designs
FAO catalogue of small scale fishing gear
FAO investigates ferro-cement fishing craft
Farming the edge of the sea
Fish and shellfish farming in coastal waters
Fish catching methods of the world
Fish inspection and quality control
Fisheries oceanography
Fishery products
Fishing boats and their equipment
Fishing boats of the world 1
Fishing boats of the world 2
Fishing boats of the world 3
The fishing cadet's handbook
Fishing ports and markets
Fishing with electricity
Fishing with light
Freezing and irradiation of fish
Handbook of trout and salmon diseases
Handy medical guide for seafarers
How to make and set nets
Inshore fishing: its skills, risks, rewards
International regulation of marine fisheries: a study of
   regional fisheries organizations
The lemon sole